SAFARI
THE LAST ADVENTURE

By the same author

Death in the Long Grass
Death in the Silent Places
Death in the Dark Continent

PETER HATHAWAY CAPSTICK

SAFARI
THE LAST ADVENTURE

St. Martin's Press
New York

Design by M. Paul

Library of Congress Cataloging in Publication Data

Capstick, Peter Hathaway.
Safari, the last adventure.

1. Safaris—Africa. 2. Hunting—Africa. I. Title.
SK251.C275 1984   799.2'6'0967   84-13287
ISBN 0-312-69657-4

First Edition

10 9 8 7 6 5 4 3 2 1

With love to my wife, Fiona Claire Capstick,
who secretly did all the work.

Contents

Author's Note

This is not a book for the complete novice to both hunting and shooting. Considering the investment in time and money involved in going on safari, the author presumes that the reader has some experience of the extended art of hunting or he or she would probably not be especially interested in examining the subject in such detail. Safari is, in my opinion, the apogee of the shooting sports and I think it fair to presume some background before assailing the heights of dangerous game hunting.

I have done all I can to simplify terms, but let me define *outfitter* and *safari firm*. They have changed over the years and are, at least in this book, largely interchangeable, especially as differentiated from *booking agent*. In the old days, one used an outfitter to arrange such matters as staff, foodstuffs and the hundreds of other items difficult to obtain at a distance from the actual hunting grounds. Modern safari companies provide all these services as a matter of course. The booking agent is generally your connection with the safari company/outfitter rather than the actual operator of your trip. The first represents the second in matters of sales and booking, although there are many safari firms who will not and do not use agents.

It has been much easier throughout the text to simply use the term *hunter* for both sexes. I use the term collectively with no sexual connotation, as my own roster of clients over the years will bear out.

Sometimes the yet unwritten text of a book of this type can appear rather as a very swift, muddy, snag- and whirlpool-filled river must seem to a tired salmon. When one tries to speak objectively in a manner calculated to be of value to the reader, who after all has paid his money to obtain the information, there are always the political, racial and sociological vortices to suck him under with little regard for the facts involved. How well or poorly I have handled this very touchy problem in a delicately fused international world will have to be your decision.

For my part, I have told the truth as I have seen it.

P.H.C.

Acknowledgments

The author would like to express his sincere thanks and appreciation to the following firms and individuals for their generous help and cooperation without which the production of this book would have been impossible. The order of their mention in no way implies the relative value of their kind contributions:

Petersen Publishing Company of Los Angeles, California, who produce *Petersen's Hunting* magazine as well as *Guns & Ammo;* especially Mr. Robert E. Petersen, Tom Siatos and *Hunting*'s publisher, Ken Elliott, for permission to use the drawings from their excellent series, *Big Game Anatomy,* created by the editors, Chuck Adams and in cooperation with Leonard Lee Rue III.

Mr. Roman Hupalowski of Safari Outfitters, Inc., Chicago, for many kind thoughts and suggestions.

Kent Klineburger and all his clan at Klineburger Worldwide Travel in Seattle, Washington, for mountains of literature and many other favors.

Pete Bellow and Dan Thimmes for their welcome additions to the material on available African areas; both of Safari Travel

International of Rosemead, California.

Jack Atcheson & Sons, Inc., for their great trouble and efforts in supplying crucial data to the text.

The entire organization of Jonas Brothers, Inc., Denver, Colorado, for their help in matters of booking, shipping and taxidermy.

Dr. Chris Botha for his kind information on his errant leopard.

Further to the agency side of the business, many safari firms have been extremely kind in sending photographic material, all of which are credited in this book. I would, however, like to especially thank the following outfitters and safari operators:

Geoff and Russ Broom of Geoff Broom International Safaris, for their generous use of photographs throughout this book, a special pleasure as I worked for and with Geoff some years ago in the then-Rhodesia.

Gary Kelly Safaris for much valuable material.

SafariSouth of Maun, Botswana, and Houston, Texas, for their many courtesies in this book's production.

Peter Johnstone of Rosslyn Safaris in Zimbabwe for all his help through extended correspondence with the author.

"Mike" Rowbotham of Hunters Tracks in Zimbabwe, an old East Africa hand who has contributed photographic material to the book.

M. Philip Kahl, for his photographs used in this book.

Bob D'Olivo for his courtesy in supplying the dust jacket cover photo.

Beth Morian for the photo of waterbuck and impala at Matetsi.

Brian Marsh, who is not only an old friend and co-conspirator in the writing game with St. Martin's Press, with his excellent novel, *The Last Trophy* (St. Martin's Press, New York, 1982), but also a generous friend who permitted some of his photos to be exhibited here.

Special thanks to Les Pockell for his usual brilliance and foresight in this, our fourth book together; and great appreciation to Kathy Babcock, assistant editor, for so much help and many valuable favors.

Lastly, and I mentioned that order didn't matter, for Fru-Fru the Zulu who managed to type the manuscript in genuine

Americanese, despite the fact I cannot convince her that the dialect is actually a legitimate form of English.

Thanks so much to you all.

Peter Hathaway Capstick
Pretoria, South Africa

Introduction

I have always thought of the African safari as the last great adventure available legally for money. Nowhere on earth—and possibly in space either—can the senses as well as the emotions wallow in a combination of stimulae such as are found in the African bush: the whine of flies, the moan of a sway-bellied lion leaving his kill in the carmine dawn, the hacksaw rasp of a leopard in the gloom, the bowel-freezing scream of a bull elephant catching your wind. The musk of sweat-lacquered black skins blending with the smoke of dying *mopane* fires; the wild, sweet decay of buffalo dung; the odd, heady cloy of cordite and the conglomerate of red, sun-raped dust mixed with the powdery fragments of crushed, dry, golden grass. The buzzing, oozing, crawling rot of meat and the whorish impact of jasmine. And visual textures too: the striped dapples of zebra in shadow, whetted steel and stained brass, the glassy ebony of a sable's horn tip, the subtle glow of ivory, the oily roil of the deep, dark river pools.

Touch is not neglected, as you'll realize after two hours on a canvas camp stool in a leopard blind, if you've forgotten the sharp-edged whine of landing tsetse and their hot, icepick gouge. Taste is one of the happier aspects of safari, where you can enjoy the world's best venison, fresh bread, biltong, crisp Cape wines and the occasional blood-warm martini to keep you appreciative. Tilapia bream *meunière*, perhaps migratory quail over a spit or whole roast warthog. Then, of course, there are breasts of francolin and guinea fowl in a dozen different manners.

On safari, there is exhilaration. And fear. There's the joy of having done a stalk properly. There's also the terror of having done it badly or of having shot poorly, bringing a blur of hurtling lion or an avalanche of elephant down on your neck in an instant, Tourist Board or no. There will be the swelter of heat, the probing fingers of cold, the pleasure of exhaustion and the dry, cicada-filled hours of boredom when it's too hot to hunt and you baste the early afternoon away in your own juices. There will be small quarrels and triumphs, frustrations and elation. And, I rather prefer "but," if nothing else, there will be adventure.

It's been a while since Clark Gable, Ava Gardner, Grace Kelly and Stewart Granger gave the popular impression of safari. You remember, the "Boys-go-no-farther-Bwana-this-Msubi-country" sort of opus that took over where Bomba the Jungle Boy and Tarzan left off. Not that the mid-century matinees were ever accurate or even remotely descriptive of African hunting conditions. Today, when people should really know better, the general public is astonished to learn that African hunting safaris are still not only available but are more popular and more important to wildlife survival and well-being than ever before.

Africa is a very shifty, tricky lady, especially if you have some strange interest in writing a safari book about her. Essentially, Africa won't hold still. What may be a fact today may be a musty memory next week, especially where politics are concerned. And since politics greatly affects the safari industry, it logically leads to the ground rules for this book.

Even if there were no such thing as inflation, it would be impossible to write a reliable book giving current prices and all details on the African safari because of the constantly changing rules and regulations, the opening and closing of different areas for different reasons and the eternally shifting situation affecting the availability of different game species. This year elephants will be on license, maybe next year they won't. Perhaps there'll be disease or political upheaval, floods, drought, locusts or merely a change in price structure ten minutes after this book is published. Africa is very, very moody.

But African hunting really doesn't change. And that is why this book takes the form it does.

I have in my library three guidebooks on African hunting, all reasonably recent and all completely out of date because they tried to explain the details of safari hunting as if they were static. They are not. To give you an idea of the problems an author runs into after a few years pass, all three books deal only with East Africa—meaning Kenya, Tanzania and the then Portuguese possession of Mozambique (Uganda is omitted), as well as the other former Portuguese territory of Angola on the west coast of Africa. This, of course, is where the action *was*. The problem is that hunting is no longer available in any of these countries, with the exception of Tanzania, and that on a different basis now, as the industry there has been nationalized.

This sort of upheaval is what has led me to decide to leave the current financial details of booking a safari to the many sources that you will find listed in these pages, rather than quoting figures we both know will not be valid much beyond the present. You'll find appendices with figures, but remember that they are given strictly as a means of getting a feel for one area as compared with another. They are not offered as current.

While we're at it, *safari* is a word with an interesting history that has only been connected with hunting in recent times. Originally from Arabic, the word was absorbed into the lingua franca of East Africa, KiSwahili, thanks to the Arab slavers largely dominating that part of the continent at one time. The Arabic is *safariya*, derived from *safara*, to travel. In KiSwahili, it translated directly as "a journey," and probably best described the slave caravans into the interior. As early hunting trips looked much the same with their armed guards, porters and bearers, the word stuck.

Most books on African hunting contain some sort of a defense of hunting, probably because the activity receives such slanted coverage from anti-bloodsport factions. Some of my own earlier works are fair examples. Nothing, therefore, could please me more than to omit such a defense for this book. The actual role of the legitimate hunter is at last being acknowledged as absolutely crucial to game's survival. As one prestigious journal, *The African Conservationist*, acknowledged in an article in its June 1983 issue on the value of sport hunting to wildlife, "Remember, conservation means wise use not preservation."

This being the case, I would like to close this introduction with the charming words of Kermit Roosevelt, who accompanied the ex-president, his father, on his famous trip in 1909, and who may have caught the sentimental soul of the real sportsman:

> We get three sorts and periods of enjoyment out of a hunting trip. The first is when the plans are being discussed and the outfit assembled; this is the pleasure of anticipation. The second is the enjoyment of the actual trip itself; and the third is the pleasure of retrospection when we sit around a blazing wood fire and talk over the incidents and pleasures of the trip. There is no general rule to know what of the three gives us the keenest joy.

Peter Hathaway Capstick
Pretoria, South Africa
February 1984

In hunting, the finding and killing of the game is after all but a part of the whole. The free, self-reliant, adventurous life, with its rugged and stalwart democracy; the wild surroundings, the grand beauty of the scenery, the chance to study the ways and habits of the woodland creatures—all these unite to give to the career of the wilderness hunter its peculiar charm. The chase is among the best of all national pastimes; it cultivates that vigorous manliness for the lack of which in a nation, as in an individual, the possession of no other qualities can possibly atone.

Theodore Roosevelt, hunter
(1858–1919)

ONE

The Great Adventure

A pretty fair case could be made that the evolution of the African safari is really a historical overlay of the past century and a half of white expansion into the interior of Africa. After Jan Van Riebeeck, South Africa's founder, pitched up at the Cape in 1652, both he and another 180 years of descendants either had too much on their hands keeping body and soul in one chunk to make much of a dent in the continent, or various colonial policies kept them from it, which amounted to white expansion reaching only a vague 150 miles inland. There were still enough elephants in the general vicinity of urban Cape Town to get settler Pieter Roman trampled and tusked to death there after he presumably wounded one with what was definitely not enough gun in 1661. That there was still little pressure on the local fauna 145 years after Roman's death seems clear from a British dispatch written by the commander of the troops garrisoned there after capturing the area in 1806, describing the "roaring of lions" after dark.

The Portuguese, who had long before established trading posts and forts on both the east and west coasts, showed even less interest in probing the secrets of the dark, dank, mysterious beauty that lay just past the bright beach sands. Ten miles inland was a long way for Portuguese influence to have any swat, even after literally hundreds of years of their presence.

It wasn't until the mid-1830s that the Cape Dutch and other elements of the people who now thought of themselves as part of Africa, rather than Europe, decided they had had enough of British domination and headed off in a series of great treks up-country, effectively changing the status quo of white tenure in Africa. Not only were there political and ethno-religious reasons for packing off to what was presumed to be the Land of Milk and Honey (bring your own cow and bee, said some on returning), but the technological improvements in firearms, resulting in more reliable muzzle-loaders, had an influence too.

These ox-wagon pioneers were to change the profile of Africa forever. It is appropriate, in mentioning these early settlers as the first major white group to enter what at the time must have seemed unlimited game fields, to indicate the huge cultural differences between these people and their heritage and that of British hunters and sportsmen who had just started to get their feet wet in African big game shooting about this time.

The Boers, as they were better known to the outside world, were essentially peasant farming stock. *Boer* in fact means "farmer." They were not sport hunters by tradition, that privilege of northern Europe having been pretty well reserved for the landed aristocracy, with some singularly unpleasant penalties for clumsy or unlucky poachers. In the new land of South Africa, though, as farmers, they tended to hunt for commercial reasons—especially elephant and hippo for ivory, antelope for meat and biltong (still the national snack of dried venison or beef) and to protect their herds and crops from animal encroachment. Any concept of preservation or conservation, at least at that time, would have seemed as strange to them as a notion that they should not kill the snakes in their homes because at some hazy point in the future the land might run short of mambas or cobras.

The first British adventurers into the interior, other than the ubiquitous missionaries, saw things differently, even though they could hardly have been commended for any particularly naturalistic foresight. Most were army officers, usually with Indian service, where they had been able to expand the love of the chase they had learned at home as boys in Britain. Asia, with its tiger beats, pigsticking meets, buffalo hunts and other sporting succulents, had primed them for Africa and its renowned wild game. One who unquestionably influenced more sportsmen than any other over the next fifty years after his book was first published in 1838 was William Cornwallis Harris. Harris started his Indian military career as a sixteen-year-old second lieutenant of Engineers and, as a captain after thirteen years of service, was ordered to the Cape Colony for two years to recover from continued attacks of severe malaria. A gifted artist, he left us not only ethereal views of the land and game of the time, but also penned the only known and surviving portrait of Mzilikazi, the extraordinary Matabele king who figured so prominently in the war and peace of the region. A dedicated naturalist, he provided invaluable museum specimens crowned by the rarest of all, a completely new species of large antelope.

Three years after he wrote his book—the version published in Bombay called *Narrative of an Expedition into Southern Africa*, and the more popular version reissued in London the following year, 1839, as *The Wild Sports of Southern Africa*—Harris led a mission from the Government of Bombay to the Ethiopian king, Sahela Selassie of Shoa, the success of which resulted in his being gazetted major and knighted. This last trip resulted in another book, *The Highlands of Aethiopia*, and closely coincided with the publication of a volume of lithographs of his paintings of southern African wildlife, which is today considered one of the rarest and most valuable of all Africana. Harris died of fever near Poona, India, on October 9, 1848. He was thirty-nine years old.

Harris' recollections of his trip by ox-wagon north from the Cape Colony in 1836–7 represents the first book on African big game hunting, and is particularly notable as Harris' reasons for hunting were sporting, not commercial. So it might be argued that he was the first person to go on safari and leave a record—although he as likely as not had never even heard the word—despite the fact that many British officers must have done considerable hunting at least near Cape Town over the thirty years that troops had been garrisoned there.

Although some of his fellow officers and relative contemporaries were mostly interested in how frequently and how quickly they could kill game, Harris was much more than just another cap-popper. Actually, his scientific interest in specimens was about equal to his joy in the sport of obtaining them. Certainly, the Zoological Society of London was the richer for his trip. The sable antelope, *Hippotragus niger*, was long known as the Harrisbuck, and that such a scimitar-horned, anthracite-hued beauty does not still carry the name of its discoverer is more the loss. How the first sable was killed is one of the best early safari tales so let's off to the remote Cashan Mountains and try to see it through Harris' eyes. . . .

It is the afternoon of December 13, 1836, pleasantly cool for the rainy season, in what is now the Magaliesberg range, near my home in Pretoria. Four and a half months out from Cape Town, Captain Harris is with a party of Hottentots, following up a wounded elephant on horseback. One of his frequent falls has bashed up his favorite 10-bore percussion rifle and he carries a cumbersome, thundering great flintlock obtained from the soon to be famous missionary, the Reverend Mr. Moffat, at Kuruman. It is a cannon firing a quarter-pound hardened lead ball persuaded rather violently along by fifteen drams of coarse black powder. As he pounds rhythmically over a dried *vlei* or marshy area, he notices a small herd of oddly dark antelope about a half-mile off in a parallel valley. Reining in, he looks them over with his pocket telescope, a shock of realization that they are completely new to science shivering through him. Instantly, he forgets the elephant among the jeers and jibes of the Hottentots, who figure that anybody who trades an elephant for an "uglybuck" like whatever those are must have been out in the sun too long. Spurs flashing, Harris rushes his shooting horse toward them.

After a hammering run, the officer is among the weird, dark antelope, two looming bulls and nine paler, buff-colored cows. Hauling up his pony, Harris leaps from the saddle only fifty yards away and sees the herd slow, then stop in curiosity, staring back at the odd white man, the iridescent purple-black skins of the loop-horned bulls gleaming like wet ebony in the summer sun. Harris takes a shooting breath, lines up the rough flintlock and squeezes the trigger at the biggest male. The smoothbore slips its hammer like a bear trap, the flint throwing a shower of sparks into the pan. Nothing. Misfire. A bull stamps a forefoot as Harris wipes the grime from his smeared forehead and recocks the big gun, centering the coarse bead of the front sight on the black chest once more. *Snap! Clash! Flash!* Silence. The antelope, now alarmed, begin to canter off, the furious Harris lining up yet another misfire. Then, they are gone.

Harris, his frustration more than he can contain, howls a curse, throws the perfidious gun on the rocky ground and re-mounts to dash back to camp where he will try to repair his own weapon.

It takes two hours before his own double-barreled, 10-bore rifle can be patched up and the hunter on a fresh horse, is back where he last saw the strange, dark antelope. Still, as hard as the Hottentot trackers work, the sun is gone before he catches another glimpse of the animals. Furious, and despairing of find-ing them again, Harris rides back to camp for the night.

Dawn is still a coy blush somewhere over the light bushveld and feathery trees of the Cashans when Harris leaves camp and is back on the cold trail of the mysterious antelope, his frustra-tion turned to obsession to collect one of the unknown, exotic creatures. For a whole searing, sweat-soaked day he and a tracker ride without a glimpse of the elusive wraiths, the black guillotine of darkness leaving them to sleep on the faint spoor, exhausted and with only tea and biltong to eat. The third day, they are again gone long before first light, cold tea and more biltong lumped like acid and harness leather in their stomachs.

The sun is high and ferocious in a sailcloth sky before the Hottentot hauls up at the edge of a series of low, broken ridges stuttered with rocky hills. At the feet of their horses is a scatter-ing of compact dung pellets near the heart-shaped hoof marks. Fresh. Harris changes the percussion caps of his rifle to be sure the dew has not affected them, eases the hammers down and removes the sling. Tethering the mounts, the Englishman and the Hottentot crab over the burning, saw-edged rocks to the lip of the emerald ravine, the officer's blood pounding in his tem-ples with excitement. Will they be there?

Through the shield of brush, Harris catches a flicker of movement and the dull gleam of arched horn where the ante-lope are resting in the heat at the end of the snarled draw. Slowly, he inches up the 10-bore, the sight settling on the chest of the big bull. *PHUTTDOOM!* The double fires, the hunter up and racing to see beyond the billowing bloom of white powder smoke. Score! The near hind leg of the bull has caught the big ball. Immediately, Harris touches off the second barrel, seeing and hearing the ball thump home into the animal's chest. No point in trying to reload as the antelope stream by, Harris watches them run out of the draw, past his hiding place, the big bull galloping well despite his wounds. The Englishman's hands are shaking as he reloads, powder, linen-wrapped ball, ram, recap. As the mutter of dust-muffled hooves dies away, the dry slither of the ramrod sliding into its housing under the barrels blends with Harris' call for the horses.

Harris and the Hottentot follow the splashes of blood easily for a full mile along a dry watercourse with no indication of the wounded bull slowing down. And then, there he stands at bay, about one hundred yards off, the hind leg given out. Harris is off his pony in a single movement, raising the rifle for the final shot. As he glances at his priming, a rumble of fear runs through his bowels as he hears a squeal and a series of low, angry grunts mixed with the clatter of hooves. The bull is charging.

Harris holds on the chest and touches off the first barrel, the quarter-pound shotput of lead knocking the black male down with a hollow thump as the big ball strikes. To Harris' growing fright, the bull scrambles back to his feet, the grunts of anger now a steady rumble of low, determined fury. Thoroughly scared, Harris slaps the wobbling foresight on the chest again and fires the last barrel. *Whock!* The bull falls and once more starts to rise to kill the man. Spilling powder, Harris manages to get a charge down one barrel, followed by a hasty ball. Still fumbling with the percussion cap, he realizes that it is not necessary. Halfway to his knees, the jet-black bull staggers, hooks his long horns twice and shudders as death takes him.

Captain William Cornwallis Harris realizes he is the first man to take the sable antelope, in the opinion of many the noblest, fiercest and most handsome of his kin on the African continent. Kudu bulls are delicately beautiful, oryx are savage and stark. But, the sable? The sable is a man's trophy.

I've often wondered if Cornwallis Harris' collecting the first sable—or Harrisbuck—just might not have been the grandest experience anybody ever had on safari. And, Harris did it the right way, spending three days to come up with his game and even taking a half-charge at the end. It's likely that he who did the deed wrote it best.

"It were vain to attempt a description of the sensations I experienced," said Harris, "when thus, after three days of toilsome tracking, and feverish anxiety unalleviated by any incident that could inspire the smallest hope of ultimate success, I at length found myself in actual possession of so brilliant an addition to the riches of Natural History."

That sort of talk makes me conclude that Harris was a pretty reasonable dude. Ah, but there were plenty of them.

It's possible that Roualeyn George Gordon Cumming might have had a chance to read Harris' book, but if so, the second major writer on African hunting doesn't mention it. A very big man for his day at fourteen stone (196 pounds), Cumming was the perfect freelance individualist, replete with a beard like a wild bushfire and a penchant for wearing kilts under any and all circumstances. Tall and powerful, he was probably everything that the well-built but recuperating Harris wasn't: Cumming was a showman who became known throughout Europe and the British Isles by the sobriquet "The Lion Hunter," while Harris was much more the scientist, zoologist and artist.

Roughly thirteen years younger than Harris, Cumming was an Eton graduate and the son of a noble Scottish family who had his first whiff of African sport on a South African stopover in 1838, the same year that Harris was back in India publishing his book. Evidently it made a lasting impression, because after a few years of wanderings through India and North America, Cumming joined the Cape Mounted Rifles and arrived back where it looked like he belonged.

In 1843, Gordon Cumming took off for "the blue" and stayed there for five years, his adventures culminating in the 1850 book *Five Years of a Hunter's Life in the Far Interior of South Africa*. An instant success, Cumming gained a reputation not unlike a combination of Dick Butkus and Tom Selleck in one characteristically shirtless hunk. Of course, he was either fearless or crazy or, as anybody who has spent any time in the African bush will likely surmise, both. His specialty was jumping into crock-crawling waters after wounded hippos, cutting slots through their hides and dragging them to land with the help of his men, one of whom, his personal servant, had been a cab driver in London.

That by himself Gordon Cumming, during his five years of bare-chested hunting in a tattered kilt, killed over one hundred elephants is not extraordinary. Some forty years later, members of a venerable Voortrekker family called Van Zyl had what was presumably a charming single afternoon slaughtering one hundred and four elephants, mostly cows and calves, after chasing them into a marsh near Moçǎmedes, in southwestern Angola. Why did they do it? I assure you that I have no idea except that it may have represented rural white mentality toward wildlife generally, or more likely, extremely, at that time. Today I doubt that anybody would come down harder on the Van Zyl party than a modern sport hunter.

When Gordon Cumming returned to Britain in 1848, he had with him a captured Bushman named Ruyter and an incredible thirty tons of trophies, including his ox wagons! This passel of loot was shown in the Great Exhibition in London in 1851 and was used to open a museum seven years later in Fort Augustus, Inverness, which kept Cumming well in the limelight as a lecturer and raconteur on African hunting. Loving every moment, he wallowed in his reputation, growing his red beard to the size of a bath towel and generally playing the unrepentant wild man with hair nets, daggers and pistols until he got a funny hunch around the middle of March 1866. On the 24th, he was laid out in the newly delivered coffin he had ordered, eccentric to the last. Pretty good. He was forty-six.

South Africa remained for the next fifty-plus years the springboard for adventure into the interior, the hunting grounds always moving farther north as man cut the bush, drove off the game and generally overbred, leaving the recently teeming plains and *vleis* of the Transvaal and other new farming areas in much the same state as those achieved through similar and earlier methods in Europe and America. Eventually, Rhodesia was opened through the rather grudging courtesy of King Lobengula and much new interest was focused there. It attracted such great hunters and naturalists as Frederick Courteney Selous, who started his career as a professional at South Africa's Algoa Bay in September of 1871, nineteen years old and with £400 in his pockets, quite a bit in those days. Selous was killed in 1917 in a skirmish with German forces in Tanganyika but he pressed a lot of mighty fine times between the pages of his life. It was he who guided Cecil Rhodes to Rhodesia, wrote a string of good books, was a close friend of Teddy Roosevelt and is generally considered to have been Rider Haggard's model for Allan Quatermain. He is often referred to as Roosevelt's "white hunter" in 1909, but this is not so. The two only met a couple of times for lunch during Roosevelt's stay.

It wasn't until the great colonial rush at the turn of the century, and especially the events of the building of the Mombasa–Victoria–Uganda Railway between 1896 and 1901 that East Africa, and with it the modern safari, found a foothold in some pretty rough terrain. The "Lunatic Line," as it was better known in Parliament, cost about 34,000 various imported Indian coolie casualties, more than one hundred of whom were taken by the Man-Eaters of Tsavo, two highly innovative male lions that shut down the entire project before being finally sorted out by an officer named Patterson, who wrote a best-seller on his experiences.

At last, though, here was a situation that physically permitted a visiting sportsman to get to his hunting grounds, possibly the finest on earth, without having to spend long weeks or months in an ox-wagon. By using the 560-mile steel ribbons, a man could land in Mombasa and actually be hunting only a few days later, often near a funny little tent town that had sprung up on some high flats, a crazy place full of crazier people called Nairobi.

True, there had been considerable private hunting activity in East Africa before this, but again along the lines of the do-it-yourself Indian shikars or the southern African shooting trips. Probably the first spot an officer or a gentleman of means considered in the 1890s was then called Somali Land. Just across the Red Sea from British Aden, it was primitive (hell, it still is!), full of game and largely still wild tribes, yet within reach of British influence.

Before the Uganda Railway came into use in the early 1900s, Somali Land was just the ticket for the man a bit tired of tigers. One of them, in fact, seems to have owned my copy of Captain C. J. Meliss' *Lion Hunting in Somali-land* (the hyphen apparently having been optional), a charming 1895 opus on shooting sport in that country. Mine is full of notes and comments by one General G. H. More-Molyneux, C.B., D.S.O., and dated Agra (India), February 25, 1901. Clearly, from his inscriptions, General Molyneux was considering a shooting trip to Somali Land. On the fly page he writes:

> In a review of this book in *The Pioneer* of July 12th, 1895, the following occurs. "To all who want good sport at a reasonable cost Somali Land may be recommended. All expenses including those of voyage can be covered for Rs600 [rupees] per month on a trip [illegible] over twelve weeks or longer, and the gain to health from living in a glorious climate is worth more than the outlay."

But, for all the joys of Somali Land, problems with the Mahdi and subsequent military expeditions dampened civilian enthusiasm considerably just at the time that Kenya was getting into gear. By 1909, the first really big East African safari was in the field. At the helm was Theodore Roosevelt, who, nineteen days before his departure, had been president of the United States.

Probably nothing in the world of hunting ever rocked the public as did the Roosevelt African Expedition, and a reading of his subsequent book, *African Game Trails*, is more worthwhile with every year that passes. Other books on the expedition give an even better insight into the times, particularly such marvelously lunatic flights of fantasy as that taken by J. Martin Miller, "the celebrated Author and Traveler," who has the African thickets hopping with Australian kangaroos and, from his illustrations, teeming with Asian tigers.

To appreciate the impact of the Roosevelt safari on the public in general and the infant safari industry in particular, it must be remembered that Roosevelt, even before San Juan Hill, had always been bigger than life. For one of the most flamboyant men of his times to hie himself off to what many thought would be sure death at the claws and teeth of—as he called them—"the beasts of raven" was a pressman's dream. Teddy didn't let them down, either. Back home, whole congregations prayed for his safety as he started off on the Uganda Railway at

Mombasa and eventually ended up at Khartoum some ten months later.

At the head of some five hundred porters, *askaris* (guards) and other personnel, Teddy carried along such oddenda as a rabbit's foot given him for luck by ex-heavyweight champion John L. Sullivan, a British double express rifle subscribed to as a gift from virtually every living author on the subject of African hunting as well as half the peerage in England and even a pigskin-bound library of classics weighing some sixty pounds and carried along with everything else on a porter's head.

He personally collected, mostly for museums, 296 animals ranging from bull elephants to Naivasha pygmy mice, the entire bag of the expedition encompassing 164 different species. From the publicity of the Roosevelt trip, safari was off to a roaring start.

At the time of the Roosevelt safari, the premier if not the only outfitting firm in Africa was Newland & Tarlton of Nairobi who, working with F. C. Selous and Edward North Buxton, made Teddy's arrangements. One of the two Australian partners, Leslie J. Tarlton, acted as "second" professional hunter to R. J. Cuninghame, a famous character. The Scottish Cuninghame's qualifications for keeping the recent president's tail away from all those snapping jaws, besides being a Cambridge graduate, included having been a professional ivory hunter, an arctic whaler, a hunter-naturalist in Lapland, a transport rider in South Africa and a collector for the British Museum in other corners of the world.

As soon as they organized their firm, Newland & Tarlton realized that they had nearly cornered what would be an institution of immense financial importance to the new colony of Kenya, whose balance of payments was still very shaky. Essentially, the company acted as agents for visiting sportsmen or naturalists by receiving baggage shipments, organizing headmen, porters, guides, cooks, mounts, tentage, servants, equipment and *askaris*, as well as virtually all the thousands of items required for a long safari. There were licenses to be bought, medical supplies to be purchased and properly packed, liquor, tinned goods, arms and ammunition and clothing to be hand-tailored by the local Indian merchants according to patterns sent ahead. Anybody arriving fresh without this preparation would have needed weeks, at least, to get an expedition into the field, and that provided they knew the local languages and conditions. A well-known Chicago cartoonist, John T. McCutcheon, who accompanied the 1909 Carl Akeley American Museum of Natural History trip, wrote that, upon merely sending a cable to Newland & Tarlton, he could arrive "with only a suit-case, with the certainty that everything would be in readiness."

The staff at N&T had style. The arrangements they put on for their safaris, perfectly provisioned and prepackaged, normally featured a hundred-plus porters, each wearing a navy sweater with N&T sewn on the front in scarlet, two pairs of new boots usually swinging from their necks. (The law required that the porters be supplied with the boots; they were rarely worn: they hurt.) The *askaris* were even snazzier in the N&T private army uniform of white knickerbockers and blue shirts. If you could afford it, nothing was too much trouble on an early "champagne safari," but perhaps it made small difference to a wounded lion or charging buffalo, which stood a pretty good chance of getting you removed from *Who's Who* without the slightest consideration for your last donation to the Fund for Animals. Despite the obvious trappings, however, there remained the fact that in no way could dangerous or elusive game be hunted without discomfort and some degree of danger—at least not if you were doing it right.

After Roosevelt's book hit the market and safari became the equivalent of the European Grand Tour, other outfitters and hunting organization firms entered the market, doing well for themselves and the colony's economy. Not all agreed with the "champagne safari" approach, though. Chauncey Hugh Stigand, elephant hunter and author, reckoned that such carryings on were "out of place" and "spoilt the charm of the wilds." Roosevelt, too, wrote that camp life "seemed almost too comfortable" for those used only to the wilder aspects of the American West and the North Woods. After a few years, most safari-goers seemed to agree with them, and the Arabian Nights atmosphere of the early trips settled down in favor of those who would rather listen to a hyena symphony than a gramophone, and prefer red stringy guinea fowl to Chicken Kiev. I often wonder when it was that warm beer usurped champagne. Probably just before I got into the business.

The early, boomtown days after the Roosevelt safari firmly established East Africa, particularly Kenya, as the classic safari country, in my opinion largely because of the incredible people who lived there from that period, overlapping one another right up until the 1960s. A dozen books would be needed in addition to the hundreds already written about the early East African hunters, many of whom penned their own or were written of by other hunters. Some were Selous, Frederick Jackson, Philip Percival (thirty-five consecutive times president of the East African Professional Hunters Association), his brother Blayney, once the only game warden in Kenya, "Karamojo" Bell, Jimmy Sutherland, "Samaki" Salmon, "Deaf" Banks, Bror Blixen, Rainsford, Dugmore, "Bwana" Cottar, Cuninghame, Carl Akeley, Sir Alfred Pease, Foran, Powell-Cotton and Stigand, not forgetting Arthur Newmann, J. A. Hunter, Fritz Shindeler, Denys Finch-Hatton, P. J. Pretorius, Pitman, Ionides and the Greys (both killed by game). Every name brings three more to mind. Outfitters like Safariland. Places like Tsavo Bridge. Hotels like the New Stanley and the Norfolk. They all meant one thing: safari. May the shades of these old ones forgive me if I have omitted many of their names. They knew who they were.

But paradise in the "Pleistocene," as Roosevelt viewed East Africa zoologically, was not to last indefinitely. Only until 1914, in fact, when the British opened fire at Bagamoyo and Dar-es-Salaam on August 8, beginning the East African campaign of World War I. War in this theatre was perhaps not as savage as the complete slaughter in Europe, but it was nonetheless deadly. Of course, all safari activities were immediately shut down, most professional hunters and ivory hunters alike either flying fighters or scouting, as did both Bell and Pretorius. Selous was killed fighting as a captain. Finally, on November 11, 1918, with the German forces poised to flood into Rhodesia, the Armistice was signed and happy days were here again. And they were, too.

From 1920 to about 1938 was the real heyday of the East African safari. Most professional hunters operated in Kenya, Tanganyika (formerly German East Africa and then British until independence in 1961) and Uganda, finding incredible concentrations of game because of the long cessation in hunting activity. Of course, upon special request, they often went into the

Belgian Congo, Sudan and Ethiopia, but the main areas were still Kenya, Tanganyika and Uganda.

One thing that vastly improved after World War I was the automobile, greatly facilitating access to remote areas. That the "motor safari" has been long misunderstood, even by the old hunters themselves, is a suspicion that continues to lurk under my balding brow. Somehow, there was a concept that taking a Dodge Power Wagon, a Willy's-Knight or even a Buick (as Lord Delamere did) on a hunting trip was in some way "unsportsmanlike," the logical presumption being that the actual hunting was to be done from the automobile or car. Well, so far as I know, there is no place in Africa where this is not strictly illegal and there is no sportsman's group anywhere in the world where such practices are considered fair chase.

When a hunter has, say, a month's vacation and has waited all his or her life for a crack at a safari, such a trip would be instantly ruled out if the hunter had to walk or ride in an ox-wagon for the full month just to get where he was going. A Jeep or Land Rover certainly doesn't help stalking; if anything it is a hindrance. It doesn't help shooting either. That's up to the hunter. What it does help is facility of access into and simple mobility through the hunting area, provided it is not misused.

It would be as logical to suggest that a man who flew from New York to Johannesburg or Lusaka, Zambia, or Maun, Botswana, was equally unsporting rather than taking a windjammer. *Of course*, hunting cars are abused. Certainly, game is killed *illegally* from them in some places. On the other hand, people cheat at marriage, cards, golf and business, too, but they rarely hang a memento of their perfidy on the wall. Like guns, knives, scissors and some drugs, a hunting car is merely another tool that can be misused but, in fact, rarely is, especially considering the stringency of the game laws and the hunter's self-imposed code of conduct.

The postwar period was typified by such work as that of Martin and Osa Johnson, whose self-avowed "objective" was "to film, more completely than it had ever been done before, a record of Africa's fast-vanishing wildlife, in order that posterity might be able permanently to recall it as it had existed in its last and greatest stronghold." That they shot tons of big game, often in provoked charges, while making their films never seemed to dawn on anybody as an inconsistency, nor would I second-guess the Johnsons who were, after all, in the business of adventure and held valid licenses.

The greatest event since Teddy Roosevelt's safari was that of H. R. H. the Prince of Wales, briefly to be Edward VIII in 1936. In September 1928, the Prince arrived and was taken in tow by Baron Bror von Blixen, "Pete" Pearson, "Samaki" Salmon, the Honorable Denys Finch-Hatton and a proper collection of knights, governors and notables for a shooting trip that lasted into December. He must have had a pretty fair time as he returned for the period January–April 1930.

East Africa, of course, realized the value of the safari trade and it's always interesting to note that the degree of game protection came directly in proportion to the amount of money spent through hunting tourism, as it should have. Price increases stayed pretty much in line with inflation, which was slight even in those days.

More and more private individuals, largely ranchers and farmers who dealt with big game every day, became licensed professional hunters, although all had to pass stringent requirements. Dead tourists were bad for business. As the years went by, firms like Ker and Downey, White Hunters Africa, Safariland and dozens more came into being, each jealously guarding their stable of well-known professionals as movie studios guarded their leading men.

World War II, of course, shut down operations, and it wasn't until the late forties that things got rolling again. With the postwar financial boom, the result was more and more Americans and fewer Europeans, particularly Britons and Germans. Still, one of the most far-reaching aspects of a war that accounted, in one way or another, for 55,000,000 dead people was the fact that for millions of other people who had previously considered hunting either the province of the backwoods or of the socially and financially elite, firearms were now a part of their lives. In the United States, blue-collar workers, who would never before their military training have thought of buying a deer rifle or pheasant shotgun, swelled sales of arms and of hunting licenses to a previously unheard-of level. Britain clung to its usual iron-clad licensing laws for guns, so the case was different there. Perhaps the whole thing culminated in Robert

Ruark's *Horn of the Hunter* (following earlier works by Hemingway), the really charming tale of his first safari in Kenya and Tanganyika in 1952, with the then almost fuzzy-cheeked Harry Selby. The book not only made Selby but cast him as the model hero, Peter MacKenzie, for *Something of Value*, Ruark's smash later novel.

Horn of the Hunter, although it sold well but not magnificently in those days, was the first message to the American hunter that safari need not be the mere musing of a British baronet. In the new opulence, many could afford their own *shauri* (work or undertaking, business, loosely used in KiSwahili) and many caught the hint, booking the outfitting companies as fully as sugar cubes in a box. In East Africa, all went well until various independences in the 1960s, especially Kenya in 1963. *Uhuru*, it was called.

I well remember being there in those days, of seeing the shift of power, which became more of a landslide. It took some years, but sure enough, in the early seventies, safari was closed one bright day, without warning to prepaid clients, in its real home, Kenya. The official reason was pressure on game. That the pressure came from poachers who moved their ivory after sale through the national airline to the Far East in what has been shown to have been direct collusion with the family of the then president of Kenya, Jomo Kenyatta, seems not to have overly impressed the preservationists who see the death of any game for any reason as totalling the same result, a simplistic and untrue conclusion. The point was that the booming safari trade was producing the funds to support an effective game department that greatly curtailed poaching and the movement of unlicensed game products. To the "heavy" money, this just would not do. Hunting was outlawed, to what must have been the resounding cheers of the preservationists and the resigned heartbreak of the conservationists, the hunters and those who really cared about animal dynamics. Kenya has gone downhill ever since, poaching—like any larceny, impossible to fight without funds and organization—toppling in two-handed ax strokes what was left of the commercially valuable animals. Perhaps it was just another example of commerce slaughtering conservation.

A fine example of how it *might* have been handled to the good of all but the poachers would be that of the Selous Game

Reserve in southeastern Tanzania, which was opened to very carefully controlled sport hunting late in 1961, and which contains the great man's grave near where he was killed at Behobeho. A full 22,000 square miles, it is the second largest reserve on earth. Whereas the whole area had been poached previously, this concept permitted hunting safaris from America and elsewhere to support three game department bases, one of which alone had a staff of more than 450 people, a dry-season track much longer than the east-west width of the United States, antipoaching posts in large numbers, three ferries and three bridges, and which still had enough of a surplus from the million and a half shillings produced by the less than one hundred hunting safaris each year to provide the government with a tidy sum for its coffers. Now, that's common-sense game management, good for the game and hunter alike, as well as for the host government.

That, twenty-two years after its opening to sport hunting, the Selous is still one of the top spots in Africa for big game clearly shows that the pressure that would have been put on the place by unpoliced poaching hasn't occurred as it has in Kenya, where sport hunting is illegal. It also shows that game management is completely viable, if only control can be maintained by responsible authorities. Those are facts, not emotion.

The example of the Selous was quickly followed in the early 1960s by other emerging countries (e.g. Zambia, formerly Northern Rhodesia until 1964, and Botswana, the Bechuanaland Protectorate until 1966). The safari industry has been one of the mainstays of development of these and many other newly independent nations. Roughly in the same time period, hunting became more available in Chad, the Central African Republic, Sudan, Zaire, Ethiopia, Angola and Mozambique as well as some of the far more specialized west coast nations such as Gabon, Cameroon and Senegal. This increased availability of sport hunting was largely the result of former East African outfitters and safari firms realizing that, although Kenya was dead through poaching corruption and Uganda gone with Idi Amin Dada, there were many other lands with sport as good and economics as needy as the Cradle of Safari. They provided the equipment and expertise. Free enterprise being what it is, there is still a wide variety of hunting in Africa for the visitor or local alike.

An especially interesting example of the economic value of safari and the concept of game being handsomely able to pay its own way would be that of the Republic of South Africa.

Not much more than ten years ago, few sportsmen would have even hallucinated about taking a general safari in the relatively "civilized" Republic of South Africa, long under the plough or grazed by domestic herds. Today, not many countries produce more foreign exchange than South Africa directly through what is locally known as game farming. Clearly, South Africa could have used a public relations firm when developing the label "game farm," which gives an impression of closely fenced pastures stocked with game that is bought and sold much as at an American "game farm," which rocks pheasant to sleep and releases quail for dog trainers to work their bird dogs. It's just not so.

The size of some South African "ranches" would make Texans blush with envy, but the point is that the only real difference in this type of hunting is that the ground is privately owned as opposed to the "block" or "concession" system used in other countries where safari firms lease hunting rights to companies over one interval or another. Not all, but much of South African hunting is as wild as you find elsewhere. There are differences, many highly favorable to a visiting hunter's purse, and there's a difference in flavor no matter where one hunts. The interesting thing is that untold hundreds of thousands of hectares and *morgen* that even a few years ago were scrub grazing for a mix of game and cattle have now been entirely allocated to game. Why? Economics, as always. Game pays its own way, eats nearly anything, is more resistant to disease and predators and generally produces a higher and better use for the land. In times of extreme drought, even game needs a hand, as it does now while I write in the African winter of 1983. Still, it doesn't have to be caught, innoculated, dipped for ticks or branded. Even the old enemies become assets to the farmer who switches from cattle to game. One friend of mine used to lose as many as thirty calves a season to leopards not so far north of the city where I live. Now, those same leopards are worth a cool $1,000 to $1,500 each to sport hunters, not a bad trade-off for animals that caused an annual liability of well over ten grand and had to be poisoned! Tell me, is that bad for leopards?

Lions were and are shot and poisoned as vermin legally in cattle country near the Kruger National Park. Now, in hunting areas, they're worth a couple of thousand bucks each. They sure aren't indiscriminately killed any longer by farmers or control hunters on lands reserved for safari. Is that bad news for lions? It was a problem when it involved $900 steers. But what game farmer would deny a pride of lions a few wildebeest at a couple of hundred dollars each, considering the fees the lions will bring just to be hunted, collected or not?

This sort of thinking is, then, the basis of the modern mechanics of the safari industry in Africa, whether in South Africa or Sudan. Once again, the elemental economic rules apply, whether to the garment district of New York City or to the wait-a-bit thorn of the Luangwa Valley or the Okavango Swamp: what can justify its existence stays, what can't must go, whether a skirt-manufacturing plant or a herd of impala. Sorry, I didn't make the rules. . . .

TWO

Selecting a Safari

Safaris are rather like snowflakes and women. No two are quite alike. Even the most elaborate and inclusive modern safaris vary widely one to the next depending on several ponderables that any potential client would have to consider before being able to choose between them. From the African side, influencing factors would include location, game density, desired specialized species and similar factors. From the client's viewpoint, time and money also loom largely. Any of these categories could be fragmented to smithereens, so for the moment, let's just look at the options of the varieties of safaris themselves.

Essentially, safaris are conducted on three classifications of land: concessions, private hunting areas and, rarely today, under the "block" system. By far the most popular are the first two as the last, the block system, has been largely phased out since the closing of Kenya and Uganda, although it does still exist in some areas of Tanzania.

The concession system works on the concept of a commercial hunting safari lease to either an individual or a safari-operating firm granted by the government of whatever country the hunting area is located in. The concessionaire, in return for a stiff financial term of lease, is also given a quota of game animals determined by the game department based upon the latest methods of game demography by which he computes his safaris' limits for the season. In addition to a responsibility to prevent poaching in the concession, maintain roads and tracks and generally preserve the natural aspect of the land, the concessionaire acts as a branch—in most cases—of the game department and with the same responsibilities. The man or company who has a hunting concession is essentially the meat in the sandwich between the client and the government. The fees he generates through licenses go to the government, the tariff he charges to clients is his gross profit.

This approach is particularly common to Zambia, Botswana, Zimbabwe and some areas of South Africa. Personally, I think it works very well and is far better than the old block system, as seen in Kenya and Uganda.

The block system was rather close to the modern idea of "time sharing" in holiday resorts, although on a one-time basis, if such a thing is consistent. There's no point in investigating closely as it's largely extinct. On a thumbnail, it used to be a short-term lease arranged between the safari company and the game department for a suitable area of predesignated safari land for hunting on behalf of the client before his arrival. The problem sometimes was that although these were large areas, the rather continual presence of different safari companies booking the better spots may have resulted in undue pressure. A fee was naturally charged for the booking of the block, just as a concession fee is charged by most governments for the use of a leased concession, above and beyond the rent paid by the concessionaire. You'll hear plenty about this later.

Private land hunting is a relatively new story, which we'll discuss in just a few minutes as it deserves a perspective all its own. For the moment, though, let's just observe that there are a wide variety of safaris available, from the classic sixty-to-ninety-day hunt to less than a week for specialized species. Varieties are as wide as your time and wallet can take.

I heard an interesting philosophy just last week from a young physician from Louisiana when my wife and I had dinner with him on his way through Johannesburg to take an assortment of what turned out to be exceptional plains game in South-West Africa/Namibia with Charlie Ward. My pal must almost be more the rule than the exception. His logic is that he wishes to take a long, hopefully lifetime, series of shorter trips on safari to accumulate his trophy collection, rather than gorge himself on one trip. Today, this is far more practical than it used to be when, in East Africa for example, a full thirty-five days' booking was required for one to even qualify for a rhino license. Now, things have opened up somewhat in different areas and a busy professional person or businessman can take a week or two and, granted some financial penalties, still be able to book a reasonable hunt for lion, leopard, buffalo, elephant in some places, and for white rhino in even fewer locations. Of course, there's nothing wrong with a week's investment in a sable, kudu, gemsbuck or any of the more impressive and challenging antelopes.

Like many modern men and women who can afford a safari, the problem is as much time as anything else. Not many professionals in any field but mine (everybody knows writers don't really work) can take off for a good, solid three months out in "the blue," particularly doctors, lawyers, accountants or the rest of the small percentage who represent ten percent of the population but pay ninety percent of the taxes. So, even though there's still a roaring bushfire business in extended trips, the drift clearly seems to be toward the shorter, more specialized safari of ten days to a couple of weeks instead of a few months, taking fewer species but with greater care for trophy quality.

A few years back, this sort of adventure was mostly represented by the client squirming through the rain forests of central Africa for a glimpse of a bongo, or perhaps the dry-tongued chance of taking a small representation of the sparsely distributed desert game or Lord Derby eland. Maybe wearing his feet off to the knees looking for an elephant with abnormal bicuspids would be his idea of a good time. Now, half the foreign visitors hunting in places such as South-West Africa/Namibia, which also has a large variety of more common game, are there merely for a good kudu or gemsbuck, the super southern brand of oryx, after they have taken representative bulls elsewhere but yearn for something exceptional.

I think that this is a very good approach to safari today, particularly considering modern circumstances. Just as John D. MacDonald's fictional hero, Travis McGee, takes his retirement in chunks as he can afford it, it's a practical and enjoyable tactic that will show a hunter a lot more of Africa than a single big trip and always leaves a little something to be savored for the future. Of course, if means are no problem, few prospects could be more mouth-watering than a series of extended trips, but not many people of my acquaintance have the time or the tax status for such a life.

Many of the shorter safaris are increasingly taking place in the form of what are called "ranch hunts," on private land, especially in former cattle country such as Zimbabwe, South Africa and South-West Africa/Namibia. In central-southern Africa, "cattle country" is not exactly what your mind's eye glimmers up for Iowa. Most of the land is anything from thick bush to light scrub and *vlei* (pronounced in the host tongue, Afrikaans, "flay"), the latter being dried-up marshes that will happily engulf a battalion of Tiger tanks without so much as a polite belch the moment it rains.

Depending on where you are hunting, the game in these private areas either belongs to the landowner, which may save you one walloping lump of loot against some countries' official fees in licenses and other financial folderol, or is on quota from the government, under an arrangement much like the concession system. Of course, some landowners have unusual ideas about the value of game. Yesterday, in a local publication here in South Africa, I saw an advertisement by a game farmer who happened to have a half-dozen Cape buffalo on his property near the Kruger National Park, in northeastern South Africa. I don't know if it was a misprint, but his asking price was 6,000 rands, about $5,500 each! Lord, you could get a valid unicorn license for that! Yet, as we'll see, determining and getting value for a safari has a lot to do with comparisons.

Another increasingly common and common-sense decision of many African countries has been to permit hunters to cull excess game from parks and reserves rather than have it done at far greater cost by park and reserve staff. To my admitted astonishment, three of the very slick conservation magazines that crossed the battlefield I call my desk last week had full-color pictures of grinning hunters and definitely defunct game animals bearing the captions that the game had been taken to the great profit of the rest of the animals sharing the reserves with them. Who knows, maybe we're making a little progress after all!

These were the last places I would have expected to have seen hunters with dead animals!

One of the big differences with most ranch hunts, though, is that you won't have to worry overly about some wandering WaNderobo elephant poacher placing your pancreas *en brochette* with something colorful like a poisoned arrow. If you believe, as I have learned to, that everything in life is a trade-off against something else, then you'll take to ranch hunting like a soft-shelled clam to sewage. I suppose it goes back to the state of mind of hunting, which tends to transcend such things as location, the complete mental focus being on the hunt itself. I never had more fun than when I was eight years old, stalking king cobras and Komodo dragons down by the local frog pond in New Jersey, totin' (one never "carried" or "packed," one "toted") my Red Ryder BB carbine with genuine rawhide saddle loop affixed to the right flank of the receiver, the entire odious outfit, if I recall, endorsed by Li'l Beaver and insinuatingly franked by Dell Wholesome Comics. Of course, having to collect one's record-book bull elk on the dividing island down the middle of the Garden State Parkway would be pushing my sensitivities a bit far.

It was in the former Rhodesia, now Zimbabwe, that I ran into the essential difference in the mental attitude of outfitters and safari firms when I first went there to hunt professionally in 1975. A completely different philosophy ruled the ranch owners or concessionaires than was the case with operations farther north. The northerners realized that most of their clients were not out on safari to live in a ranch house. They wanted as much stick-between-your-teeth Africa as they could get. Staying in somebody's house while not hunting, listening constantly to the code rings of a forty-party phone line while the *wheeze-thunk* of a power generator raised knots on their skulls wasn't their idea of getting as close to Karamojo Bell as they could afford. Nor is it mine. But it is understandable how these misinterpretations come about.

Let's presume that you have spent your whole life in the bush. That any client would want to pay a lot of good money to come and live on a scale much lower than that which you've worked twenty or more years to build up to, with stereo, sometimes television, a hammering generator and a whanging pump flushing water into rushing, gurgling holding tanks, may seem idiocy and apparently often does to proprietors of ranch hunts. The point is that the concept of safari, camping out and all the attendant living experiences, makes little sense to a rancher who has spent his life trying to make his home into a good copy of the lobby of the Hotel Pierre rather than the grass-hutted local village.

When I started off in Rhodesia, I tried to get this idea across to the gentleman with whom I was working. He agreed that I could go ahead and build a "grass camp" on the Dumba River, similar to those used in the Luangwa of Zambia, ten miles away from the electronic pleasures of headquarters. Well, you could pull a lever and flush the Dumba for the size of it but it was still a gorgeous place, the spot chosen being under an *Ngamo* fig that wouldn't have fitted into Yankee Stadium. It swarmed with green pigeons (which are apparently cleaner than that species that hangs around statues in public squares, or maybe I just didn't notice) and was alive with bushbabies and assorted fauna at night as well as by day. Just across the small stream was a wide *vlei*, yellow as corn with twelve-foot grass stems as thick as your thumb, tufts as high, windy and white as a spearman's plume. In the mornings, reedbuck tiptoed and simpered near the edges while impala drifted ghostlike through the shadows of the late afternoon; the buffalo, lion and the lone sable bull haunted it at night. There was usually the eerie, ethereal, broken-flint keening of jackals, which always seemed to be learning to call, and the tortured bedlam of the hyenas, especially if the lions had been lucky.

The huts were spacious, their sides neatly nipped and their roofs as shaggy smooth as a lion's flanks, supported by new *mopane* poles sunk well into the black bottomland and wired together at their junctures by a grinning, sweating Gladstone who twisted the thick, soft iron cords with the broken head of a pick until they bit and sank squeaking into the dry, dark bark and pink-lined white wood. The floors were the traditional mixture of mixed cow or buffalo dung and mud, which smells as sweet as a new-mown field when dried hard, smooth and as solid as terazzo.

There was a *chimbuzi* too, a snail-spiral of matching grass baffles, and a real toilet seat bolted (rather precariously, I always thought) to the chiseled-out top of a fifty-five-gallon drum, the deep hole for the long drop—as such facilities are un-blushingly called in safari camps—dug out with a sliced orange juice can lashed to the end of a twenty-foot stick and operated by Elias, whose personality suited the excavation perfectly.

The shower was a masterpiece. It had a ten-gallon tin that had once, certainly before UN sanctions in Rhodesia, contained olive oil, to which a nozzle and connecting pipe had been welded or, more likely, affixed with Pratley's Putty, the ubiqui-tous adhesive cement that kept that country going for years when nothing else was available. I know that whoever Pratley was, he should have gotten the Grand Cross of Valour, at least in the opinion of most ex-Rhodesians. The highlight of the shower, particularly since it was my idea, was the giant bamboo stall and floor under the toggle valve, which had once seen duty as the business end of a bull watering can. Though bamboo is not a native grass—bamboo *is* grass—there was nonetheless a magnificent stand, possibly transplanted from the Congo, some five miles away at the crumbling site of the house of an early homesteader. Lashed with the smooth white inner fiber of the *umkukubuyu* tree, the dark green of the bamboo made the stall look like a neat type of gazebo. A nearby heating point ran a constant low fire, giving mixed warm water whenever it was needed.

The kitchen was centered around an old antheap that we cut off and used to support the wood stove, much like one I had had in Zambia previously. Although it had long lost its asbestos insulation to lovelorn mice and rats, it nonetheless proudly pro-claimed in bas-relief: Welcome Dover 1902. I'd far rather have that one than a gift of the newest microwave.

To quote the late General George S. Patton, commenting on his proposed design for a new tanker's uniform featuring for-est green trousers, red piping and a gold football helmet, "Son of a bitch, but it was beautiful. . . ." It was, too, but the camp on the Dumba was never used. The outfitter just couldn't be-lieve that anybody would want to listen to bushbabies and hyenas, pad around on cowdung floors and miss the evening news, the client given an option. Well, he was the boss, the con-cessionaire. Thus passed my only potential contribution to the betterment of the southern safari mystique. Dumba Camp was burned to the ground, as I understand, shortly after I left the country. Too much of a potential attraction to traveling terrorists without reservations elsewhere.

The point of the last exercise was to advise that you should make yourself completely aware of exactly what type of accommodation you're likely to encounter, depending on whose firm you decide to book with. Hell, there's nothing wrong with the vast majority of client accommodation on ranch safaris, many are a pure delight with nearly every possible amenity you might have found in East Africa in the old days. Just make sure there's no misunderstanding before you book.

Exactly what duration or length of safari you should choose can only be determined by you yourself. If you're an avid hunter but will probably be able to save up for only one such jaunt, I would try to make the hunt as long and inclusive as possible. After all, the airfare of repeat short hunts is a bit rough. I have not in recent years heard of anybody booking for sixty or ninety days, but I suppose it does happen. In most places you'd be out of business well before halftime because of license limitations unless you were to shift countries. The average major safari today is generally twenty-one days, and most safari firms normally quote this period for securing a good general selection of trophies. We have already spoken of the shorter trips and the growing trend toward them.

If price were no object, I think I would start off with a twenty-one-day trip to one of the classic areas. This would be plenty to give you a strong taste of the flavor. After taking a representative bag, you can always rebook the same area and hunter or push on to different countries or regions for a wider variety of game that you haven't gotten the first time around. This period of time will be sufficient to determine whether you wish to return at all, but if you're as entranced as most hunters are with Africa you will still have had good exposure. It will also give you a reliable basis for planning your next trip.

One of the fastest growing areas of specialized safari—which I specifically discuss later in this book—is that of bird shooting and/or fishing, both of which are so fine in Africa generally as to practically ruin a Beaverkill fly-fisherman or plantation-owning Georgian. Since bird shooting is the more popular, let's wade into that first.

Virtually anywhere that there is big game hunting, there is bird hunting too, but the reverse is not necessarily so, and that leaves the glaring obviousness that there's one stack of a lot more bird shooting than big game hunting. Until perhaps twenty years back, there weren't a couple of dozen people a year who traveled all the way to Africa just to hunt waterfowl or other gamebirds, but it's certainly not the case now. Bird shooting was always one of the nice frills on safari but normally took place either after a client had collected his major species or far away from normal hunting areas because of the noise factor of disturbing big game. That it was so good and under nonexistent gunning pressure in most areas stuck in many hunters' minds, and I know a fair busfull who made their second and all subsequent safaris only for feathered game.

Since, as we have probed pretty thoroughly, all safaris are a matter of economic logic and financial reality, it's understandable that a concession holder doesn't put his main emphasis on shooting birds when he has a finite season and a limited number of clients he can accommodate at top rates on land that costs him a great deal of outlay to provide his ultimate income. This is the same reason that you'll almost never, ever see a strictly photographic safari in a hunting area; the income generated just doesn't justify the outlay in staff, equipment and time. So it is with birds or fish—unless an outfitter is a specialist, or has come to realize that, by acquiring bird shooting or fishing rights in lands within reach of his operations, he is adding financial icing to his cake. After all, what fisherman will concentrate on trout when he's paid the equivalent of a down payment on the World Trade Center for a week's beat of classic salmon river? It's sort of the same if you're comparing elephants and guinea fowl: they're both fine game, both African, but the monetary considerations give them a very different priority.

I don't want to get into particulars of bird shooting overly at this point when we will cover it in a "What-Every-Young-Girl-Should-Know" form later. Much the same with fishing. It's just that since we're delineating the different essential options of safari, you ought to be aware of the possibility of a feathered safari, usually combined with sightseeing, perhaps fishing, certainly game watching and such. It's not a bad idea, either, to get an easy whiff of the real Africa. You can always come back.

The main differences between the overall structures of hunting and photographic safaris are as follows: the former are conducted on lands reserved for hunting, whereas photographic trips are nearly always limited to parks and reserves—usually parks, as reserves generally have no tourist facilities.

I suppose most African hunters are asked, when they espouse the concept that killing is merely the logical terminus to the hunt and not the direct object, why they don't hang up their guns and take up photography instead. And a logical query it is, too, if you don't know a great deal about both.

In the case of photography of wildlife in Africa, especially that of dangerous big game, there is a gaping, yawning, echoingly vast difference between leaning out of the roof hatch of a parks board Land Rover and snapping a picture of a Cape buffalo or a bored lion surrounded by a ring of radio-advised Land Rovers in some sanctuary or other, and tracking either species up in the dense hunting cover of a concession for a rifle shot.

Unless a person is a practicing black-belt idiot, the circumstances of camera "shooting" are less hazardous than those of rifle hunting if for no other reason than that very close confrontation with dangerous game that might damned-well charge is generally not part of the script. Also, the most common denominator of disaster is nearly eliminated: game is not confronted while wounded, unless by accident.

Somebody once wrote that hunting big game with a camera was similar to kissing your sister. Maybe not quite; let's make it a rather voluptuous cousin. It's great, but it deserves its own label.

I wasn't long in Africa before I learned that there is just no way a person can hunt big game and take photographs at the same time, certainly not action pictures at least, which probably further points up that these are allied but different arts. Most photographers would go mad with frustration in a hunting concession trying to take the usual ho-hum shots of grazing impala that swell the film magazines of most tourists' Brownies and Instamatics in parks where the game is used to playing Bambi before hordes of vehicles. Don't forget, what you're paying for on safari is to get *away* from the game park traffic jams (they're more common than you might think!), so you can't expect the game to react as it does after, in many cases, generations of being completely protected and sheltered by man. It may well be African, and any hunting client ought to arrange for a day or two in a major game park or reserve for the experience itself, but the first forty-eight hours of actual hunting under really natural conditions will point up the differences in spades.

These, then, with the exception of scientific expeditions, those organized for groups with particular interests, and other special-purpose trips, are your options: the three-to-six-week big trip, the slice of retirement trip, the bird or fishing safari, or maybe a combination of the last two. Each is a grand experience for its own sake.

THREE

Man in the Middle

Could it be you've gone and done it? Made the decision? Deep down in that brooding, savage heart of yours you probably always knew you would, even though you haven't quite found the precise diplomatic instant yet to have advised your wife that an investment in your very soul, your psyche yearning to be free and—don't forget this—your *common* happiness, is far better served by a deposit on an African safari than on such transitory things as a new car, an addition to the house, a face-lift or some sinful jaunt to Paris. After all, little Brunhilda's teeth aren't all *that* snaggled, and Krugerrands don't look like such a good buy anyway. Look at it this way, with all the wonderful, exotic and exciting African shoulder mounts you'll be bringing back, you won't have to redecorate the house after all! Isn't that great! Not only that, those special rifles you buy now will be worth a fortune in a few years. Just think of inflation! By golly, you should have thought of it earlier. . . .

It's absolutely heart-warming to see that your lady embraces the idea with the same unshammed enthusiasm as you do. You know her sneakers are good for at least another winter and, anyway, she has a coat and some matches. Those spontaneous comments about scrubbing floors and selling her gold tooth are touching but unnecessary. Point is, what's the next step?

Booking a safari isn't all that unlike contracting for a wedding. You supply the money and the main participants and somebody else will be delighted to do most of the work of putting the whole show together. The consequences of a bum safari are a little less far-reaching, but about as much care needs to be exercised with the undertaking.

The guy you're looking for is the safari agent. He's actually a specialized travel agent who performs as a broker between outfitter and client. He's the specialist for the hunter who doesn't know where, when or whom to contact in Africa, and he will perform the same services for the sportsman as a general travel agent would for anybody booking for a European or Far East tour. The difference is that he knows the pitfalls and solid ground of the shifting technical terrain of safari.

I have heard some hunters speak in less than kindly fashion of their agents, but such performances are quite rare. Of course, anybody can get the name of a safari company out of the back of a magazine, write them, book a trip and live happily ever after with all his *Rowland Ward's* record-book trophies. Many hunters do. Having been an agent, an outfitter and a professional hunter, I flatter myself that I may comment without bias on the strengths and weaknesses of doing business directly or through an agent. For the first time, unblooded bwana, the advantages of using an agent far outweigh the drawbacks.

The first thing, though, will be to *find* an agent. Most lurk quietly in the "Where to Go" sections of the outdoors magazines such as *Petersen's Hunting, Field and Stream, Outdoor Life, Sports Afield* and other hunter's magazines of the same persuasion. Possibly a better representation might be rooted out of such highly focused periodicals as those of *Game COIN* (Game Conservation International), *Safari Club International* and like publications of groups purely interested in this type of hunting. In any of these, however, you'll find ads for various parts of Africa, usually placed by safari firms' representatives in the United States and elsewhere. Pick a few and either write or call them, asking for literature and giving as much detail as possible concerning your requirements. If you're completely unfamiliar with what you want, for heaven's sake tell them and say that you're considering a first safari for a general bag and what do they recommend? The more dope they have to go on in terms of your ideas, the better they can serve you.

After a few days, an exciting series of fat folders will arrive, and you can begin the process that encompasses the essence of safari: daydreams that are anticipation now and that will be memories later. The accumulation of safari literature is important because it is timely. You and I both know that nothing written in this book in terms of absolutes concerning licenses, per-hunter prices, flight connections or any other static items will necessarily be valid even by the time this goes to press, given inflation, currency fluctuations and politics, let alone a dozen other factors. But that's not important, as every year that passes will be updated in the brochures to reflect actual changes in charges and other variables in that season's tariffs and new license schedules. The way that elephants, for current examples, are coming off and are being placed back on general licenses would make you wonder, in similar fashion, whether the country you decide to hunt next year will have the same name as it did at the time you booked. Recent historical precedent suggests that it's dicey that it will. Perhaps there's a secret deal with the geographers and atlas publishers to ensure that no matter what edition you buy, it will always be slightly out of date.

Before we get stuck into the nuts and bolts of comparison booking to enable you to choose one area or country over another and one safari firm over another, let's stick to the agent and the reasons for using him.

Just to make things pristine, I am no longer an agent, nor do I have any connection whatever with any safari firm in any part of Africa, or anywhere else, for that matter. So it seems to me that when you can buy the genuine, unbiased opinion of anybody for the paltry price of this book, you're way ahead. Granted, what you are getting are my opinions, but they weren't drawn out of a hat.

An agency receives, or in fact, holds back its commission for the services it provides from deposits and monies paid in by the client, crediting the outfitter or safari firm with the difference. This amount may vary, depending on the usual laws of supply and demand. A new hunting company may have to give a higher percentage to be represented by a top booking firm, while the opposite is true with a safari group that can pretty well pack the aisles on its own. Figures for commission run roughly between 7½ and 15 percent on the daily fee and exclude costs for licenses and extras, with stops in between. You will notice that some, if not many, brochures are printed in cooperation with a major airline, normally an international carrier, which gives the booking agent a slightly better percentage on the commission of the sale of the airline ticket through an involved formula that, in effect, packages the ground portion—your safari—with the air fare. The clue is a code beginning with IT, followed by five numbers and letters. This also means that virtually any travel agent may sell the trip, although they know as much about safari as I do about gemology. Don't worry about it. You will not be thrown into a group tour. It's simply an internal travel agency method of getting better distribution as "tour operators" and thus a better couple of percentage points on the air ticket commission. This should be no concern of yours anyway as you are not eligible for a commission discount on your ticket unless you are an accredited agency. The airline and the agency, by the way, tend to cooperate to one degree or another on the production costs of the brochure.

Okay, the agent makes his money on a percentage from the safari firm and a percentage on the air ticket. Thus, he works for you free, because if you don't go, he gets no commission from the other side of the deal. Of course, he encourages you to go, but rarely in any way other than by helping you solve the many problems requiring exotic answers, which he normally has in his bag of tricks. The one thing he doesn't need is dissatisfied clients, and he usually works hard enough to make this very clear.

One of the pluses of the agent is that, if you live in America, he is near enough to contact. If you're like me and want anything that you covet and can afford delivered yesterday, this skims a bit of anxiety in awaiting air mail from Africa, which can take weeks even if your answer is processed immediately. Don't expect the agency's switchboard operator to have taken a Botswana sitatunga (aquatic antelope), but you'll find in most cases the only way agents get to be agents is to have been on safari in the areas they represent and to have learned the nickel-knowledge answers to clients' questions through personal exposure. For the most part, they know some if not all of the professional hunters personally, have spoken at great length to returning clients whom they have booked regarding potential or real problems, and are themselves hunters or they wouldn't be in such a crazy business.

Besides their services being free, with smaller representations they frequently can advise immediately of vacancies or openings in this or next year's schedule; failing that, they can have a cable answer within hours or a day.

The agent who is well established can—with huge importance to the potential client—give the names and addresses or phone numbers of previous clients willing to be quizzed on their impressions of their trips. Most clients who have been pleased with their safaris are happy to do this for no other reason than that they just love to talk hunting.

Possibly nothing is so singularly important in booking a trip as to check references. Insist on whatever number (be reasonable!) of references you feel is fair, and contact each one to your satisfaction. Most outfitters who run a clean ship are delighted to give these names, permission to use them having been obtained, because nothing sells a safari better than an enthusiastic former client. You'll also pick up opinions and bits of diamond information from them that somebody always forgets to stick into a brochure, especially if you and the reference are countrymen and tend to see things roughly through the same glass.

A rather more sinister aspect of using an agent is that, if you happen to have problems with your safari company, no matter who is right or wrong, there's a lot of very wet real estate between you and Africa, and complaints or even litigation are very difficult to implement when jurisdictions and distances are so great. Far better, if a trophy shipment has been mis-shipped, to work through the original agent than to attempt pressure on the safari company out in "the blue." This sort of thing is very uncommon, but misunderstandings and outright dishonesties do happen. And it's far better to have somebody in your home country to whom you can complain or with whom you can negotiate or arbitrate. Don't forget, from the agent's point of view, he represents *both* you and the safari firm, no matter what the technicalities of the law. His bread is buttered on both sides.

I very well remember an instance in which, as a New York agent, president of Sportsmen International, Incorporated, I had a complaint back in the 1960s about a tiger shikar a client had taken. To be frank, the gentleman had certainly not received the services to which he was entitled and had contracted for. Understandably, he was upset. Although it gave my finances a double hernia, I completely refunded his money, several thousand dollars, to keep the integrity of my firm despite the fact that I was not reimbursed from the shikar firm. This was an extreme case as, even though the man did get his tiger, he did it without a cent's cost. Still, from my viewpoint as an agent, realizing that he had been given a bit of the shaft on the Indian side, I felt the good name of my firm as being reliable was worth the money to maintain.

As an aside, there was a famous case of a man who went tiger hunting with a well-known brand of rifle in caliber .375 H&H, also in the 1960s. One wonders if this wasn't a "con," but the claim and the resulting lawsuit stated that when the time came for the hunter to fire at the tiger, the rifle either wouldn't fire or misfired. Upon his arrival home, he sued the arms company for the cost of his trip and, if I recall correctly, his own time also. Rather than incur the negative publicity that the suit would have generated, the arms firm settled out of court.

This was, at least in my opinion, ridiculous, as the plaintiff claimed that he had never fired the rifle before the moment when the tiger appeared.

Who, with the slightest knowledge of firearms, would attempt to shoot a tiger with a rifle he had never fired? It had, according to the plaintiff, never been zeroed with either iron or telescopic sights. One wonders if the preservative was even out of the bore! Well, the man won the case by default, probably on the advice of the gun manufacturer's legal staff or perhaps their public relations department.

Let's not be naïve: your booking agent wants to sell you a safari. And this can be an advantage to you if you think about it. If you deal directly with an outfitter or a safari company, you will only have a choice of their product. Not so with the agent. He gets paid no matter which firm he books you with, maybe a bit more or less, but he still makes his cut. He also is most interested in your having a whale of a time, based upon his recommendations, so you will come back to him again and book your next trip. Although most reputable safari firms run better than a fifty-percent repeat client factor because of the relationships built by weeks in the field between professional hunters and clients and the resultant loyalties, many safari companies prefer the client to keep working with the agent because of the "detail" problems it saves them from a distance. Remember, they're as far from you as the other way around and it's usually worth the commission from both viewpoints.

Obviously, because he's usually been there, the agent is familiar with the best way to get to the various hunting areas and the best airline connections or hotel stopovers. I had a personal experience some years ago, when I first changed over as a professional hunter from Zambia to Botswana, which brought this home to me. Getting a cable requiring me to arrive in a very short time to meet incoming clients, I asked a simple garden-variety travel agent to book my airline passage. This they did, on a round-trip basis from New York to Johannesburg to the little Batawana village in the Okavango Swamp of Botswana called Maun, the main safari terminal for the rest of the country. Unfortunately, because one ticket clerk or another knew no better, I was given an "open" return, single coupon ticket to New York, and—my own fault as I didn't closely check the tickets, nor did anybody on the senior side of the agency—found myself obliged to purchase for cash a full-fare, highest rate nonexcursion ticket to get home after the season, which just about depleted my earnings for the previous several months. Refunds, lest you happen to otherwise find out the hard way, are normally obtainable only from the agent where you bought your ticket in the first place, and you'll need a separate coupon for each segment. Point is, if you're going to Africa, go through somebody who has a remote idea where it is and how its airlines run.

There are several categories of agents that you should be aware of. The largest, and you'll generally know them from the fact that they can afford larger ads, are full-service travel agents of which the safari branch may or may not be a specialized arm. These are normally members of IATA, the International Air Transport Association, sometimes of ASTA, the American Society of Travel Agents, and of more numerous self-policing local associations. In many cases, these act as general agents for various safari firms, handling all their bookings, say, in North America, and keeping reservation books for the hunting outfits.

Other African safari firms are represented by a wide number of agents, mostly smaller ones in smaller places. Others are "library" or "recreation room" operations that keep no airline ticket stock but are run and staffed by hunters who are semi-retired, are of some means and wish not only to do some hunting every year but to deduct the costs thereof from their income taxes. Oh yes, it can be done and with complete honesty, too. The IRS doesn't say you have to make a profit!

Some safari agents, mostly individuals, have deals in which they have the safari company merely credit their commissions on the company's books until they have earned enough to come back over and shoot off the credit balance! Works very nicely for some people, many of them outdoor writers, editors and such, who are frequently asked to set up safaris.

I don't mean to give the impression that if a booking agent works out of his cellar, he's not competent to do a good job for you. Nor is the obvious counterconclusion valid, that an agent with a swish address is better qualified. Thus, I expand my previous warning and recommend that you ask the agent to give a few satisfied customers' names and phone numbers, too. If he doesn't want to or can't, he's either brand new, in which case you must rely on your own judgment, or he has few if any satisfied customers. The laws of commerce haven't changed since early Roman times: *caveat emptor*.

Of course, there can be reasons to deal directly with your hunting firm, particularly when you've been with them before and are in a position through experience to say exactly what you want to hunt, with what professional, when, how and so on, based upon your earlier trip. But, hell, you don't need this book for that. I'm sure to say this will endear me to few outfitters or agents but there used to be a couple of safari firms that would rebate the agent's commission on a safari if you booked direct and asked for the rebate. But they weren't usually the sort of people you would have wanted to hunt with in any case. Pretend I never said that. You'll be better off.

FOUR

The Price of Paradise

Presuming that you have now received those enticing packets of literature from several sources, the decision as to which country to hunt in and which safari firm to book still looms. As you will have noticed, most items in brochures are pretty crisp, neat lists of license fees, starched schedules of services included and those not, liability disclaimers and such. Not the masterpieces of adventure writing that they might be. You'll also have an interesting time with those safari companies who quote fees in South African rands, Zimbabwe dollars, Botswana pulas and so on, for which you will have to perhaps consult the *Wall Street Journal* for exchange rates. Ah, well, that's part of the fun of it all. What else could you do in the line of great adventure that would require payment in pulas, for God's sake?

Perhaps the best place to start concerns the time you will have available, as this will directly influence where you end up going. There are no shortages of major considerations in choosing a location, but the one that immediately comes to mind is most concerned with the equator, which rudely divides the continent about in the middle. The seasons are, obviously, reversed from the Northern Hemisphere but don't forget that this is only in direct relation to how far one *is* from the equator. It took me a long time, being a New Jersey boy used to calculating my position while hunting by the sun, to rewire my brain to realize that although the sun still comes up in the east and sets in the west, it doesn't get there by the same route. It travels in a northern rather than a southern arc, which can get you lost in one hell of a hurry until you are used to it. For a North American or a European, southern Africa is really a mirror image. Most countries drive on the left, water taps are reversed, light switches are flipped down rather than up for "on," and even the basin drains in the opposite direction from whatever it is up north, according to some because of the Coriolis force of the earth's rotation. I never paid that much attention. Still, why they haven't gotten round to Christmas in June is quite beyond me. In any case, be advised that the seasons for hunting are quite different in northern and southern Africa.

The most prevalent influence on safari seasons, which are generally never closed as are American seasons, is rain. During the rainy season, hunting is largely impractical because of impassable rivers, mildewed camps, crocodiles in your soup and such. Hey, when it rains in Africa, you'd better lash down the tiller in most places. Happily, most rain in Africa can be counted on, at least in terms of time of year. Nearly every segment of the continent has a wet and a dry season so far as safari hunting is concerned. South of the equator, the dry season is roughly from May through October, some places being open for hunting from as early as March, despite the heavy vegetation, and a few others waiting until June. This would be typical of Zambia, Botswana, Zimbabwe, South-West Africa/Namibia, South Africa and, before they became "people's republics," Mozambique and Angola. Naturally, because of elevations and other climate-modifying factors, rainfall in these countries varies to some degree, but the May-through-October rule holds very solidly. The old safari grounds of East Africa had two rainy seasons. Although Uganda doesn't look as if it will settle down in the immediate future—North Koreans are training troops there as I write this—and Kenya is still *verboten* for hunting, it's still safe to mention that the Tanzanian season is July through December, but the local conditions will vary as much as the game in sections of the country. Tanzania has a dividing line between the distribution of "northern" and "southern" species, the northern area holding game typical of Kenya and the southern half those more akin to Zambia and other Zambezi countries.

In the north, the present area of activity is largely Sudan, the biggest country in Africa, which operates from December 1 through May 31.

These climatic comments are purposely general, as exact details of seasons will be provided by outfitters or agents. For example, in Ethiopia, because of altitude and other variances, you'll run across such wide differences as these: in the Omo Valley of the southwest, the season runs from October 10 through March 1. In the Harar, Afdem and Gawane regions of the east, the season is October through June 5; in western Ethiopia, February to June 20 and, down where I used to hunt in Borana, just across from Kenya's Northern Frontier District (NFD), it's August through April. See what I mean?

The point isn't to try to give mean temperatures and rainfall for every bush and rock, just a rule of thumb that can be relied upon under reasonably normal circumstances, whatever *they* are.

There is a further consideration in choosing an available date that really must be a matter of personal choice. In the concession and private areas of Zambia, Botswana, Zimbabwe, South Africa and South-West Africa/Namibia, for example, the question is always whether or not a hunter will generally do better at the beginning, in the middle or at the end of the season. And there are definite factors to consider.

In March, April or perhaps early May, the trade-off is between the fact that the game in the area hasn't been hunted since the past November and is far less skittish than it will be late in the season after quite a few safaris have been through, and the negative aspect that the vegetation in most places will be very thick, green and high, as the sun hasn't had a chance to dry it out since the rain quit. The big herds of buffalo won't have had a chance to trample it down yet either. Visibility is essentially lousy, even though the game is much less nervous.

Logically, at the end of the season, the opposite is the case, as you'll be able to see forever, even in *mopane* groves, but game will be much more alert. I suppose that, like most choices in life, one is as good as the other, but the really "cream" months tend to be May, June and July in most southern areas, as much because of the perfect weather as anything else. The early season will be colder, the later warmer, but don't think you can't start a prize-winning collection of first-issue chilblains in Botswana or Zimbabwe in July! I've seen it 12° F. in the Kalahari in that month, and frost is common every night in Maun in the Okavango.

Just for the record, the Central African Republic has had some excellent hunting over the past years and is still open for business. The Aouk and Manvovo River areas are hunted from January through the middle of May and the rain forest regions of the Ouarra and M'Bomou rivers from the middle of June to September 15. Zaire, formerly the Belgian Congo or portions thereof, also has some limited hunting, particularly in Kivu Province for jumbo, in July through August and again in December through January. Since this is quite a bit off the beaten track, it would be extremely wise when dealing with small local outfitters, through an agent or not, to most closely question previous clients so you don't run into any "surprises."

There are limited safari operations in a couple of West African countries but I do not recommend them for the first-time hunter looking for the classic safari experience. Later, fine. Sorry, tourist board.

So the rule of thumb, provided the earth doesn't shift its poles again, is roughly May through October for the south and, up north, December through May.

Right. Having figured out when you will be free, the next consideration seems to be determining the type of safari that would fit you best. Since we've already discussed the essential options in vague terms, let's get down to the hog jowls and black-eyed peas.

Beyond the fact that price will probably have something to do with your selection, the first item you will have to decide is whether or not you want a simple, representative bag of reasonable male animals or want to really concentrate on the chance of taking a whopper or two. Certainly, in the case of the "plains game," which is a safariism meaning antelope or gazelles generally and omitting the "Big Five" as well as other carnivores, you can have a safari that will decorate your trophy room beyond your wildest (excuse me) dreams for about half of what it will cost you to try to take the whole works. You may also go the other way and spend six cheerful weeks playing a local version of masochism involving the pursuit of a log-tusked elephant with vital statistics better than a hundred pounds a tooth, with the odds on finding him running roughly the same as your being elected Playmate of the Year.

I have had two clients return three times each with me to continue their pursuit of a hundred-pound jumbo. One finally did score but the other was not fated. Another came back twice for a record-class bushbuck, hardly a major species, and probably spent well over $50,000 before he finally caught up with one. Oddly, when I had other clients out, these weren't all that rare to find with a bit of work, but they seemed to evaporate like ectoplasm whenever we were out together. At last he took a very fine male, which was the big gap in his spiral-horned special trophy collection.

Seeing that the only things common to most safaris are the general convention of services included in your fees by the hunting company, not to be confused with government licences, taxes and extras, we might as well have a look at what you'll be getting for your daily fee or prorated total cost of accommodation.

Services, lest I overgeneralize, *do* vary between companies but follow a general rule. One outfit, operating in Zaire, includes even airfare from Brussels to Zaire in their fee (plus licences and ivory taxes), whereas others limit even mileage on their hunting vehicles, charging past a certain figure on the odometer. Each brochure must therefore be read carefully, particularly concerning extras such as local accommodation while off safari, charter flights and rifle rental. Some really great safaris have gone to vinegar on their conclusion because the client didn't read the full services and exclusions.

You can normally expect the following unless otherwise stipulated: a licensed professional hunter, a full staff of Africans including gunbearers, trained skinners, cooks, waiters or personal servants, trackers and casual labor to keep the camp in proper trim. You'll also get accommodation, whether a neat grass hut, a ranch house or a tent; toilet facilities (of one sort or another, usually quite acceptable); camping equipment, including beds, mattresses, mosquito nets, tent furniture, linen, all table utensils, usually a paraffin (kerosene) fridge or freezer or both, a medical kit and snakebite outfit; all normal food; trophy skinning and preparation while in the field and as many vehicles as necessary to properly accommodate the client and the rest of the safari on the trip, including trucks, if necessary. In a phrase, everything you will need to be comfortable and to keep the safari mobile except for items of personal requirement such as booze and other variables.

It's probably more important that you be clued up concerning what *not* to expect rather than what you will get for your fees, as this is where most unpleasantnesses arise, despite the fact that financial conditions are usually laid out clearly. Think of things this way; you're paying for the basic comforts of life and services necessary to expose you to the game from point of arrival at the jumping-off location and return to the same point. Beyond these items, which, considering the rawness of the bush, are from ample to luxurious, anything else is normally paid for with your approval by your safari company and put on your tab, which you are expected in good faith to settle before you leave, in the same manner a fine hotel would handle things for you.

For starters, you can rule out anything before or after the contracted dates to be included in your tariff. If you arrive at the starting point a day early, not a bad idea, don't expect the safari firm to pay your hotel bill or feed you. The same for the way back home. Most safari firms will designate a starting point for the trip, which will usually be the same place—not always— where you will settle up at the end of the trip. How you get here is for your own account, unless otherwise specified.

Government game or hunting licenses and concession fees are separate from your basic or daily charges, as is logical, although your safari company will nearly always obtain them for you and expect to be reimbursed before you go hunting. After all, there are interest rates even in the African bush. The cost of alcoholic beverages will usually be run on a "tab" for your account to be settled when you have finished your trip. More on this later.

Ah, like Texas, everything in Africa is a bit bigger than life. All booze is charged to you and it is highly customary to instruct your outfitters to request the professional hunter to lay in a stock—at your expense—of whatever he normally drinks. I have never heard of this being abused so don't worry that you will be taken advantage of. If you've read Ruark, you're probably familiar with the old comment used to designate a safari gone wrong or friction between hunter and client as one in which the professional "was still drinking the client's whiskey." Except for imminent confrontation at gunpoint, this would be the absolute last thing to break down, the thought of the professional hunter paying his own bar bill completely unthinkable.

The same convention applies to wines, beers, mixers, soda, Cokes, tobacco and really anything else of a personal nature, which the firm will be happy to supply you at a charge. Should you plan on hiring your rifles or shotgun from the safari firm, also expect to be charged a daily fee plus the cost of ammo. Most companies will cheerfully credit you with anything left over of ammo or liquor, probably some of which you will prefer to leave as a gift with your professional in any case, but this is up to you.

Should you decide, which I doubt you will, to ship your arms and ammo and personal effects over before your arrival, the costs for having the stuff cleared through local customs by an agent are your expenses also. You can usually arrange to have your hunting company take care of this and then pay your agent, which will be put on your bill.

Some of the most important costs you should appreciate before you even get past the point of paying your deposit are those of the dipping, crating, shipping, clearance and mounting of those field-prepared trophies you may collect, no matter what the year may be when you read this. The laws of all countries I know of require that trophies, before import, be dipped in a solution to kill any possible pests that might otherwise be transported. Obviously, this is not just a dunking, and appropriate documentation as to this process must be enclosed. The packing of your trophies to ensure that horns, tusks and delicate parts won't be damaged or box-worn is an art in itself and will be done on your instructions and at separate cost advising destination. The shipping expenses are also formidable, depending on what you choose to have mounted, and you mustn't forget that most consignments of trophies will have to be cleared through the customs of your home country either by you or by an agent, although many large taxidermy firms have this down to a fine art on behalf of their clients.

The best advice I can think of for someone going on safari is to obtain price lists for different mounts from a variety of taxidermy firms and, with an eye to where you might wish to display them, try to decide before the fact how you want your trophies field-prepared. It's too late to decide on a full body mount of an antelope if it has already been caped for a head and shoulder mount. Give some thought, if you're taking an elephant, as to just what you wish to use of the trophy. A wall hanging of an ear? Gloves from the same leather? How do you want the ivory displayed? From chains hanging from the wall? Teak or elephant leather bases flanking a doorway or fireplace? Do you want the tusks merely cleaned, leaving a lot of the natural discoloration of wear, or do you want them polished up like a giant set of new dentures? Do you want the tail just salted and dried to hang from the wall or do you want elephant hair bracelets knotted from it? This last item will almost certainly be done by your gunbearer. I'm the only white person I know of offhand who does them personally, but there are surely others.

The same applies to most everything. If you have the luck and skill to take a leopard or lion, how do you want them displayed to best advantage? Full-head rug mounts? Flat full-skins? What color felt backing, if any? Antelope, too; if a shoulder mount, which way should your sable face? Obviously, you don't want him staring into a blank wall or corner.

I'm not going to get into a discussion of such extras as mileage over the normal safari allowance, as some firms have no such stipulation while others do. If there happens to be some landmark you wish to visit that is out of the normal operation areas—or if you wish to spend a day or two in a national park or reserve, for instance—don't forget to ask if there will be any additional charge for the transportation or service.

Charges for aircraft charters should be fully understood before you contract for either the necessary flights or the safari itself. To take a typical situation such as Botswana, where most firms have hunting arrangements in both the Okavango Swamp area of northwest Ngamiland and also in the Kalahari, far to the south, it is common for the client or clients to take a company or air service charter from one area to the other while the professional hunter drives the safari crew and equipment by road. This is normally not included in the general tariff unless otherwise stated. There would usually be no additional charge if the client decided to motor along with the professional, but it's one hell of a drive and most are well advised to fly if they can afford it. The larger safari companies have their own air services, using light twin or single-engine aircraft much in the manner of the Alaskan bush pilots. In some locations, however, it may be necessary to contract with another carrier to make your connections. Just make sure you establish—in writing—how much the service will cost and what the precise arrangements are.

Gratuities and tips are a very difficult area when it comes to recommendations. In terms of the black staff, most firms have a policy of the division of a recommended amount of money among the personnel, which is normally divided by the professional on behalf of the client, based on the importance of each man's job and sometimes his seniority. The African personnel most deserving of tips are those who work the hardest and who must take the most skilled decisions toward their work, with direct benefit to the client. Here, we think in particular of the skinners, gunbearers, trackers, the cook and the personal servant or waiter. Those who are employed casually in situ by the professional to carry wood and water, dig latrines or pack the client's camera cases and personal *katundu*, rank not nearly so high in anybody's eyes as the permanent staff. In tipping, don't forget that you're not ransoming yourself into a corner table at a posh New York restaurant; rates are much lower, and you either spoil your hunter's staff or embarrass the next client in camp by overdoing it. Listen to your hunter's recommendations.

A personal aside: I believe it's a good practice to be present when, at safari's end, the personnel are tipped. It's an appreciated way of saying thanks for the grand job on the elephant-hair bracelets, or for the five hours tracking after your wounded kudu that finally got him. Most rural staff aren't quite sure what tips are, understanding them as some sort of payment they weren't expecting until they realize that you are just saying thanks. They also understand then that the money comes directly from you.

Another aspect of recommended tips to African staff is that you must understand the strict hierarchy or pecking order that tends to exist among them. The first gunbearer is generally the most senior, his assistants and/or trackers coming next. He often won't eat with the man under him, any more than the cook would deign to take a meal with the kitchen *toto*, the teenager who carries water and does much of the washing up. Democracy is not the way of things, at least not to the understanding of most American or European clients. Nor should it necessarily be according to our presumptions of what local values ought to be. You are now in their land, and their way of doing things will influence your existence more than seems immediately apparent. Africa runs on power, which is frequently a by-product of seniority, despite United Nations pronouncements to the contrary. Interestingly, the Amero-European concept of "one man, one vote," which has caused so much bloodshed in Africa over the past decades, is the farthest thing from political logic in the tradition of the African tribesman. The concept of a common villager making a political decision that has always traditionally been made by his hereditary headman seems insane to them. How, they reason, could a common man be expected to have the wisdom of decision required of a chief or headman? Well, this is not a political discourse but if you're going to live for weeks or a month with bush Africans, you might as well know the ground rules.

I've often wondered what I would write in a book of this sort if asked for advice about how or if to tip a professional hunter. We will explore the unique relationship between a professional and his client later on, but for the moment let's observe that after the length of a safari, living in each other's pockets, the atmosphere is usually that between trusted friends, not that between buyer and seller, hired hand and boss. To many hunters, the idea of tipping their professional is much like offering money to a good friend for a small favor you have asked of him. Still, nobody must lose sight of the fact that your professional is with you, if not entirely, at least essentially because of the fact that he must earn a living. Not much of a living, to be sure, but he must support his family, too.

There really isn't an answer or a formula as to how much you should tip your professional hunter, if you decide to give him a gratuity at all. I have received such amounts as $500 in cash (for two days in which I got two men a very good lion), fine rifles worth much more, $20 for a month and often nothing at all. Certainly, any client who figured as richly as ten percent of his ground accommodations would be lavish indeed.

As far as I can see, there are three ways to make your decision. The first would be to leave nothing at all. If you didn't like the bastard, this will probably be your decision. Next, you can make him a gift of cash. The amount should be based upon what you can afford, how hard you think he worked for you or any other factors you consider pertinent. How much? Well, the way inflation is going, I wouldn't like to make any specific suggestion, but no full-time bwana, after a good performance on a three-week trip, would be anything but deservedly grateful for as much as it costs to buy a reasonable bolt action Winchester, Remington or Ruger rifle back in the States. How much would you tip a headwaiter for a couple of hours' service? Remember, your professional works or is at your call twenty-four hours a day throughout the entire safari.

The third option would be to give your hunter a gift. In many cases, this would be one of the tools of the trade, usually a rifle or other decent piece of equipment. Normally the formalities of transferring ownership aren't too much trouble, depending on where one happens to be. I recommend against sending your hunter some gift later for the simple reason that he will have to clear it through customs when it arrives and undoubtedly have to pay duty on it. At the moment, merely as an example, the duty on an imported firearm for a South African resident is more than sixty-five percent of the invoiced value.

By the bye, I should mention that I would not have my Model 70 Winchester .375 H&H caliber rifle were it not for a technicality of this sort. Built as one of the very rare ones in 1943, it was taken on an Indian shikar by the father of my late good friend, Dean Witter, Jr., and presented to the professional hunter, or shikari, at the end of the trip. When the professional had the unmitigated gall to then send Mr. Witter, Sr., a bill for the customs duty, the old boy hit the proverbial roof and demanded the gun back. Dean, Jr., gave it to me shortly before his death in July 1976 and it has been my "working" rifle since.

Many clients are more than pleased to have their professionals back to the United States or Europe as their guests, sometimes in connection with hunting conservation meetings, and this can also be a pleasant way to say thank you for a job well done. Or better yet, a chance to flex an elbow or two and relive the trip over a few relaxing days on the client's turf for a change.

To determine the precise cost of a safari before the fact is rather like figuring out the length of a piece of string with only one end in sight. To some degree, each safari is unique in that each client will take different species, incur different expenses in transport or shipping or have more or less personal extra requirements in terms of food or liquor. This being the case, the only approach is to have a good look at those expenses that are likely to be incurred as a matter of course.

The overall costs of a safari are included in the following, taken in the order you'll likely encounter them:

1. Airfare
2. Daily or basic safari rate
3. License, trophy fees and special taxes such as on ivory
4. Change-of-area fees
5. Gratuities
6. Dipping, packing, shipping of trophies and equipment
7. Personal extras, including liquor, special foods, customs duties, arms rental, extra mileage, transit accommodation and anything of a private nature
8. Taxidermy

Before breaking these items down, please bear in mind that the amounts shown are for comparative purposes only, essentially to indicate that there are large differences in costs between one safari firm or country and another.

Airfare is an area where a good agent can really help you, being familiar with all the details of air travel to weird places where a hunter is likely to go. Having done something like fifty-five round trips to and from Africa to Europe and the United States, I'd like to offer a few ideas that might be of practical help.

Whatever your mode of transport, don't forget that the east coast of America and the west coast of Africa are still a reasonable distance apart, certainly enough to have you consider stopping off for a day or two either in London or Rio de Janeiro to rewind your body clock. Normally this can be done with no problem of extra airfare or expense beyond your interim accommodations. If you're carrying your guns, which is likely, simply leave them in customs bond until you return to the airport to leave.

An important thing to consider is whether or not the airline you book as your carrier counts its baggage allowance by the weight or the number of suitcases. There is still a variance, which could cost you a hefty penalty. In the old days, and still on some airlines, the rule was forty-four pounds per economy passenger (twenty kilograms) and sixty-six pounds per first-class traveler (thirty kilograms). Today, the rule is to allow the economy-class passenger, beyond his stipulated hand luggage, a total of two bags, no matter what the weight. From New York's Kennedy Airport to Johannesburg, I can assure you, is an overcharge of $75 U.S. dollars per extra piece, which seems reasonable to me, although details should be carefully checked as to policy before you actually fly. I can well recall clients stuck with up to $4000 in overweight through one doodad or another!

So, in the matter of airfare, check with your agent or an appropriate carrier that services the country where you will hunt, and work out the best deal for yourself.

The daily fee or basic cost of safari is one of the widest-ranging major items of expense you'll come across. It's the price, quoted either as a per diem in terms of how many clients and professional hunters are involved or as a lump sum for a specific safari length, which represents the rock-bottom cost of your trip. It will be spelled out in terms of what it includes and what it doesn't, as we've already discussed, and it is the platform from which the other financial obligations you will incur are structured.

The most important thing to look at, once you have determined that two, three or four reputable companies are offering more or less the same inclusive goods and services for their fees in relatively similar areas, is the basis of the client-hunter proportion to costs. Also some safari outfits will offer a discount for safaris contracted for very early or late in the season.

When it comes to saving money on your safari, this is the first place you should investigate, because, with the right firm, provided you're willing to spend some time along for the ride, you can whack a large chunk off your costs by forming a joint venture with a hunting pal and sharing many expenses, including that of your professional hunter. Here's how it works:

Since most safari costs that involve the outfitting firm are fairly fixed, they try to expand their profit by sort of splitting the difference with the client who is willing to share his hunt with a second person, or a third or fourth. By law, no professional hunter may take out more than two shooting clients under his auspices, but since camp meals are largely game and the cost of sticking up another tent is negligible, both you and the outfitter can benefit. Thus, you'll nearly always see prices, whether daily or lump, reduced *per person* when clients share a professional. As a practical example, let me cite the following rates:

In Botswana, for the 1984 season, you can save the difference between a one-PH (single professional hunter), single-client rate of $750 per day down to a per-client rate of $475 a day if two clients share the hunter. A net saving of $275 a day is $137.50 a person a day, which seems a fair compromise for hunting along with a pal. If you can get four clients to share two professionals, you'll only be tagged for $425 a person a day. So, the more the cheaper, and hopefully, the merrier.

Not all safari firms will reduce the tariff so dramatically as the previous quotation, which is from SafariSouth of Maun, Botswana, and you'd be foolish to share a hunt with another person to save but a couple of bucks a day. Better to book two pro hunters, one for each of you, and spend the small difference in enjoying the exclusive services of the professional hunter.

A lot of practical thought should be given to the idea of sharing safari costs with a friend. There are obvious financial advantages but drawbacks, too. Sharing hunters normally flip for first shot at a trophy, the next shot going to the loser and so on. As long as inclusion in the record books of soaring heads isn't a requirement and you know your partner, it should work out well. If, however, there is any jealousy likely to arise, better give the whole thing a long second thought. A professional can service two hunters for the most common game, but considering the time element in taking leopard, lion and elephant, it wouldn't be reasonable to expect a full double bag of the more difficult species from one professional on a shortish safari with two shooting clients. But then, you wouldn't have been paying for exclusive shooting either.

Before we get directly into licenses and other costs of this nature, this seems a good time to explain that there is a direct relationship between how long a safari period you contract for and what game you'll be permitted to hunt. In some countries, this can have a bearing on whether or not you share a professional hunter with another client. Botswana is a good example, and to quote the brochure of one firm there: "Lion, sable, leopard, sitatunga and eland are not available for hunts booked less than 21 days. When two clients hunt with one PH (professional hunter), only one sable, one lion and one sitatunga are allowed between the two."

Nearly every safari area in Africa has one or another variation on this theme, depending on the make-up of the local game population. In some places, this ratio of time booked to licenses permitted is declared by the government, in others it's merely common sense on the part of the concessionaire who doesn't want his rarer, low-quota animals collected by those clients who do the least for his bank account. The lower the numbers of a particular sporting species on the safari firm's quota, the higher the price and the longer the safari you will have to book to hunt them.

For all the good this policy does for game management, it still has some inherent drawbacks that once got a good pal of mine into a compromising and possibly downright dishonest situation when he was hunting for a large safari company in central Africa. As was the usual procedure, the season's safaris were booked based upon the two prime factors: the numbers of various animals on quota and the reasonable assessment of the ratio of success for each particular species. Since the problem was with lions, let's say that the trips booked were arrived at in this way: the concession was given a quota of thirty lions that year, the same as the season before. Since twenty-nine had been killed the year before by a total of fifty safari hunting clients with lion licenses, it was reasonable to presume that booking the same number this year would give just about the same roughly sixty-percent success ratio. Only it didn't. It was either a great year or a bad year, depending on your point of view. By September 10, the last lion on quota had been taken and only forty lion-licensed hunters had been involved. The safari firm had sold fifty licenses and booked another ten clients still to arrive to go lion hunting, with the shooting of any more *Simbas* pure jailbait for anybody involved, had they known it. My pal had nothing to do with decisions of this type and, frankly, he needed the job. Somebody in management elected not to advise the rapidly impending clients and to just try to ignore the whole thing.

In the field, this meant identifying huge pug marks, so fresh they practically steamed in the early morning, as "old," "female" or "I know this one—no mane at all." To spend days on end with a paying client who thought he was hunting lions while the pro was all the time praying not to run into one didn't do much for his self-esteem. The hunter resigned immediately after the safari but still didn't dare talk about the fraud for fear that the "old boy" system might get his professional hunter's ticket pulled, which it can be in some areas for no reason at all. Some chief game officers don't like folks who rock the boat.

The hunting company should, of course, as soon as it saw that the lions left on quota were evaporating, have advised the clients of the situation and given them the option of canceling, having their lion-license money refunded (it would have had to be covered by the firm; once it's bought from the government, that's it) or rectifying the dilemma in some other manner. Perhaps the financial risk was too great, perhaps it was just too late. Whatever, it could be called no less than fraud and my friend was an unwilling part of it. In any case, the devil must have been on duty as none of those hunters ever saw a lion, although they otherwise did extremely well, more than half of them rebooking for the next season. I hope they decided to go early. . . .

There's really no way to protect yourself against this sort of thing when booking a safari, but I dare say it was a rare incident. Most outfitters are as guileless as cherubs, of course, but it might not be a bad idea to ask for confirmation in writing that, where applicable, all species you have contracted to hunt will still be on quota and available during the period of your safari.

Because it pertains to this general minefield zone, here's

another caveat when running down lists of available species.
Look, in bringing up some of these matters, I'm not trying to
say that the safari firms are gilding lilies or making misrepresen-
tations in any way. They're giving hard facts. *But*, don't presume that because a particular species is available on license in a
given area, it's left a single footprint there since the last Ice Age.
Possibly to give the sales impression of a tremendous selection
of game animals, you'll notice the inclusion of such less than
classic lords of the wilderness as the porcupine. Now, who on
earth would shoot a porcupine on purpose and then pay between $20 and $35 for the questionable privilege? But when you
see the porcupine in the lists of game available, it's no lie. You
can shoot a porcupine if you're so inclined. I wonder if they
charge backwards?

A good bit of the "padding" is unrealistic when thinking of
the licenses you will purchase beforehand. When I was hunting
in the Luangwa Valley of Zambia, I always used to wonder what
I would do if I saw a bushpig, *Potamochoerus porcus*, or a
grysbok, the elusive little twilight antelope of the deep bush.
Both are still on license in Zambia, but in a long, long time I
never saw either. After what is now about a decade and a half in
areas that harbor both, I haven't run across a wild example yet.
Had I been a client, it would have irritated me to have bought
nonrefundable supplementary licenses of about $200 for these
two species without any real chance of bumping into representative examples.

You'll also see quite a few smaller predators lumped in to
fatten the list, but unless you have some personal or scientific
interest, you're as well off not to buy supplementary licenses
where required for such fare as serval cat, civet cat, bat-eared
fox, caracal, baboon, genet, wildcat and other minor-leaguers.
Some, such as the serval or the caracal (lynx), do make attractive rugs, but larger-caliber rifles don't do much for their appearance and they are rarely encountered anyway. Like my
bushpigs and grysboks, they tend to be strictly nocturnal, and
night hunting is illegal anyway.

One of the essential reasons for contacting previous clients
is to check with them the current situation with any species in
which you have an interest. Waterbuck come immediately to
mind because I got into a hell of a row with a gentleman I

worked with in a central African country by observing to a well-known outdoor writer client that, in four months, I hadn't seen one. In retrospect, I see that it was a severe faux pas and a grand example of the results of not engaging brain before putting mouth into gear.

Because, some years back, two or three very good trophy waterbuck had been killed on this gentleman's concession, they were proudly offered as one of the best trophies available. Well, for sure the game department was happy to sell you a waterbuck license, and the safari company equally charmed to ferry you about in your quest of one. The only problem was that there weren't any. Nearby, on other properties, yes. Not where I was. I had hunted the place hard for months and never even cut spoor, so unless they had taken to climbing trees, the conclusion was obvious. Madder than a snake, the gentleman took me off the safari and personally conducted the writer, a good friend of mine, on a waterbuck safari to prove me wrong. Obviously, since there weren't any, they not only didn't get one but found not so much as a secondhand dropping. I must say that the incident didn't do worlds for our relationship.

About two years ago I was asked to evaluate a new safari company and its concessions in southern Africa, as a nonpaying guest, except for licenses, for anything I especially coveted. Since all I really wanted was a decent jumbo—I had never taken one for myself—I only killed a couple of impala for camp meat. For the rest of the trip I spooked about for a big elephant with the normal results and generally just looked around. On the way to the concession, I had stopped by with the owner to pick up the new brochure he had developed and I found it most attractive. It listed large and exotic varieties of game animals, specific maps and boundaries and details of services. However, after five days in the bush, I began to wonder if the place hadn't been mixed up with somewhere else.

One perfectly beautiful *koppie*, which overlooked gorgeous bush that should have been seething with antelope, left an oddly empty impression. With a spotting scope, I lay for a couple of hours trying to see something, any game at all, but with no luck. A day later, I found out that although it was regularly hunted—for what I can't imagine—it was in fact the impact area for an army mortar detachment who practiced their 81mm ordnance there three days a week!

Half the concession was a firing range! If I had been a paying client who had read the brochure, which somehow did not mention this, and then booked expecting a fair hunt, I would have been less than pleased. The brochure, incidentally, was also riddled with offerings of other species peculiar to areas more than a thousand miles south, with no mention made that they were not found wandering cheek by jowl with the northern stuff.

Other items of, uh, questionable validity, were the cases of elephant and lion, the two animals I was especially interested in as they are rarely available in this particular corner of the world. Lying between ranching/farming land and a national park, the concession indeed did offer both, although not exactly as you would have guessed. Because of game fencing, lions didn't tend to come through much from the park, and if they managed to get into the concession from the ranch lands, they had to pass through a "flak alley" in which they were declared vermin because of their depredations on cattle. A lion or two *were* taken every year, to my surprise, but it wasn't what you would really think of as lion hunting, often done at night despite the law. Dozens were killed by ranchers on the outlying cattle lands, though, which wouldn't make you too pleased to be on the wrong side of the fence at $400 a day.

Elephant hunting consisted of driving along the boundary fence separating the concession from the park and trying to catch one that had broken through during the night for greener pastures before he got back into sanctuary before dawn. Rather a bloody game of ring-a-levio. What would Karamojo Bell or Jimmy Sutherland have said?

It really wasn't a case of humbug, the owner being no hunter himself and not realizing that he was being criminally misleading in his offerings. Actually, fewer than half the species he offered were even found in his concession. A short chat with a previous client would have told me this, although I did enjoy the trip. Had I come from America or Europe, though, with a long-saved wad of traveler's checks for my lifelong ambition of a proper safari, I strongly suspect my sense of humor would have been strained.

Before getting completely away from basic fees, a mention should be made of deposits and the conventions associated with them. Perhaps there are safari companies that don't require deposits on booking, but I've never heard of them. Normal deposits required to confirm your safari run between twenty-five and forty percent, depending on the firm. Most safari outfits will require you to complete a booking form that states clearly what you're paying for and what is extra, terms of cancellation and other appropriate items. I would personally not be inclined to deal with any firm that asked for more than forty percent deposit on your basic fees—not licenses or extras—as it would seem to indicate some cash flow problems that might possibly leave you holding a leaking bag.

Deposits are usually required to be paid at least thirty days before the safari begins and, like all payments, must be in a form that is negotiable. Personal checks are frowned upon, and you'd be amazed how many safari companies have gotten stuck by really high-profile people over the years. Most firms will let you settle small, personal service items by noncertified check, but not the main expenses. There's too much involved.

Cancellation, should you be forced to do so, can be a problem. A rule of thumb, but by no means a firm rule, unless spelled out in your contractual documents, is that a safari deposit is not refundable within six months of the departure date *unless* the professional hunter can be rebooked for the period. Be certain to ask about cancellation terms and details before paying your deposit, and get it in writing. Some companies have a strict schedule of refunds.

The payment of a substantial deposit for a safari is not unreasonable if you consider the position of the company. A cancellation at short notice leaves them with the nearly impossible task of trying to fill the same slot in time, which means a waste of valuable season days as well as of the professional and all his staff, who have to eat too. The outlay for purchase and upkeep of equipment in environs as unforgiving as the African bush are pricey, and goods such as tinned food, perishables and a load of other essentials must be laid in. Don't doubt that your deposit is being put toward the things you'll be using and enjoying on your trip. The logistics of a good safari are amazing.

The balance of the basic safari fees, in nearly all cases, must be paid either before the client arrives or before the safari leaves home base. As you will know from your contract, that's *it*. No hunt now, pay later, unless it's through your bank.

A couple of points remain that could cause friction and, to my most definite knowledge, have done so because no understanding was reached before the start of the trip. The big one is the problem of breakdowns.

I really don't know where the moral obligation lies here, with the safari company or the client. If a vehicle, which the client is directly or indirectly paying for as part of his contracted services, breaks down (and count on it that it will to one degree or another), it will require anywhere from minutes to days to fix, depending on the severity of the problem. On one hand, the client *is* paying for the use of vehicles assigned to his safari and any reliable outfitter warrants that the best practical care is taken to see that he won't lose hunting time because of mechanical failure. A professional hunter is—or should be—an accomplished bush mechanic, although I would have to admit that this was always my weakest area. On the other hand, I was always lucky, which I would far rather be than a good auto surgeon. Yet the very nature of safari travel dictates that one must expect minor to fairly serious problems during the course of a safari out of reach of a proper garage. Normally, even in the case of near evisceration of the hunting car—mine was once tusked several times through the pancreas by an angry cow elephant—something can be rigged up, a vehicle can be borrowed or some other remedy patched in until the car is right again. And the client should realize that the firm and professional will do their best *within reason* and *as is possible* to make it right. Of course, to be out on your second day and have the car engulfed in a warthog subterranean condominium and be advised that the rest of the trip will be on foot wouldn't exactly be acceptable either. It is the safari firm's or the pro's vehicle and their risk, and they are obliged to do their best to provide the transport as stipulated in the agreement.

So perhaps before you go drawing any certified checks, you

might inquire, requesting a letter in answer as to what the firm's policy is on *extended* breakdown. Forget flats, boil-overs and small-fry problems. That's part of the game.

Besides your basic fees, the financial factor that will most influence your choice of an outfitter or even a country will be that of licensing structures and taxes. And in some places, it can be a wasteland of barbed red tape.

Like most things in Africa, nearly every country seems to see things differently, so what applies in one would draw a jail sentence in the next. Ignoring the dozens of different titles applied by different governments to licenses of different types, try to envision the following varieties:

- Concession, tourist or game management taxes
- General hunting licenses
- Special licenses
- Extra trophy taxes or head fees
- Health certificates, export taxes
- Gun licenses

Happily, not all safari countries will assault your wallet for all of these items, some being quite reasonable. But to get an idea, let's first have a look at these expenses and how they work.

The concession tax is an overcharge levied by the government on safaris that normally take place on concessions leased by them to your safari firm. Consider this for an indication: Botswana will charge you, right off the top, between $600 for fourteen days in the Kalahari and $950 for twenty-one days or more, combining the desert with the Okavango region. The Luangwa Valley and Kafue areas of Zambia have a game management area fee of $800 a throw. Sudan has a tourist and development tax of $800 per hunter, and concession fees will also stick you with an extra $8 to $10 per day to pay a government game scout to keep an official eye on you. At the moment, neither Tanzania nor South Africa makes any charge for concession fees, although a few South African outfitters do make a nominal charge of their own. South-West Africa/Namibia has some concession fees but these are usually covered in the daily fee as they are quite nominal. Zimbabwe, on some lands, will cost $600 for a twenty-one-day trip.

General hunting licenses are familiar to most Americans, as that is the way things are handled in the States. You qualify for and buy a license and you go hunting under the terms of the law. Of course, the federal government confuses the issue with the addition of a migratory waterfowl or duck stamp, but things are still pretty simple. Not so in some African locations.

A general license is usually at the bottom of the heap of potential fees that may be extracted from you and, where it is required, may be seen as a sort of warrant to buy other and more specialized licenses. The more common game is usually represented, most frequently in such a manner that the general license permits you to hunt it in the first place, a second or even third fee being payable if you are successful. Normally, anything rare or especially desirable will not be found listed here as, consistent with the concept of game being able to pay its own way, heftier fees are charged for the "plum" species.

Not all countries require the purchase of a general license before allowing special licenses. In fact, you can hunt in quite large areas of South Africa with no license fees at all, paying only for what you shoot on a straight-schedule per-animal basis for trophy fees.

Obviously, if you are price-conscious, you want to keep your eyes open for countries that require the least in the license rigmarole. Not the most advantageous of systems but far from the worst would be Botswana. Their way of doing things is to let you elect the species that you want to hunt and pay an up-front fee for the privilege of hunting it in the first place. Of course, this is again influenced by the amount of time you have booked for, but you can, as of this writing, still take, on a safari of only fourteen days into the Okavango, two buffalo, a leopard, a lion, a sitatunga, a kudu, an eland and one each of bushbuck, croc, duiker, impala, red lechwe, reedbuck, steenbuck, tsessebe, warthog, plus two wildebeest and two zebra. The cost of all this for the prepaid license to hunt would be $3,082. If you were one hundred percent successful, the trophy or head fees, to be dissected in a moment, would run from a high for the lion at $1,000 for a general license and another $1,000 for trophy fees, to a low of $7 apiece for game licenses for duiker, steenbuck and warthog, and between $25 and $50 each for these species for trophy fees. The grand total for this half comes to $5,870, and the two totals combined, $8,952, not exactly cheap, but then how much is the experience of a lifetime, including three members of the Big Five and some of the top glamour game, worth to you?

Just before moving on to head fees, remember that no results are guaranteed on safari and that the odds on your being so lucky as to collect male members of all the species represented on license, thus incurring the whole list of trophy fees, would be pretty slim. If you're not that interested in a lion, you can save $2,000 off the bill right there. If wildebeest don't turn you on, you can pass them up and save $430 just on the licenses alone, never mind the shipping, dipping, packing and taxidermy. Will you want two Cape buffalo or is one enough? Take off one of the two you're permitted and you'll save $530. As I said, all safaris are custom trips.

From a client's point of view, the best license deals are in those countries that permit a hunter to take a wide variety of game without incurring a financial commitment that is nonrefundable if he is not successful in getting some of the trophies he wants. Zambia is rather in the middle of the road, requiring prepayment of all supplementary licenses and then simply charging an export license of $600 (as of 1982) for the lot. If you don't shoot it, you pay for it anyway.

Probably the most lenient in this regard are South Africa, Tanzania, Zimbabwe and South-West Africa/Namibia. In the case of South African hunting farms, where safaris are conducted on private land, the viewpoint is that the game belongs to the landowner and not the state so, varying according to which provinces of that country you hunt, license requirements will be minimal. The main charge will be for trophy fees, determined individually by the landowners on a competitive basis and only payable if you have been successful. Some of the best bargains, provided you don't insist on a bedroom view of Mt. Kilimanjaro, are here. Much the same result is obtained in Zimbabwe, even though the government is more active in licensing. On most South African *jagplase*, or hunting ranches, you will only pay a very low fee per day and the main expense will be made up from the fees for what you decide to shoot. Services are less. Still, the whole bill will be a mere fraction of what you would spend elsewhere with a full staff and a professional hunter.

Since the widely varying prices charged by different governments for the same species of game will have a ground-zero impact on how much you ultimately pay, because they are common in one territory and rare as emeralds in the next, perhaps the best way to illustrate how important it is to select between the license fees as carefully as you would between basic or daily fees would be to take a small groups of game animals and see, irrespective of other costs, what their licenses and attached fees would be in different countries.

Since they are found in many hunting areas, let's figure on the 1983–84 costs for a collection of one each of greater kudu, lion, buffalo, zebra and impala. Hardly representative, but still covering the range of license costs for some of the most popular, widely distributed and prized animals.

The chart on the following page should give some idea of the discrepancies in license fees, but a few words of explanation are in order so that it doesn't give an inaccurate picture of the whole. All prices are as I gathered them from agents or outfitters and, in many cases, combine more than one type of license cost, where required, to come up with an accurate total in U.S. dollars. In the case of Sudan, where it was so structured as to make this impossible, the total fee for the five animals includes a charge of $350 for a general license. The fees do *not* include basic costs, export licenses or, in fact, any cost beyond those of merely the hunting licenses and trophy fees.

Actually, I was quite surprised at the outcome of some of this material, not expecting Tanzania to have the lowest cost and South Africa the highest. The difference, though, is reflected in the unappended fact that the basic fees are only a fraction in South Africa of what they are elsewhere, the bulk of the safari charges being trophy fees, which look expensive but are largely made up for by lower daily costs.

In some countries, I have given a range of prices from different safari companies that represent largely their own fees for game on private lands either with or without licenses, as required.

Because the combination of greater kudu, lion, Cape buffalo, zebra and impala is not found all over Africa, just as a matter of interest I have listed the members of the quintet that are available in locations where they don't all occur together.

Representative License Costs per Country in U.S. Dollars

	Kudu	Lion	Buffalo	Zebra	Impala	Total
Zambia	660	1100	330	440	135	2665
Botswana	695	2000	530	430	95	3745
Zimbabwe	300 450 650	1200 2000 1500	600 750 1200	275 450 400	60 100 100	2435 (low) 3750 (med) 3850 (high)
Tanzania	370	735	135	150	40	1430
Sudan	500	550	175	350	50 (Grant's for impala)	1975 (includes $350 general license fee)
South Africa	350 500	1900 2200	1100 1400	350 450	45 90	3745 (low) 4540 (high)
South-West Africa/Namibia	270 (low) 350 (high)	—	—	300 (low) 400 (high)	150 (low) 200 (high)	—
Central African Republic	—	1000	250	—	—	—
Ethiopia	325	412	—	175	—	—
Zaire	—	1000	350	—	—	—

I saw no reason not to directly substitute a Grant's gazelle in place of the impala to be able to get valid five-species totals.

From this license schedule you ought to be able to see right off that if, for example, a Cape buffalo is one of your dream animals, you probably won't want to pay the extra money to shoot it in South Africa, where the species is quite expensive, when you can go to Zambia or Botswana and take one for half of the same license fees or less, everything else being equal. Actually, the license fee in Tanzania is only about a tenth of Zimbabwe's high. Again, don't take these prices as being up to date, as they will surely have changed by the time you read this. They are for comparative purposes only.

Another important license-related fee is that applied to the exporting of your elephant ivory after the normal hunting and trophy fees. Today, finding a good elephant is one of the most difficult orders, as many countries are opening and closing elephant hunting almost on a yearly basis, depending on annual assessments of the herds and population in general. Zambia closed elephant hunting in February 1982 for five years to study the situation more closely. Botswana has also closed ivory hunting as of this writing. Elephants are, however, still available in Zaire, Zimbabwe, Tanzania, parts of South Africa and Sudan. For the moment, then, here's a badly chewed thumbnail sketch of the various regulations if you want to take an elephant:

Zimbabwe: License and trophy fees, $2,500 to $3,500 plus a government levy of 20 Zimbabwe dollars per kilogram of ivory in excess of forty kilograms (eighty-eight pounds). The Zimbabwe dollar is worth about 90 cents in U.S. currency.

Sudan: License costs $400 plus approximately $35 per pound tax for ivory.

Zaire: License and trophy fee total $1,000 plus approximately $85 per kilogram (roughly $39 per pound).

Tanzania: Trophy fee of approximately $1,220, no additional tax.

South Africa: Not widely available, normally only near the Kruger National Park. Trophy fee only, in the area of $3,500. No tax.

Change-of-area fees are not normally encountered except under those circumstances necessitating a complete move of the safari from one location to another some distance away. A typical case would be that of Zambia where a safari planned to hunt both in the Luangwa Valley and farther north, in the Kafue area. The normal charge for this shift is $500 per client, which sounds stiff, but there's a lot of work involved. Another example where an additional charge might be incurred would be that of Botswana and a switch between the Okavango Swamps and the Kalahari Desert for different species such as a gemsbuck, the big southern oryx.

Gratuities have largely been discussed. The amount you choose to pay is really up to you, but suggestions will be supplied by the safari company upon request.

The dipping, packing, shipping and general treatment of trophies can be a large expense item and many companies handle their charges differently. At least one leading Zambian firm charges a flat $750 per client to take care of the job, no matter what the size. On top of this, there's also an export license fee per client of $600. A similar charge is the $500 per client found in some Sudanese operations, including shipping of all the trophies from Juba to Khartoum, collect forwarding, customs clearance and all documentation. The government here will cheerfully charge you an additional total of $17 per animal for veterinary certificates and export tax.

Other countries and operators will use a local taxidermy house to ship, dip, crate and document your trophies and forward them to the taxidermist of your choice. Some of these smaller firms do very fine work on their own and many clients elect to have all their mounts done in Africa and shipped to them upon completion. The brochures will carefully spell out particular arrangements. The subject of taxidermy itself is so absolutely personal in terms of individual taste and requirements that it would be impossible to discuss it in depth here.

Personal items are essentially those expenses that include anything other than those goods and services spelled out as being included in the basic tariff. One point to remember, though, is that you should advise your safari company of any particular likes and dislikes you have in food. I know of a safari not long ago where the professional and the client were hardly on speaking terms with each other after one week. The client was outraged that the camp had run out of salted peanuts! He hadn't mentioned beforehand that he himself ate more than a pound of them a day, and it wasn't long before the snack box was bare. They were in the middle of nowhere and it wasn't reasonable to expect the catering arm of the company to have known of his quirk. Had they had a clue, it would have been no problem. If you are excessively fond of any ordinary food or get the dry heaves even thinking of others, just say so before you arrive and your taste will be catered for as well as is possible. After all, you're paying for it!

Although they're not major expense items, the matter of your gun licenses, permits, visas and other formalities are as crucially important to the success of your safari as is your understanding potential health hazards and preventive medicine. Let's get them out of the way right here.

African countries take varying attitudes toward the importing of firearms and ammunition by tourists, but most realize the value of the safari industry to their economies and are not inclined to create dramas at customs, provided the necessary documentation is available and in good order. Fifteen years ago, in Ethiopia, it used to take up to a week to get your guns clear of customs in Addis Ababa, and that only with a liberal spreading about of baksheesh.

There are some rules in gun importing that are almost universal, though, and the first would cover the types of guns permitted under most circumstances in the majority of countries. If you want to bring in a semiautomatic rifle or an autoloading shotgun, forget it. These are mostly seen as too applicable to military purposes. Most countries won't consider the importation of a pistol or revolver for the purposes of your safari, notable exceptions being South Africa and, until recently, Zimbabwe. Don't ask me the logic that permits elephant guns and rules out popguns.

In many parts of Africa don't try to bring in a rifle in caliber .303 British or a .22, the former being a military designation and the .22 considered too valuable to poachers should it be lost or stolen. The numbers of rifles or shotguns you may import temporarily and the amount of ammunition you may bring in also depend upon the country in question, but your outfitter and your agent will each be able to advise you completely in plenty of time to take care of the formalities. Since these regulations change with greater frequency than you might think, anybody in the safari business keeps on top of them.

Normally, those countries requiring pre-import documents will need the most obvious information including make, type, caliber, serial number, the number of cartridges to be imported and their caliber. Photos or a police certificate of good conduct may be required in some of the more remote areas, but it's not usual.

Visas are a matter best handled by whoever takes care of your air tickets. Considering the red tape of some African countries, this seems to be another excellent reason for using an agent rather than trying to arrange things yourself. Most agents keep visa and entry permit applications on hand for every place they represent. This can save a very sweaty brow and a long phone bill trying to coax them out of a few embassies I have dealt with. Since there is little in common between one visa application and another, and since considerable time must be allowed to have your passport suitably stamped or inscribed after it has been sent off, this is one of the first things to be attended to, *certainly before* you pay for one or another penalty-refund air ticket that might be no good to you if, for some weird bureaucratic reason, you are turned down!

FIVE

Uniform of the Day

It's interesting that it would be one of Britain's leading early sportsmen, the author of *The Compleat Angler*, Izaak Walton, who wrote, "Look to your health; and if you have it, praise God, and value it next to a good conscience; for health is the second blessing that we mortals are capable of; a blessing that money cannot buy." Perhaps Havilah Babcock, the great writer of southern American quail shooting, put it as well when he observed that "My health is better in November," when the quail season opens.

Africa is not quite so simple.

You may well need some inoculations, if not for the place you are going to, then because you'll require them to get back into the United States because of possible exposure to an area that is still subject to a particular disease. Again, your agent will advise you. Don't worry about taking a bit of his time, he's paid from the other side.

The big thing to remember in African hunting is that, except for being eaten by something unsociable that might otherwise be shot by your professional, you will have to look out for your own health. Africa is not exactly the leech scene from *The African Queen*, and very few clients in my experience have any difficulty at all. But, you're not around the corner from the family sawbones or the pharmacy and if something goes wrong other than by luckless injury, it's usually your fault because you forgot to take one or another pill or otherwise protect yourself. It probably won't do much for safari sales, but you had better be aware of the possibilities before you pay your deposit.

The three major problems that could possibly develop into rare serious illness are malaria, sleeping sickness, also known as trypanosomiasis, and bilharzia. It is with the greatest pleasure that I announce, ladies and gentlemen, that you'll have to work very hard and be very dumb to have a tiff with any of them.

Make no mistake, there is sure no shortage of malaria in Africa. It's simply that medical research has reached the point that there is no reason for contracting it severely, any more than there is for blaming the fact you forgot your pill for becoming slightly pregnant. I think I'm the best example I know of how far we've really come in malarial prophylaxis tablets. Since 1964, twenty years back, I have been hunting professionally in severe malarial areas such as Nicaragua, Brazil, the former British Honduras, Mexico, Zambia, Botswana, the former Rhodesia and some other quite questionable locations. I have never had malaria. Not in any form. Last night, I tried to think of some-body I knew who was a professional who hadn't. No luck. The difference was that I started playing bwana about the time the really effective earlier preventatives, beyond quinine and atabrine, came in, my first recollection being Aralen phosphate, which I took with religious regularity. Today, preventive medi-cine is pretty slick. It's not claimed that the newer compounds will positively prevent one of the several forms of malaria, but they will make the attack much less severe than it would other-wise have been.

In passing I should say that, in the Luangwa Valley, I once thought for sure that I had caught it, and a proper dose, too. I fell into a raging fever and was brainless for about a day and a half, confined to my camp bed, the only two days I have ever lost while on safari. Hot, cold, legs in a paper roller. You know the movies. But about noon the next day, I awoke and was liter-ally fine. We took a record-book leopard that same afternoon. Don't ask me, I don't know what it was. At least it has never come back.

The most important thing you should do before coming on

safari, and I don't care when or where it is, is to start on a course of preventative antimalarial prophylaxis tablets *well before* you leave on your trip. This means several weeks to a month beforehand. Since a prescription is required, see your doctor and advise him of your plans. If the brochure does not state so, tell him as a matter of course that there may well be more than one form of malaria in the area; some prophylactics don't cover all varieties, such as cerebral malaria. Should you tend to be forgetful, tie a string around anything prominent to remind you to take a tablet each week on the same day to preserve your "protective envelope."

Right, unless you are bucking for medical history, you need not fear malaria if you follow the regimen of preventive treatment. To stay out of the way of sleeping sickness, you've got to be a touch trickier, but then it's rare in most of Africa.

"Tryps," as it's commonly called in the bush, is not nearly so hairy a fate as it used to be. I've written elsewhere that it has a terrible reputation for fatality because those indigenous blacks who contract it heavily in very remote areas don't ever see treatment until they are comatose or worse. In fact, SS, as it's also called, can be quite easily cured, provided it is recognized and treated as soon as possible.

Now look, I'm no physician and I don't want to make an irresponsible statement. So I won't. I shall merely observe that to catch SS you will have to be bitten by a tsetse fly that dined off a carrier or sufferer under certain conditions. As a raw rule, most of the best hunting today in Africa is where there are large concentrations of tsetse (*Glossina morsitans*, one of the bad ones), because they carry nagana, a similar disease fatal to all domestic animals and birds that haven't had generations of conditioning to the trypanosomes they inject. Logically, where domestic animals can't live, game thrives. In the old days, a "salted" horse was one that had recovered from the disease and was thus worth about ten times its normal price, as it could be ridden into the tsetse-infested interior without the certainty of the owner walking home.

Both Zambia and Botswana have SS but Botswana has a worse reputation for the disease because it has more "carriers" in the form of indigenous Bushmen, particularly the Masarwa of the Okavango. It is still found elsewhere as well.

The normal symptoms of SS are at the site of the bite itself, an inflamed swelling developing like a carbuncle or boil. Headache and swollen glands are also typical, although your professional will certainly know what to look for. If you don't feel a hundred percent, for God's own sweet sake, tell somebody. It may well only be a thorn infection.

The course of treatment is so relatively simple that bitten clients who have become infected may be back on safari in less than a week. The normal procedure, at least when I was there, was to fly the suspected victim to a well-known clinic in South Africa specializing in tropical diseases. Of course, they were set up to handle problems that an American or European physician would simply never have a chance of even seeing. I know three American friends who had picked up malaria here or there and went more than a year before it was diagnosed by their family doctors. This is not an indictment, just an observation that American doctors don't necessarily look for malaria or sleeping sickness.

Bilharzia either.

I've been told that bilharzia, also known as bilharziasis or schistosomiasis, is the most prevalent potentially fatal tropical disease in the world. I wouldn't know about that but it is certainly the scourge of large areas of Africa. It's a waterborne disease which follows the cycle of a parasite that passes through man and freshwater snails, hosted in each and contracted usually through the pores of the skin where it may take up highly active residence in a variety of organs, including the human brain. It's a long, slow and very debilitating illness that is only cured or arrested by poisoning the body to the point that it kills the snail flukes yet leaves the carrier alive, although the course of treatment usually makes the sufferer wish he weren't.

If you want to be completely safe from bilharzia, follow one simple rule: stay out of the water. Most of the ponds, streams and rivers of semitemperate, semitropical and tropical Africa are infected to some degree because of the continuation of the schistosome cycle through untreated human waste containing the flukes. The most dangerous conditions are still or "dead" water, but it can be contracted in swiftly running water, too. So if the crocs aren't enough to put you off a dip, think about the risk of bilharzia. It ain't worth it.

Drinking water on safari is always filtered, boiled or both, which removes any potential residents before they get to you. A filtration system using porous "candles" as the medium is the most common. In Hemingway's day, dysentery was common among clients, yet I can say I have never had it nor have I ever had a client pick up a dose. Like every other aspect of staying healthy on safari, use common sense. Don't drink water unless you're sure it has been treated. While on the subject of tummy bugs, I have never noticed any particular problem with clients becoming ill from eating locally grown green vegetables, such as is often the problem in Central American locations. Greens are carefully washed, but in any case, they don't seem to have any inbred penchant for causing clients to beat a path to the long drop.

Although not precisely related to health problems, several items that should be in your shaving kit or cosmetic box can make worlds of difference to your comfort. If you're hunting in the dry or winter season when 95 percent or more of safaris are conducted, you'll find the atmosphere as parched as Teheran on Saturday night. A dispenser of Chapstick—no relation—or other lip balm can save you the real discomfort of sun and wind-cracked lips. I spent the whole of my first season smearing my smackers with a slab of rancid zebra fat and was happy to have discovered it. In fact, I have seen the dry wind factor combined with cold so bad that the watering of my eyes used to cause the eyelids to crack, split and bleed unless coated. No fun, especially when it's so simply prevented.

For women, or men too, I suppose, a container of some moisturizing cream for parched skin is a basic requirement. If you are in Zambia, Botswana, South-West Africa/Namibia, South Africa or similar areas from June through September, you'll see when you're hunting that the atmosphere will draw the juice out of a beetle. Just look at how quickly a piece of meat biltong cures. It's exposed to exactly the same factors as is your skin, only less so. Biltong is dried in the shade. You'll be dried in the sun.

With the sure knowledge that you won't be able to drop by a pharmacy, you had best bring anything that might be required. I've listed these in the appropriate appendix but shall quickly run down the list here. Those items I have found useful are aspirin or other painkillers, antacid, topical disinfectant for scratches, antibiotics such as penicillin in tablet form, Lomotil or other antidysentery medicine, Dramamine, Bonamine or other motion sickness tablets, Anbesol for tooth or gum irritations, and a small container of talcum powder for chafing or itching. Eye drops are a must, as wind and dust irritation are a constant factor. I sincerely hope you won't need any of these things, but take it from anybody who has been there, better to have and not need than the other way around.

In addition to the drying aspect of the sun, you'll want to add sunscreen with a PABA base for sunburn, perhaps zinc oxide if you have particularly sensitive skin, and anything else you've found effective. The southern African sun is bloody tricky, the shade of a tree almost uncomfortably cool and the sun harsh through the thin, low-humidity air. Chris Pollet, the late and well-known hunter in Zaire, and I once did a trip together in Ethiopia in January when he was so badly burned that he spent half his time in bed in agony. By the second day, the little diamond where his shirt opened at the top of his buttons was as raw as cube steak, seared right down to the meat. He carried the scar until his death. I'll tell you what he would have told you: Don't fool around with the African sun.

The object of this advice is not to make you a traveling dispensary, but all these remedies are low-bulk and can always be left behind for the next unfortunate soul who may have forgotten something. Should you need any of these things and there are none in camp, you'll be damned glad you brought them.

You also might want to consider the value of getting a tetanus shot before you leave. Should you be cut or punctured, particularly from an animal source, you might require one, and that could cost you some time off safari to get it. In some areas of Africa, the permanent front teeth of black children are removed so that they may be fed milk if lockjaw is contracted. Another consideration would be a buttful of gamma globulin by injection as a precaution against such remote possibilities as jaundice. Your physician can best lecture you on the advisability, but don't discount it offhand.

Before closing out this section, some thought ought to be given to insect repellent or anti-itch dope. Personally, I never use the stuff for tsetse but that's my quirk. In fact, most of the major brands are effective. A problem to look out for is that some types of insect repellent on the skin can cause severe complications with sunburn. The smell is also considerable when tracking, as anybody who has recently fought in a tropical bush war will confirm, but I suppose that any animal capable of smelling repellent would have no trouble winding you, in any event.

A separate item I didn't mention earlier (and that we'll look at more closely later) is one or another form of antihistamine to prevent or remedy allergic reaction to local pollen, especially grass-seed reaction. Grass and weed seeds during the winter hunting seasons are a problem to some people's systems, the sharp ends of the seeds being hooked and caught in socks and pants cuffs and from there irritating the skin. One client I had in Zambia scared me half to death by coming down with a simmering fever from the inflammation caused by this problem. A common antihistamine cleared up the trouble, which was apparently an allergic reaction to the strange irritation. As I tend to a lesser but still poor reaction to this seed infection, I hunt in shorts and sockless shoes, but that takes a bit of getting used to.

I hope I haven't scared you off your safari with this recitation of the salutary joys of Africa; I didn't mean to. The odds of your developing any medical problems at all are fairly slim, but the point is that you must know what to expect and be prepared.

Most hunting clients going on safari bring far more clothing and personal items than necessary, although the right choices for the area you will be hunting are essential. Every safari firm and booking agent will supply you with an accurate list, which is normally quite general. The reason for this section is to try to give some of the missing detail, based on my own and my clients' experiences.

Clearly, the first consideration is where you will be going. If you're hunting the South African Lowveld at reduced rates in February, you sure won't need the same things that you will thirty miles away on the Highveld in June. Still, since there are differences in local weather from one camp to another, let alone from one country to the next, let's approach this thing from the basis of normal weather in most places, broken down into time of year and location.

In normal safari season, rain is rare nearly everywhere unless noted as being otherwise. Some outfitters, obviously to increase slack season business, proclaim that one may hunt all year. To sucker anybody *unknowingly* into a rainy season safari would be criminal, at least in my opinion, although it's worth the discomfort to some for the substantially reduced rates one may be able to negotiate. I have hunted in the rain on many instances, especially when working with one or another game department, and would far prefer to simply be soaked and remain so than to swelter under a raincoat or foul-weather suit. In any case, for our purposes, rain should be considered as extremely unusual, a light windbreaker in your luggage normally being adequate. Since every outfitter will supply you with a general idea of what to expect, why don't we simply start at the soles of your feet and work north with some suggestions.

Shoes or boots are probably the most important items because you will spend the most time in them. I am constantly astonished by clients who, despite personal letters begging them to do otherwise, arrive with nearly or completely new footwear that has not been properly broken in. To try to walk the miles involved in collecting a representative bag on feet that are sore is like doing the Bataan Death March for fun. Whatever type of shoes you choose, the first iron-clad rule is to do whatever is necessary to break them in before you arrive. You'd think that was unutterably obvious but you're wrong. Equally apparent is the fact that unless you are a professional marathoner, you'll be walking far more on safari than at home.

I had an experience in 1981 that changed my mind quite a bit about footwear, when we had two unseasonably rainy days while I was hunting buffalo in southern Africa. I was wearing the type of gum-soled shoe typified by the Clark's Wallabee model and those made by Hush Puppy and others, a rounded-toe model I started wearing because of tendon problems from an old jaguar bite. I still wear them daily but not for hunting. The first problem was that on the terrain of scattered rocks the low-cuts gave me no ankle support, and when it started to rain, they stretched to the point where I could almost turn my feet around in them, so slick and stretched had they become. No criticism of the shoes. I love them but not for hunting buffalo in the rain.

Some safari clients have extolled the virtues of the newer

style jogging or running shoes, usually of European or Japanese manufacture, and although I've not tried them, my good pal Clive Siegle of Abercrombie & Fitch in Dallas, the *fundi* on such matters, does not approve of the choice. After many discussions with those who have tried them, he advises that they are constructed for running, not necessarily walking. The difference in balance and reinforced areas is not appropriate for safari walking and hunting, says Clive.

The choice is, naturally, yours, but the best general bet covers the following: comfort, light weight, ankle height and either composite or gum soles.

Considering the worry most people have about snakes, a word is in order here. The Gokey reinforced snakeproof boot is a lovely piece of work and is highly recommended for the quail fields of Texas or Florida where rattlers are as common as Ohio tourists. Yet the chances of your being bitten in Africa, especially in the winter months when you are most likely to be taking your safari, are very slight. Searching the balding expanses of my brain, I cannot remember hearing even a questionable "sea story" about a client being bitten by a poisonous snake or any other for that matter. I'm sure it has happened and wouldn't have been spread around for reasons that are in themselves clear, but it would be a very strange occurrence. Snakes are largely dormant during the colder months, which doesn't mean you can't get unlucky. It also doesn't mean you won't be run over by an ice-cream truck before you leave.

The worst snake, at least statistically, is the puff adder, which kills more people in Africa each year than cobras and mambas put together. He's common, hard to see and delivers the traditional adder toast of good cheer with a big bite and economy-size belts of venom. He's not outwardly aggressive and mostly fangs barefoot Africans whose vibrations he doesn't feel while catching a bit of warmth at dusk on a dirt trail. Until stepped on, that is. Being lethargic, he doesn't move off until it's too late. But even with his bad record, it would be highly unusual for you to even catch a glimpse of one in most areas. Don't sweat your whole trip stumping around in knee-high snake boots. It's not worth it. Even if you do roll "snake eyes," every camp has a kit as well as antivenin.

Besides your shooting shoes or boots, you'll want a pair of

"comfies" for lounging around camp at night, padding off to the loo and other such extemporaneous expeditions. Because of the dust, I wouldn't recommend an open sandal or even a shoe that has to be polished, but some kind of a casual slip-on that covers your foot and that doesn't have to be laced. I favor an old pair of Sperry Topsiders that are laced loosely enough so that I can slip into them like a moccasin. This is the classification of shoe you'll still see on traditional safari brochures as "mosquito boots."

Before I leave the subject of footgear, permit me to donate a fervent confirmation of one of the first things your professional will tell you: don't put your feet into shoes until you're sure they're unoccupied. You'd think from all these warnings that the place is literally crawling with scorpions, centipedes and other democratic assortments of what are generally called *goggas*. It isn't, but you had better treat it as if it were. You go spontaneously sharing your right shoe with a big scorpion and you'll wish you'd read this chapter more closely!

Although I don't wear them when hunting, I would recommend that a half-dozen pairs of athletic-type socks be brought along. I don't like them because they pick up grass seeds and burrs as well as other vegetable garbage that slips off your skin. But then I don't wear ankle-high boots either. You might well remember the old army trick to prevent blisters, should you have indications of a coming crop. Wear an underlay of silk or synthetic socks, which will prevent the slightly rougher material of the athletic socks worn over them from rubbing.

The most important aspect of choosing socks is to be sure that they don't protrude over the tops of your boots where they will be exposed to seeds. If they can be tucked into the top of the footwear, they'll be shielded and you will be much more comfortable. And make sure they fit. A "bunch" that gathers in a lump against a sweaty foot on a long hike is trouble.

The question of pants or shorts is pretty much of a toss-up. I have always worn shorts but there have been plenty of times when I wished that I had had pants on with stovepipe fronts. Because of personal preferences, a definite pronouncement can't be made, at least not by me. Let me try to point out the advantages of each.

Shorts are cooler, which is no light consideration early or

late in the season when days are warmer and the sun downright mean. Although the skin of your legs will be scratched by thorns such as the wait-a-bit with its fish-hook design, and by bush in general, they will at least not hang up, in most cases forcing you to stop and unhook the material from the thorns. You'll be scratched by plenty of thorns right through most trouser material in any case, so if the complexion of the skin on your shins is your living, better think about a salmon fishing trip instead. Another point, especially considering the thorn and bush problem, is that shorts are much quieter to stalk or walk in than most trouser cloth, which magnifies each little snag with a sound. I know of at least one lion with a rock star hairdo that would be in Oklahoma right now had my client been wearing shorts and not gotten hung up.

Trousers, unless you don't mind shins like frozen lamb shanks, are more comfortable in an open Land Rover, with no doors, window or windscreen, roaring along through the fresh hoarfrost of a Zimbabwe *vlei* near dawn. They protect from the hot sun, even at the price of coolness, and are certainly preferable to shorts in fly country, which is no minor consideration. I don't mean just tsetse either. Africa has a complete smorgasbord. The advantage of a bit of cloth over sore knees when crawling after game is not to be despised either.

Lest I be pegged as unreconstructed, let me advise here that I am speaking of women as well as men. Generally, safari skirts or culottes, despite their racy, "authentic" design, are best left for camp wear and, at least according to most of my lady clients, women are more comfortable all round in trousers, certainly while actually hunting. I take their word for it.

I simply can't bring myself to write of anybody else's underwear except to say that you'd better make sure that it doesn't ride up or chafe despite the anatomically unlikely positions often achieved while stalking.

Belts aren't too important except that they be sturdy and able to support whatever you want to hang on them. I wear a plain leather one, not much different from most, that takes my belt knife and an ammo carrier. I used to favor a U.S. Army web pistol belt over the pants belt, which had ammo pockets originally made for Garand clips but that took eight rounds of .375 H&H beautifully. I could also attach a canteen and stick other odds and ends in the ammo pockets, such as a small snakebite suction kit, water purification tablets, a little plastic bottle of wound disinfectant and other eccentricities. I left it somewhere or other at the end of a season and never had a chance to get another one.

Shirts, like pants or shorts, should be of a neutral color, my best choice usually darkish khaki to loden green. *Do not* bring camouflage clothing to African countries without first ascertaining that it's legal. In Zimbabwe, South Africa and South-West Africa/Namibia, it's strictly *verboten*, as camo is the standard uniform of terrorists and the security forces. You can do without a couple of extra nostrils. Most places where camo is illegal will have this pointed out in the literature but don't count on it. Check yourself.

The type of shirts you favor should be loose and comfortable. I never have all that much to put in them but I somehow like the idea of lots of pockets just in case I someday get lucky. The bush jacket type, provided it's not festooned like a stale Christmas tree with buckles and odd contrivances seen by designers as essential for Hollywood, if not Africa, is a good choice, as it has pockets on both breasts as well as hips and sometimes on the sleeves.

Speaking of colors, stay away from white or any other bright expression of fashion—it scares the hell out of game. I once "test hunted" (evaluated) a farm in Rhodesia where I was escorted by the rancher, now a professional hunter, who was that day resplendent in a shocking electric blue shirt that would have embarrassed an Amazon butterfly in the mating season. That the most we saw was an apparently color-blind impala at about eight hundred yards evoked only his amazement until I mentioned the problem. It had never occurred to him.

There was and still is a fashion some bush hands swear by that says that a pale smoky blue hunting outfit will not attract tsetse flies. I never gave the stuff a real empirical test, but so far as I have witnessed, there's nothing to it. I would say that tsetse hunt by both attraction to motion—as is clear from the way they swarm a moving car—and, I suspect, to some extent by scent, as do mosquitoes. In any case, pale blue never slowed them down in my observation.

Along these lines, I can't resist a short tale about tsetse and my shaving kit. This was in Botswana, where I had bought a zebra-covered tackle kit from Peter Becker at Botswana Game Industries in Francistown, my old one having developed the same symptoms of bush wear that I had. Each day, when I came in from hunting, I had to spend a few minutes in my tent tracking down and swatting the tsetse that had come in while I was away or they would ambush me as soon as I undressed.

One day I left the shaving kit out on the bed by mistake and, on coming home, saw that it had a half-dozen tsetse on it, trying (I presume) to bite through the cured hide. A single spritz with a can of pyrethrum spray and they were annihilated without my being asphyxiated in the process. This was the case each evening, every fly in the place always on the zebra skin of the shaving kit. Clearly, they recognized either the pattern, color or hair texture, maybe even the residual smell of the zebra as food, even though it had long been tanned. I never drew any scientific conclusions from this, but I had a lot fewer tsetse bites.

Your choice of short- or long-sleeved shirts will have to be made on the same logic as that of shorts or trousers. Probably a couple of each, considering that long sleeves can always be rolled up, is the best bet.

One thing I always look for in a hunting shirt is a breast pocket big enough to take my small hunting binoculars. By far the most comfortable way to carry them is on their lanyard around your neck, but tucked into this pocket when you are stalking or crawling. To have them swinging free like a pendulum is a pain in the neck, almost literally.

Most hunters would never think of including a pair of leather gloves for an African safari, but they are more than a little useful. A dawn ride in an open Land Rover in central or southern Africa in winter is a chilling experience, particularly if you're holding the cold metal of your rifle to boot. After a few miles, my hands without gloves feel as if I've been setting out broadbill decoys in Chesapeake Bay in January. You won't need heavy, fleece-lined ones, but plain leather to keep the awful chill off is a must for winter hunting.

For the same reason you will need a lightweight but snug jacket to keep your body warm. I have a quilted goose-down shooting coat for Land Rover travel in winter and, although not a real arctic design, it would be appropriate for December in

New York. For warmer times of the year, remembering that there's a nasty chill factor early and late in the day, I like the vest-type quilted windbreaker, leaving the arms uncovered. A light nylon windbreaker that can be folded to take up a small space is an excellent addition.

The subject of hats in Africa is one of the most charming aspects of the history of the white man's folly. The British colonists in the East African Protectorate, which became Kenya Colony in 1920, were nearly psychotic over the supposed effects of the sun, possibly since sunlight was such a rare commodity at home in Britain. At the turn of the century, it was seriously doubted that white children could even be raised in Africa. A member of the Foreign Office, passing through a bit of Kenya in 1902, sagely advised that "White labour under an equatorial sun, no matter how high the elevation may be, is impossible."

Winston Churchill, five years later, wrote that "Although the skies look so familiar with their white, fleecy clouds and passing showers, the direct ray of the sun—almost vertical at all seasons of the year—strikes down on man and beast alike, and woe to the white man whom he finds uncovered."

Frederick D. Lugard, the giant of Ugandan colonization, was even more suspicious than Churchill or the officials of the Foreign Office. "Removing the hat [to adjust it] in the sun," he wrote in this same period, "is a folly I see daily perpetrated. . . . If it is necessary to remove the hat, even momentarily, it should be done under the shade of a thick tree." Don't you just love it!

The British colonial terror of the sun extended well beyond the supposed effects of solar energy on the brain, to the extent that any early pioneer wore, as a matter of course, a thick fabric "spine pad" to protect that tender portion from unknown radiation. Some went so far as to wrap their simmering stomachs in scratchy flannel cummerbunds to, as Lugard put it, "protect the stomach, liver and spleen."

So suspect was the unknown effect of solar radiation that even thick pith helmets and solar topis were double-lined with cloth, colonials faithfully wearing their hats in their living rooms in the sure knowledge that their thick corrugated iron roofs were not in themselves proof against the relentless sun.

It probably took until World War II Pacific experience before it was fully realized that, although the sun was not to be disregarded, it wasn't absolutely deadly either.

Everybody has a vision of the "safari hat," a wide-brimmed, sweat-rimmed floppy affair with, in the case of an old Hollywood hand, vague bloodstains, the odd bullet hole, roosting bats and, of course, the inevitable partially moth-ingested leopard-skin band. I've often wondered if it was invented for Stewie Granger by Edith Head and perpetuated by some joint effort of Abercrombie & Fitch and Bob Lee's Hunting World. The design is actually from the "terai" Indian style, sometimes featuring a "double terai," which has two brims, one over the other, for additional protection from the sun. The design is, in fact, quite good for practical purposes, if protection from the elements is the primary consideration.

Today, if you want to stand out as a "dude," the best way to do it is to show up in Africa with a leopard-skin hat band. I know. Years ago I did it and I can still hear the chuckles. If you want to be a super dude, arrive with a fake leopard-skin band. Of course, that's only my personal viewpoint. Suit yourself. You could always emulate the late ivory hunter John "Pondoro" Taylor, who wore no headgear but a turban!

I don't like hats very much and don't wear them unless there's a practical need. In very dusty conditions, I favor a military beret simply to keep a couple of pounds of daily topsoil from polluting the near dazzling shine of my pate. My favorite low-sun headgear was a leather visor in dark brown, a style I acquired years back in Rhodesia, which nicely shades early and late sun yet lets cooling breezes play. A hyena or a bushpig ate it one night and, since Rhodesia is no longer Rhodesia, I no longer have a visor.

As with all safari clothing, keep your headgear toned down in color and weight. I have had a lot of clients arrive in the commercial advertising caps that appear very popular at the moment, the billed-visor variety extolling the assorted virtues of Caterpillar tractors, Sierra bullets or Red Man chewing tobacco. These are a good, light, practical outdoor design, but I can't say as much for the colors. If you can get a grip on a nice dull one, it would do fine. Whether you're choosing hats, shirts or anything else, you don't need anything bright.

After you have spent a few days on safari, it will strike your curiosity that quite a few of the blacks you'll see in the bush are one-eyed. This, in itself, is a pretty good ad for wearing either dark or shooting glasses. I'm pretty much a believer, particularly when bird shooting. I know of two professionals who have lost an eye to a client's pellets, and I have been hit by spent shot quite frequently. It might be "spent" if it hits your clothing, but it would sure ruck up an eye pretty badly. The only problem with glasses comes in the use of binoculars, but modern ones now have rubber eyepieces that permit you to place the eyepieces against the eyeglass lenses. The danger of a stick whipping back or a sharp grass stalk catching you in the squinters is not all that minor. When you can, wear protective eye gear. It's better than a sharp stick in the eye.

Under odds and ends, we can probably lump handkerchiefs, sweaters, pajamas, kikoys and swimming trunks. There is always a good use for a few bandana-type hankies, whether to mop off or to cover a spot that's gotten a bit more sun than you had in mind. A sweater of the lighter variety is very handy for around the camp fire at night or whenever the weather is a mite too warm for your jacket. Personally, on bitter nights, I sleep in a cashmere sweater and find it perfect. The kikoy is very popular with most professional hunters, and clients seem to like it too. Basically, it's just a wrap-around piece of cloth hailing from Arabic East Africa, not unlike a tablecloth, which is wrapped around the hips and worn casually around camp whenever it's hot, rather like a male sarong. Your professional should be able to put you onto where to buy one or two.

A bathing suit is also a good thing to stick into the corner of your suitcase, as you might be in an area where there is no bilharzia and, in any case, will likely spend a day or so at a game lodge or other place that has a swimming pool.

Check the appendices for quantities of clothing to bring, but don't overdo things as daily fresh laundry is a standard item with every properly run safari company. Generally speaking you should not need more than three complete changes of basic hunting clothes, and could easily make do with two. Although it doesn't necessarily apply to safari, it is customary in Africa that a lady washes out her own undergarments if the laundry help is male. Probably just a missionary colonial leftover, but you ought to know this custom.

Personal equipment to bring on safari can be as simple or involved as your own personality, but some items are particularly suited or completely inappropriate for safari use. Knives are a good example and a perfect place to start.

Most first-safari clients bring along a largish bush knife, suitable for hamstringing a bamboo thicket, which is completely unnecessary, considering that the people who will be doing the various chores of cutting are better equipped than a shipwrecked Hoffritz store.

There are two primary requirements of a knife on safari, if you are the client: cutting bites of biltong and looking authentic. I don't mean to be flippant, as some visiting hunters enjoy pitching in and helping the skinners in the field. If this is part of your repertoire, by all means here's the chance of a lifetime to test some of your custom or commercial knives under circumstances that would require a hundred seasons of deer hunting in Pennsylvania to equal. But unless you know what you're doing, leave the work to the skinners, who are paid for their artistry. If, however, you're not especially interested in immersing your elbows in effluvia, don't bother bringing a Smithsonian Bowie or an Arkansas toothpick.

If I had to pick a single chattel that I really doubt I could get along without on safari—or at home, for that matter—it would have to be my Swiss Army knife. You know the kind, a bull penknife with all sorts of gadgets and doohickies that delight the soul of any small boy, possibly not the least attraction of which is the red plastic handle.

I'd as soon go on safari without my rifle as my Swiss Army knife. I have skinned out impala often, and once, on a bet (provided I was permitted to sharpen it twice), caped a bull buffalo, using only the large 2½-inch blade. Essentially, I love Swiss Army knives the way I love double rifles. My favorite is now about twenty years old, having been purchased on a happy whim at Newark Airport, and we have shared more adventures than Tom Sawyer and Huck Finn. With this I have executed such critical errands as carving a new wooden *mekugi* holding peg for the handle of a newly acquired samurai sword out of a coat hanger in my suite at the Plaza Hotel; sawing, filing and finishing a new warthog ivory bead for an Evans .470 Nitro Express; extracting wood splinters more than an inch deep against the bottom of my foot bones; cutting the heads off one rattler and one Egyptian cobra; probing a bullet wound (not mine); drilling sling-swivel holes in solid walnut stocks and a host of other minor Herculean labors. There's practically nothing you can't do with one, and if it won't do the job, you can use it to build the tools that will!

Mine, a stainless model that I strongly recommend as your choice, has a large 2½-inch blade, a smaller 1½-inch blade, a pair of folding scissors just when you want them (who carries scissors?), a hook disgorger and fish scaler, a three-sided rasp/file, a rip saw that will cut through a buffalo's thighbone in less than a minute, a bottle opener/screwdriver, a can opener and fine screwdriver, a Phillip's-head screwdriver, a drill/leather awl, the best pair of tweezers I have ever used, and a genuine imitation ivory toothpick! They're not cheap, the prices rising as the models get more involved, but if you don't have one, I strongly recommend your picking one up, and not just for safari.

Like most Americans, I am childishly fond of gadgets, although I probably couldn't explain properly how a bottle opener works. Before I forget: if you want to appear seasoned, remember that on safari in the field, all bottles are opened on the hidden bottom curl of the dashboard on the passenger's side of the Land Rover. The metal is finished off in a perfect loop that pops caps better than if designed for it. Or maybe it *is* made for it. . . .

Since your professional will have a fair assortment of tools, you may find that one of those "pocket workshop" tool kits with a master handle and a bunch of different inserts for odd screw and Phillip's-head sizes is handy. Some have hammers, awls and all sorts of surprises. They're not expensive but, if you need one of the attachments in the bush, nearly priceless. They're also literally pocket-size.

Every professional carries a tape measure, usually a steel one with increments in both inches and metric. You'll get tired of constantly borrowing his, so include one of your own.

Your tent or hut will surely contain some sort of light, but on the off chance that one isn't enough or you don't want to fool around with lighting a lantern every time you get an errant urge, bring along one of those very compact disposable flashlights that are sold at so many cigarette counters or stationers. Don't get the "penlight" sort, that's underkill. The ones about the size of a 100-millimeter cigarette pack are just right and will last the life of a month's safari. Incidentally, they're a marvelous gift for the local people, since they are not only useful but also convey huge status. That they will be conceived as eternal, never being shut off until they burn out, does not diminish the value of the gift!

One of the more interesting experiences I had when I first came to Africa was in having brought along some four dozen butane disposable cigarette lighters, which I reckoned would be great presents for the bush people. Let me make it clear before I proceed that I imply no stupidity to these tribesmen whatsoever; hardly, considering that most whites would die of starvation under wilderness circumstances where they would have to start watching their cholesterol. The difference is some sort of cultural-mechanical gap that lets them make fire easily with a hardwood spindle, a soft base wood and some dry bark fiber scraps with palm friction when they cannot master the idea of holding down the gas-release lever while striking the flint wheel of the lighter. On several instances, I tried teaching them, without any success, until my thumb was raw from spinning the striker and demonstrating how it worked. But as I grew to learn the basic languages, I suspected that the concept of butane looking like water was what made them implicitly believe that it would only perform for a white man.

I know that this sounds crazy if you're sitting and reading it in Sioux City, Iowa, or London, but it is true in my experience. There was no way I could get my gunbearers, skinners, trackers and the rest of my staff to properly operate one of these lighters. They did, however, make marvelous ear lobe inserts where such was the style. Well, you're not going to Africa because you want to duplicate Secaucus, New Jersey. *Vive la difference*!

When it comes to sharpening those knife blades, don't forget to take a pocket steel such as the Gerber. Of course, many blade purists will recoil in horror at the idea of touching up an edge with a steel, but I just don't have the time or talent for using an Arkansas stone and, frankly, I prefer a steel anyway. A fair piece of advice if your choice is to bring along your favorite belt knife skinner: Don't, under any circumstances, lend it to an African skinner to see how he likes it. These people are used to working with very inexpensive and purposely soft butcher-style blades that, when the previously dragon-toothed edges have been worn away, are sharpened by rubbing them across a fallen hardwood log sprinkled with sand and earth! It does a great job on their knives too, but I doubt you want that treatment on yours.

One of the problems in skinning big African game, especially buffalo, hippo, rhino and elephant, is that the skin is so impregnated with dried mud and dirt that it would dull a laser in two cuts. Much better that you save your better blades from such a fate!

What must be remembered is that when you are on safari and offer modern and prized equipment to men who aren't used to it, you can't expect it to be treated differently from the most basic item. I recently swallowed an attack of apoplexy when a pair of antique sterling silver candleholders were "polished" with a thorough rubbing in flint sand and followed up with coarse steel wool on the "stubborn" spots. They sure did shine! But the fault was mine. I hadn't said *not* to do it that way. The difference is *not* racial. It's cultural.

Some of my most treasured memories are on cassette tapes. If you don't bring even a modest recorder to Africa, you're missing a dimension of your safari. Although I have no commercial interest in any brand names, I must say I have rarely seen any problems with the various better Japanese makes, such as Sony, which offer both plug-in and battery-operated modes, usually with capabilities for battery recharging. Before we proceed on this point, you'd better be reminded that there is no similarity whatsoever between most African electrical current and European or American varieties. Happily, we do have the alkaline batteries, which last so long and well as to preclude a lot of the troubles of even twenty years ago.

The smaller cassette recorder/players will not only give you the opportunity to record local music, such as impromptus put on by your safari staff on the occasion of killing an important trophy, but to run footage of those incredible early morning bird symphonies. Notes, recorded letters with all the proper background sounds and other audio projects are beyond value when you have been back home for a couple of years and want to recapture a touch of the real thing. Don't forget, also, that a good-quality low-volume recording of African chanting and singing is an impressive vocal backdrop to any slide show.

In choosing cassettes, I would not be inclined to bring those with a longer playing/recording time than C-90, which is forty-five minutes a side of recording. The C-120s are very convenient but I've found them to be a touch delicate and, if they snarl up, they may break as they're being repaired under safari conditions. You don't need sophisticated equipment but, if you want better results from bird calls and animal sounds, you might consider a directional microphone. Bring plenty of batteries, although a triple set of fresh alkalines should be plenty, including one set in the machine, for the length of an average safari.

Should you want camp music, you should also bring along some prerecorded tapes. But don't forget that if you're listening to artificial music, you may miss the real stuff in the African evening. I rarely play "canned" music in camp, and most clients agree with me on this. You can listen to that anytime. This is the same reason I don't ever use a portable camp generator. It spoils the real, natural night noises that you're really paying for.

And on the subject of electrical gadgets, unless your electric shaver or electric toothbrush is battery-operated, you're wasting your time and space. Safari is getting *out* of the bright lights, not bringing them along with you. . . .

I'd prefer to give photography its own space later, but this is a good time to suggest the possible inclusion of a Polaroid, Kodak or other instant camera for less formal hunting and camp photography. Few things are more pleasurable than being able to see the print right away, and definitely nothing besides money or meat is such a treat for the indigenous people to whom you may wish to make a present of an instant portrait.

Tape is always a good, lightweight and small item to have with you. I like to bring a roll of nylon-thread-reinforced packing tape, a small roll of silver-colored duct tape and a small spool of bright yellow cloth tape. If you don't need them, all the better, but if you do, just like the pharmacy, the hardware shop isn't next door. A tube of good glue can be invaluable and it wouldn't be a bad idea to throw in a little blister pack of one of the new "super glues," which will apparently bond right to wrong if properly applied.

Although most casual sewing repairs will be done by the camp staff, I like a little "bachelor's friend" sewing kit to lurk somewhere in the bowels of my gear. Over the years, I have found that for hard-duty-wear button repair, nothing beats waxed dental floss as thread. If there's space, stick in some extra shoe or boot laces too.

Seems to me that I didn't mention it when we were speaking of medical supplies, but if you decide against the Swiss Army knife, by *all* means bring a good pair of fine-edged tweezers. I'd be hard-pressed to think of where you won't find thorns, the plucking of same from your quivering corpus every night being as much an institution as the "sundowner." At least, the wait-a-bit or *wag-n-bietjie* thorns, fish-hooked for efficiency, are not long, although they will break off in your meat. There are far more impressive African thorns such as the camel thorn, but they're more intimidating than dangerous. Sisal, used for rope making, is a bayonet-tipped plant with each leaf armed with a steel-hard point. They're murder but at least they don't normally break off.

In fact, I would say that Africa is far more forgiving in the thorn department than such areas as Marajo Island, in the Amazon Delta, where I have hunted the descendants of imported Asian buffalo. The thorns there are absolutely murderous, being largely of palms and brittle as glass crystals. We used to carry as much alcohol for disinfectant as for the popular use. Some, though, were completely painless, so smooth and sharp were they. Eleven months after I left Marajo, I was watching television one night—Walt Disney, no doubt—and happened to notice an odd lump on my forearm. I gave it a squeeze and out slid a 1¼-inch-long thorn that had been there for nearly a year without my noticing it. I have been told that these palm thorns will "travel" and sometimes hit the heart, which I guess might tend to cancel most of your life memberships. Don't worry about it, though. You're going to Africa, not Brazil.

I didn't say it before but if you wear eyeglasses, be sure to bring an extra pair. The same goes for sunglasses.

Some of the most interesting and fun times I've had have

been the result of throwing one or another gadget into my bag. An example of this was the small case that is offered by some tackle manufacturers and has a combination fly/spinning rod, reels and the necessary addenda for a sneaky salesman to knock off an hour or two and still look respectable. Sure, you'll be run out of your local trout or salmon club on a rail by the purists but you'll get a touch of African fishing! Most of the smaller species such as bream and bass will take flies and lures, so an off-afternoon waiting for your leopard to feed can be well filled-in here.

Perhaps the best ever of my gadgeteering was that involving the "cold" light sticks now popular and widely available. If you're not familiar with them, they're a light-transmitting wand of plastic about ten inches long and containing a mixture of chemicals. When the stick is bent, the chemicals mix and create chemical light, a fairly bright greenish glow. There's no heat and no danger, so far as I know, unless you are inclined to eat one. Bush Africans purely love them, and if you drop a couple into your kit, you might have some fun one safari evening.

SIX

Tools of the Trade

Facts make me nervous. Essentially, they're shifty, saber-toothed little brutes that, weasel-like, emerge in the dark of the moon when least expected and, with a single cynical slash of mossy fangs, eviscerate a whole covey of prize, home-grown Assumptions. For many years I was the proud owner of one of the finest bunches of Assumptions you ever did see, some of them having become so tame they had nearly begun breeding Conclusions. So pleased was I with this collection that I decided to bring them all to Africa with me. Within months, the whole herd was wiped out, decimated, annihilated. African Facts are among the most savage.

One especially attractive Assumption I remember well was that to be properly armed in Africa, the hunter should be toting a rifle of a caliber that equals at least four times his hat size. The logic was that of Dodge City and the grizzled gunslinger asked by a dude reporter why he carried a Colt .45. "Cause they don't make a Colt .46, sonny."

Ruark confirmed this in an anthology brought out after his death at forty-nine. "Use Enough Gun," pontificated Bwana Bob. He was right, too. But not quite. Most men use too much gun.

Since the British double express nitro calibers seem to have all but disappeared into the vaults of Texans and Maharajas, things have gotten a lot simpler in the choice of a big bore for use on large, ugly and rapidly impending African animals such as elephant, buffalo and rhino. Today, they would be the .458 Winchester Magnum and the .460 Weatherby Magnum. Sure, there are plenty of others such as the British .404, the .505 Gibbs and the .416 Rigby, but for purposes of this powwow, let's just say that they're not common fare for Americans. Ammo is very difficult and expensive to obtain for all except the .404. In any case, they're roughly in the same class. If you *must* have a .416 Rigby and can afford it, fine. But not a fraction of one percent of the people who read this book will take that option, so let's stick with the main theme.

Before another syllable on big bores, you must first decide whether you will take your own guns or rent them from your safari company. I strongly recommend you bring your own for a couple of good reasons, not the least of which is that you'll then have a chance to be familiar with them (or it) and this will greatly improve your chances of doing well.

When professional hunters meet on safari, one of the most common answers to the standard "How's it going?" is, "Nice guy, but the poor bugger just can't shoot." Your shooting on safari is the most important aspect directly relating to success, and your degree of skill will correlate precisely with the quality and quantity of your bag. I'm not talking about missing an elephant twice at twenty yards—although I've seen it happen—but the tough shot at a record-book kudu at 225 paces, as it pauses for two heartbeats at the edge of a bush-choked ridge. The man who can pull off the hard ones with any regularity has it all over the client with a rented rifle, fixed with a scope he wouldn't have chosen and which probably doesn't fit him in any case. He'll also be completely unknowledgeable about the holdover for the gun or windage allowance because he likely doesn't know the caliber and its practical field characteristics. After all, if he used the caliber regularly, he'd bring his own.

If you can afford a safari, I suspect you can afford your own rifle, the choice of which I'll get to in a bit.

Since we're starting at the top of the commercially available Big Berthas, let's have a look at the .458 and the .460, as they've developed into premier monster-stoppers.

Winchester whelped the .458 Mag in the mid-1950s in a very successful attempt to duplicate the ballistics of the grand .470 Nitro Express, one of the best giant killers of the double calibers. The idea was a 500-grain bullet in "solid" or nonexpanding configuration and a 510-grain soft-point thundering up better than 5,000 foot-pounds (fp) with each load. That's a lot of thunder! Velocities are about 2,130 foot-seconds (fps). Obviously, somebody at Winchester in those days foresaw the demise of the Anglo twin-tubes and made provision for the vacuum that would be created.

I somehow doubt that Roy Weatherby, the Viceroy of Velocity, prays for me daily, as I've written some rather faint-praise comments on his products. Actually, as I have tried to point out, the Weatherby concept of ultra velocity in bullets is quite as impersonally valid as any views I may hold, being completely verified by the exclusive use of Weatherby rifles and calibers by many of the world's absolutely top big game trophy hunters. I'm not knocking Weatherby products; it's simply that we have a classical and basic difference in our philosophies of optimum bullet performance, his being that of hydrostasis, in which a "shock" is imparted by extremely fast bullets, and my experience being that, within reasonable bounds, it just ain't so.

In any case, if you wish to kill a very large animal very dead, you will do nicely with a .460 Weatherby Magnum or a .458 Winchester. As an extension of the "Colt .46" theory, the Weatherby is the most "powerful" shoulder-fired commercially available caliber you can buy. The only problem with both the .458 Winchester and the .460 Weatherby, though, is that very, very few nonprofessionals shoot either one very well. And this, when accuracy of bullet placement is of such great importance on dangerous, large game, is not so hot.

The reason is a combination of rifle weight and bullet weight, which equals eye-crossing recoil or good old-fashioned kick. Although both these calibers throw bullets of the same weight and diameter, despite commercial designations of implied caliber, and although both are savage on the face and shoulder, the Weatherby is worse in recoil, giving about twenty percent more than the .458 Winchester, which isn't exactly a cream puff either.

It's long been a fashion in American rifle design to feature lightness, which is rather the opposite of the concept in classic British arms. Consequently, a decent double comes nowhere near thumping the shooter the way a .458 or .460 does; it rather pushes than slams. Of course, the answer is found in the most basic of the laws of physics, something to the effect that "for each action there is an equal and opposite reaction." Reaction is what you catch in the chops from a heavy caliber in too light a rifle. Big bores bite at both ends!

Look, *if* you are thoroughly experienced with the heavy rifles and can shoot them well, then bring one. But don't take a .458 simply because you reckon that bigger is better and that African game can kill you. You simply don't need it. In fact, you'll live longer with a "medium" bore you shoot better.

I never got around to figuring out just how many safaris I have been on with clients but I do recall that I never—with one exception, a professional gun writer—saw a single one of them really do good work with the .458. Essentially, and with some good sense, they were afraid of it. I don't mean that they didn't do passably on elephant and perhaps less so with buffalo, but I have never lost the feeling—developed through my own experience—that they all would have been better off with rifles they shot better with and thus had more confidence in. For my money, that's the .375 Holland & Holland Magnum, a long-bearded old classic that harkens back to Blimey in 1912. How phenomenally good it is, is clearly demonstrated by the fact that it's still a standard chambering for most any make or model of American big game rifle.

I once, when first starting off as an African professional, kept a notebook in which I then reckoned would germinate the seeds of the Great African Novel. Among the odds and ends scattered therein were the responses of eighteen professional hunters to such questions as "What do you prefer your clients to use?" and "What's the most important performance factor for an African safari rifle?" With one exception, the responses were, respectively, "The .375 H&H" and "Penetration." Penetration is a matter for the chapter on ammunition, but the election of the .375 as the *beau ideal* of the safari hunter is based on a lot more than theory.

As we noted, the .375 H&H was spawned by the gnomes in the collective innards of Holland & Holland, who are to British gunmaking what Rolls Royce is to automobiles. The .375 caliber, particularly in the 270- and 300-grain bullet loadings, seems to be the absolute compromise of a cartridge that can efficiently kill the largest of land animals yet spare the shooter ringing headaches or displaced retinas. Probably because they had hyperactive public relations officers, combined with amateur ballistics theoreticians, there was an old law in some East African countries that a caliber of over .400 was required for buffalo, elephant and rhino, but in my opinion and that of most of the professionals who blatantly ignored it, it was the typical product of so much bureaucracy. Lion and eland might be taken with the .375 H&H, it was pronounced, but not the really big game. Of course, the rule, where applied, was and still is ridiculous.

That's not just my view of things.

John "Pondoro." Taylor, son of a Dublin physician and author of several African hunting books based on his decades of experience that culminated in his probably being the last of the genuine big-time ivory hunters and poachers, had a particularly soft spot for the .375 H&H. In his 1948 work, *African Rifles and Cartidges*, Taylor singled out the .375 as "undoubtedly one of the deadliest weapons in existence. It heads the list from the point of view of its caliber, and in the opinion of many hunters ought easily to head it from the point of view of its power also."

Pondoro Taylor worked up a set of theoretical "Knock-Out values" based upon his practical experience and calculated upon the chamber pressure in tons of the load, weight of bullet, muzzle velocity and muzzle energy, formulating the whole thing into a value expressed in correlated numbers. The .375 H&H with a 300-grain bullet only came out on the theoretical chart at 40.1, compared with the .600 Nitro Express at 150.4. But even Pondoro realized this was approaching the ridiculous. The 900-grain .600 bullet was so unpopular among elephant hunters because of lack of penetration compared to the .577 Nitro that fewer than seventy-five rifles in this caliber were ever made by all manufacturers! As Taylor wrote: "Altho my formula gives this rifle a Knock-Out value of 40 points, I must regretfully admit that it does not really do full justice to it." Taylor owned five .375 rifles, two doubles and three magazine guns, and put more than five thousand cartridges through them. I completely agree with him.

The beauty of the .375 H&H is simple: you can take every animal on earth with the caliber without ever being over- and only rarely undergunned. I temper this comment as being meant for the amateur hunter, as there are plenty of specialized situations where I would rather have a .470 double, such as in elephant cropping. Still, I spent five seasons backing up clients with the .375 H&H and never had a problem; well, not any problem relating to my rifle or its caliber. For a safari client it's more than enough gun for two reasons: first, it will kill any African animal you hit properly with the right type of bullet and, secondly, you will tend to do this well because you won't be flinching in anticipation of the brain-scrambling thump of the .458 or the .460.

When, in my ignorant later youth, I was cropping elephant and buffalo in central Africa, we were issued a bunch of Winchester .458s in the Model 70 "African" variety, a slightly beefed-up version of the old Winchester standard magazine rifle. At eight and a half pounds, the gun was essentially far too light for the recoil of the cartridge. After fifty to seventy-five rounds, these guns would consistently develop shears and splits at the pistol grips. Facing a very angry herd of jumbos with one's rifle in two pieces didn't do a great deal for the old Winchester's local image, but in fact, most other brands had the same problem. If a .458 doesn't weigh at least ten pounds, as does the Colt Sauer, it is just not enough rifle for the cartridge.

The advantage of using the .375 H&H for *everything* is reflected in the old saw about being wary of the man who has only one gun: he probably knows how to use it. With solid ammo, the .375 is perfect for smaller antelope, killing neatly without excess damage, while still being first class life insurance for dangerous game. You're not a professional and won't need the same things out of a rifle as he will. Sure, there's an edge to the bigger calibers in the types of eyeball-to-eyeball things he'll get into but if his client were using a rifle he could shoot well and delivered his shot properly, there wouldn't be a hairy confrontation in the first place.

I wouldn't comment that I've shot everything on the African continent with the .375 because nobody has. Still, from elephant to steenbuck, if you can come up with something better, I'd love to hear about it.

If you're a gun buff, there is certainly a case for bringing a lighter rifle for smaller species. In my experience, the "super" .300s are the most popular, such as the .300 Winchester Magnum, the .300 Weatherby Magnum, the .300 H&H Magnum and related calibers. The 7mm Magnum, as bred by Remington, did some very good work for me in Ethiopia, but this is largely because of the long shots through very open cover, which are by no means so common farther south. Heaven forbid that I start a couple of thousand ballistics buffs foaming at the mouth, but there's not all that much between this class and the .270 or other typical calibers. I think the .243 Winchester as well as the other 6mm loads fit some beautiful notches for long-range sub-100-grain work, but they're better left home, as a good .30 will cover a lot more ground.

If I were to do it again, and I did the last time I came out to Africa as a nonprofessional, I'd opt for the .30-06 as a second rifle. For one thing, the case capacity, compared with the .308, is large enough to duplicate the 250-grain .318 Nitro, one of the premier lighter elephant calibers of its day and a favorite of "Karamojo" Bell. As with the .375 H&H, the varieties of bullets are marvelous, although in the case of the .30-06 most of them are available in commercial loadings down to 55-grains in the new "Accelerator" Sabot load and up to 250-grains in hand-loads.

Because models will change over the life of this book, I think it appropriate to speak mainly of types of rifles for safari purposes.

If you take my advice and choose a .375 H&H, you'll most likely be best off with a bolt action, although this is largely up to you. This is by far the most popular and the strongest action, although you may decide to opt for a Ruger No. 1 Tropical Rifle in single shot. The "flanged" version of the .375 is, of course, available in double rifles but the ammo is rarer than sympathy, being specially rimmed to be caught and held in the chamber.

It probably wasn't reasonable of me to completely rule out the possibility of your acquiring a double rifle. There's a great deal to be said for them, despite the cost. Even the grand old

British makers will churn one out for you if price is no object—and I mean no object at all—and several European firms make them regularly. Thus, a few comments from what is rapidly getting to be twenty years' field safari experience. Many of the continental double rifles are over/under, which are not to be despised but they have a major drawback compared with the traditional side-by-side British guns: they require several times the angle to break and load than does the horizontal configuration. Maybe not a really big deal but something to think about, as they are slower to load and must, of course, be completely broken to eject the empty shells.

I have a very bad impression of the doubles, especially the new ones that use belted rimless cartridges, such as the .375 H&H and the .458 Winchester. The problem lies in the cartridge's lack of a rim, which means that one or another type of metal "finger" or pawl is located at the rear of the chamber to catch and hold the round in position so it won't fall into the chamber with the extractor behind it. I have twice had clients with these rifles who have gotten a cartridge past the pawl or retaining lug, where it is very difficult to fish out again, particularly when you're in the middle of a herd of highly unhappy elephants. Another of these rifles was particularly queer. It would not handle Winchester and Remington .458 ammo equally, one of them—I don't remember which—absolutely freezing the action despite the fact that they should have been rounds of precisely the same diameter and measurement. I had to kill a very angry wounded elephant on the banks of the Munyamadzi once when this happened with a European client. Since it was charging, I suspect that had the man been alone, with the action of his rifle "frozen," he likely would have been killed. This is not the sort of nonsense you pay for in a double rifle.

So tightly stuck closed was this gun that we never were able to open it on the safari, as I feared shearing the breaking lever. Actually, it was just as well. The way the client had been shooting the double, he couldn't have hit an elephant from the inside. When he used my spare .375 H&H Mauser action, he really started to connect.

Should you be a real traditionalist, insisting on a double-barreled rifle, pick your caliber carefully. Eley/Kynoch, the Im-

perial Chemical Industries branch that made most of the nitro
express ammo over the years for the British doubles, has cut
back to a shadow of its former production. Today, with prices
for nitro express cartridges so dear to collectors, let alone
shooters, a single .600 round bringing better than $100, you're
going to have a real problem with all but two calibers, the .470
Nitro Express and the .500/.465, of which there are still good
original supplies and new American sources such as BELL,
Brass Extrusion Laboratories Limited, filling the gap. Certainly,
if you're going to have a rifle built, pick one of these two rounds
if you ever want to shoot it.

Books a lot longer than this one have been written on the
choice of a safari rifle or rifles. You'll enjoy much of the work
by Col. Charles Askins—a dear friend but a velociphile with
whom I do not ballistically agree—Jack O'Connor, with whom I
don't agree either, Karamojo Bell, with whom I do concur, Pondoro Taylor, who seemed to have his head screwed on properly,
and Elmer Keith, whose old book *Safari*, while it is a nightmare
of zoological misinformation, is spot on when it comes to calibers and rifles, if you believe in heavy artillery.

To summarize, if I were going on a first safari, I believe you
couldn't go wrong with a decent quality .375 H&H Magnum by
either Winchester, Remington, Sako, Ruger or a host of lesser
known names. I'd choose either a standard commercial American or continental bolt action, such as the Mauser, in a weight
of at least nine pounds and with a magazine capacity of at least
three rounds plus one "up the spout." The more the merrier.

Metallic sights are largely a matter of opinion and familiarity. I haven't used the peep type since I was in the army when
they were still using the Garand rifle, but would agree that there
is a lot to be said for the peep. Personally, I like the wide V of
the old British express sights with a fairly big bead as a foresight. The hinged-hooded night sight, as found on Mausers by
Continental Arms of New York, features a thumbnail lift-up
enamel or ivory white night sight that nestles into a recess when
not in use. I normally used this when cropping elephant as it was
highly visible and, although more coarse than a fine bead, lined
up instantly.

I would strongly advise you to stay away from rifles that

have a series of flip-up rear "leaf" sights graduated for different ranges. Older Mausers are typical of this type and so are many of the Mauser-action British-magazine rifles of some years back. My intimate friend and constant companion, Mr. Murphy, founder of Murphy's Law, claims these were his original idea. I wouldn't doubt it in the least. Since anything that can go wrong will, the more "leaf" sights that are available on a given barrel to get caught by branches and grass and make you shoot over your target, the more *will* be caught. Since each leaf is progressively higher, you may have taken a fifty-yard shot with the four-hundred-yard leaf and wondered why you completely missed a buffalo's chest or worse, wounded the damned thing.

You'll hear a lot of different opinions on this, but I like my .375 to be zeroed in for one hundred yards, which puts the point of strike about six inches low at two hundred yards and about two feet low at three hundred yards, all this with 300-grain bullets. Six inches and two feet are easy to remember and I believe it's far better to hold over rather than adjust sights for the allowance.

The whole thing is for you to *shoot* the load you select at one hundred, two hundred and three hundred yards, and see for yourself exactly how high or low you must hold at longer or shorter distances. I can recall only once having had to take a shot at better than three hundred yards, and that was at a wounded roan antelope in Zambia, which was in a pause between second and third gear at better than four hundred paces. I held more than a body ahead and a body thickness above his back, and he crumpled up like dynamited cardboard.

Of course, and this isn't a how-to book on shooting, remember to hold a touch *high* at extremely short range, then lower at mid-range to the zero, as your bullet will still be rising to the line of sight, then above it, and back down to your point of zero.

Probably nothing has done so much for practical conservation, in terms of saving wounded game that would have otherwise been lost, than the telescopic sight. Yet one still hears the strangest comments about scopes from nonshooters, who have some idea they're somehow infallible or, failing that, unsporting. If there are people who shoot better without scopes at longer ranges, I haven't met any of them. But I can think of a recent incident to illustrate that even some fine riflemen are sufficiently unfamiliar with scopes as to believe that somehow they are unreliable.

My friend is one of the top shots in South Africa but, until a few months ago, had shot only Bisley-style competition, which is strictly with iron sights. He had it in his mind that telescopic sights were some sort of gimmick, a concept that grew over more than twenty-five years of shooting. I suppose this is understandable as he'd never even looked through one! Well, after a few sessions on the range with modern sniping equipment, he realized that there was just no comparison between using a scope and using iron sights at any kind of reasonable distance. Seriously, this was three months ago and I hear from a mutual pal that he's actually thinking of writing a manual on the subject!

Before we discuss my ideas for a good African scope, let me pass on a bit of inexpensive advice. *Don't* ask your professional hunter to "zero" your rifle for you. It's just not done. You are probably completely aware of this, but on the off chance that you're not, almost nobody can regulate a scope for another person because of differences in "hold," facial contour, trigger control, and even parallax, which is the apparent change in the direction of an object, especially as seen through a scope, caused by a light shift in position such as that produced by a tiny difference between the way the rifle is held and the way the target is viewed through the scope. The crosshairs may be in one spot for your eye and in another for the next person's. You will also immediately advertise that you're either afraid of your rifle's recoil or that you simply know very little about shooting. Of course, if you don't know anything about shooting, you're unlikely to spend the fees required for a safari, but should such be the case, let your professional know and he'll work with you.

There are circumstances when a scope is most inappropriate, especially in the hunting of dangerous game at close quarters, where the field of view is obscured by the magnification. Another odd place one sees scopes is on some double rifles, since, even ideally, both barrels shoot to the same rough point of impact only at a specific distance for which the barrels have been regulated during manufacture. Basically, I think a scope on a good double is akin to the proverbial female appendages on a boar.

Most experienced writers will advise a single-power 4x scope for an all-round rifle. Personally, I favor a variable power, which will give me greater magnification and light-gathering properties when the light is poor, and it doesn't get much poorer than the early evening in a leopard blind.

Even a few years ago, variables were frowned upon because some didn't hold their point of zero when the magnification was screwed up or down, but I think this problem has been largely solved. I used a German 2x–7x for a couple of years in Zambia with good results and, since then, have gone to a 3x–9x with coarse crosshairs around a finer set in the center of the field of view. I find the three-post tapered styles clumsy, and they cover far too many minutes of angle at even one hundred yards for fine work.

The reason I like the variable-power scope is that it is the most adaptable, coming down to 3x and up to 9x with a twist of the fingers. Of course, it should always be kept in the lower positions for normal field carry, as a fast target would be hard to pick up at close range with the tiny field of view, and this could get you killed if the close animal was a charging lion or buffalo.

As important as the scope itself is the mount that attaches it to the rifle. The advantages of a detachable or "tip-off" mount in my opinion far outweigh the drawbacks because of the flexibility offered. A model I like is the Pachmayr Lo-Swing, which offers three positions. The scope may be in position for use over the receiver, swung away and down to the lower left of the action or completely detached by unscrewing a thumb knurl. This offers an almost instant choice of open metallic sights or telescopic tube in less than a couple of seconds. The mount and the scope are held in position by a spring clip when in use, and they swivel on two pivots to clear the iron sights. When in thick cover, I completely remove the top half of the mount and the scope itself so it won't somehow get hung up in the bush, leaving me the express sights, which are all I'd want at close quarters anyway. One of the best features is that the Pachmayr, when reattached after the scope tube has been completely removed, holds the original zero perfectly.

The claw-type mount is also fine, a lever attachment tightening the scope in position for use, although it doesn't usually offer the option of carrying the scope still on the rifle but out of the line of the iron sights. One thing I don't like about some of the European rifle designs, sometimes seen on continental doubles, is that the claw mount is an integral part of the rifle's receiver and offers no real option for any other type of mount. The claw, however, is very reliable and holds zero well.

Over the past few years, there have been quite a few new types of scopes, especially those that appear to project a glowing dot at the point of impact when seen through the lens. I've not had much experience with them but suspect that if they are sufficiently recoil-resistant, they might be excellent for the cave-mouthed .458s and the .460s. The big question, though, is whether or not they can take the sixty to eighty foot-pounds of kick the big bores generate. You might want to bring one along for a tryout. . . .

Probably the best advice to offer is that if you've done a lot of deer hunting or such back home, stick with what you're used to in scopes. If it's fixed power and a standard mount, that's fine. It's just that you get a touch more flexibility with the detachable mounts and the variable scopes.

One of the major problems I have had with my clients' shooting has been the common failure to use a scope properly when game is located and it has been decided to try for a shot. I can't emphasize this point strongly enough. The most common fault occurs when the shooter raises his rifle to sight through the scope and loses the target. The reason for this among even fairly experienced hunters is that they tend to look *at* the scope rather than simply fitting it between their eye and the target while not taking their focus off the animal. The big trick is to keep both eyes open, never varying the point of focus of the eye from the target. A scope should really be used with both eyes open, otherwise the stereoscopic depth and angle aspect of the shooter's sight is lost. It might feel awkward at first but try to get used to the idea. The master eye will take over, I promise you faithfully. Once you've located the target, don't take your eye off it, simply raise the rifle and fit the scope between the eye and the animal. The rest will come naturally. So often the shot is lost when the shooter glances down to look at the scope or the rifle, loses sight of the half-camouflaged game and points the rifle all over the area trying to pick up the target again. The same applies to the use of binoculars, although less critically. Should you be completely uncomfortable using a scope with both eyes open, I wouldn't tell anybody if you closed one as you started your trigger squeeze. But to locate the game through the scope and get the crosshairs on in the first place, just remember to keep both those peepers wide.

One of the most dangerous aspects of the magazine bolt-action rifle to the man who uses it on potentially vindictive game is the magazine release plate and button on the bottom of the forestock below the action. Doubly interesting is that the heavier the caliber, the more likely this catch is to release on the first shot, kicked free by recoil, dumping the nice, shiny contents of the magazine with gentle thumps all over your boots. Perhaps this characteristic of recoil-released extra rounds has led to the increasing popularity of the clip or separate magazine designs of which I see so many lately.

I have had several unnerving incidents involving the mag floor plate, all, oddly enough, with buffalo. One client brought out a borrowed .404 custom rifle on a Mauser action and, because he was using single-loading to zero, he placed no "stacking" pressure on the staggered load of rounds that would have been in the magazine under field conditions. When we came up to within about ten yards of a very fine *macho* buff in cover thicker than excelsior, my client fired and the catch released a brass bomb load of .404 cartridges into his pants cuffs. It had been a good shot too, but we were just a bit too close. The bull swung toward us and flipped on his afterburners, giving me just enough time to stick a .470 solid below his right eye. Happily, he'd had enough. Other circumstances were not quite so hairy, but all had the potential of becoming unquestionably hirsute.

The point of the exercise is to make certain that the retaining catch of the magazine is strong enough to take the recoil of the caliber. When you zero in, use a full magazine as you would in the field, even though you'll get a certain amount of deformation in your soft-point cartridges as the kick throws them against the front of the magazine. There has been some improvement in this deformation problem as well as the problem involving solid bullets where the slug is driven back into the neck of the cartridge past the cannelure, creating in effect a compressed round. I wrote in *Death in the Long Grass* of nearly getting the Ultimate Relief with a .458 that did this when I was cropping elephant. Not an ad, but if you're using soft-points, the Winchester Silvertip is especially resistant to this problem.

Rifle slings with detachable swivels are, in my thinking, a great addition to your hardware. The greatest common mistake under ordinary field hunting conditions is to let a gunbearer carry your gun for you. I can't even dream of how many trophy opportunities have been lost by the client's not having his rifle within reach even if not in his hands. African hunting is of the very nature that anything may literally pop up from under your feet, and if I can't see clearly for at least two hundred yards in every direction, I carry my back-up gun personally. Considering most of the terrain of southern Africa, this means eternally.

As we'll see, timing to get a shot off before the chance is lost is of crucial importance. If more than half the time is taken by having the client's rifle transferred to him in the first place, there's that much less time to do the deed. Still, in very thick cover, a sling can easily be removed by unsnapping the swivels and sticking it into your pocket, probably along with the scope.

Besides the ordinary method of carrying a rifle slung over a shoulder, I would suggest another way to carry it when there is a possibility of a shot being offered that will have to be taken in a hurry. If you are right-handed, sling the rifle over your left shoulder, the muzzle up, but the sling strap behind your shoulder instead of in front and the underside of the rifle pointing toward you in a vertical position, your left palm pushing out lightly against the balance of the middle of the gun. It's comfortable, held by the tension of the weight of your left arm against it, and, most important, can be brought into position with a firm ready sling hold in far under a second. Just shrug the left shoulder to release the sling and it will slip just behind your elbow, steadying it for the shot. I like this position so much that I've had all my shotguns equipped with slings and rarely miss at least a chance at a rising bird because of the speed of the trick.

Muzzle brakes and muzzle porting, which dissipate recoil

without hurting accuracy, are increasingly popular and have even become standard equipment in some of the really heavy-hitting calibers. I've not used them on my own rifles, but see no reason why this should not be considered as a way of reducing recoil. Recoil pads are usually included in most of the bigger-caliber rifles and, if yours doesn't have one, consider having one added.

Before moving on to bullets, let me again reinforce the idea that you'll be better off with a .375 H&H than with a .458 Winchester Mag. Although the .458 bullet at 500 grains is 40 percent heavier than the .375 at 300 grains, the latter has about a third less recoil while producing muzzle energies only 14.1 percent below the much heavier slug. This makes your recovery from recoil of the first shot much faster and hugely more pleasant. In my experience, the .375 H&H in a 300-grain solid bullet is a far better penetrator than the more tissue-resistant .458, and this is no little matter when speaking of the performance of African bullets. So, in a phrase, don't use more gun than you can handle.

SEVEN

A Solid Suggestion

Any rifle is only as ultimately effective as the bullet it fires. Today, when there are more different types of bullets on the market than hair-coloring products, the choice you make can have a lot more impact on your future on an African safari than merely making the wrong selection for an American deer hunt. It can get you killed, and very messily at that.

African game animals vary in size from antelopes not much bigger than toy poodles to elephants, the largest land animals. Considering that cartridges are commercially loaded and marketed in such types as hollow-points, round-nose soft-points, pointed soft-points, bronze-points, plain lead, teflon and bronze, alloy-tipped, H-partition and a dozen other forms from truncated cone to bluff-nosed—not including the military and law-enforcement options of tracer, armor-piercing, incendiary, ball, explosive, spotter and Glaser—it would seem inconceivable that one single type would be safe to use on all members of this huge range of targets. Obviously, a 130-pound impala doesn't require the ballistic persuasion of a 2000-pound Cape buffalo. But in the deep scrub of much of Africa, who can say what will appear and when!

Happily for the hunter in Africa, amateur or pro, there is an excellent trade-off that, although not absolutely ideal for all circumstances, will kill any African animal deader than the nickel cup of coffee. It's the solid, and, since the late 1800s it has become the standard, stalwart round in most professional hunters' chambers.

As discussed earlier, you'll have to cover an awful lot of ground to find a seasoned pro who doesn't think that bullet penetration is the most important function of a rifle-cartridge combination. Your first few days on safari will show you why. There's one hell of a lot of difference between the TV wildlife shows that depict game animals in parks and the facts of hunting them in concessions or safari areas. Safari is not like most of the telescopic-sight ads, showing elk, moose, deer and bears always broadside, offering a clear shot at the boiler room. Often only a small portion of the animal is visible and, if a bullet can't penetrate through nonvital bone and meat to reach paydirt, it's worse than foolish to fire at it in the first place, as you'll only cost yourself more expensive time following up a nonfatally wounded animal. With equal frequency, you'll have to take one degree or another of a "Texas neck shot," either raking from a hip forward or directly up the back. The soft-point of any type, even those supposed to "wade in deep" with "controlled expansion," just can't penetrate far enough to be effective, especially at longer ranges. The solid, also known in days of yore as "full-patch" bullet, works on the exact opposite principle: it's designed to penetrate through whatever animal matter it runs into, in an undeviating line, as far as is physically possible, given its caliber, weight, striking velocity and resistance encountered.

Probably because solids aren't commercially loaded in America for calibers other than those obviously for African use, they are often not appreciated because they're simply not used by Americans. When millions of dollars are spent on advertising campaigns to promote one or another patent style of expanding bullet and its reliable, crushing performance because of one notch or another between bullet and jacket or alloy tip, most men who haven't tried them get the reinforced impression that nonexpanding solids simply "zip right through game animals doing no real damage." Now really, think about that!

Who could believe that a 300-grain .375 H&H Magnum solid bullet, with a diameter of better than a third of an inch, traveling at a speed to thump into your waterline at nearly 2,200 foot-seconds at one hundred yards would simply "drill right through" with no immediate damage? Anybody who believes this has never seen solids at work.

Not only will the properly designed and constructed solid slug put a lovely hole through any organ it's correctly directed at, it becomes triply deadly if it touches bone, because it will smash it and, with the imparted velocity, turn the shattered chunks thereof into the biological equivalent of grenade fragments.

Of course, the solid is recognized as most effective against the real heavies that would otherwise disrupt a soft-point expanding bullet by the weight and resistance of muscle and bone tissue. The solid is the classic dose of medicine against elephant and rhino as well as buffalo when not in a herd situation. But if it's so acknowledged to be effective against the really big game, why would anybody apply the backhand, topspin logic to conclude that it would be less so against smaller game with less resistance? It makes no sense, theoretically or practically, as your first experiences with nonexpanding ammo will demonstrate.

I have no idea whatever how many thousands of smaller antelope plus lion and leopard, I have shot with solid bullets. Not only has there never been a problem, the meat damage and skin disruption have also been minimal. As a professional who only shoots if a client's animal has been wounded and looks as if it may give us the slip—or in the case of a charge—I find that most of the angles offered me have been less than ideal, usually going-away. A soft-point just wouldn't have been enough in most situations, whereas a solid nearly always is if I do my job. Only two cases come to mind where the solid did not seem effective, once on a puku, a heavy-set, deer-sized antelope in the Luangwa, and on a warthog not long ago. I shot the wounded puku four or five times through the shoulder with .375 solids before it piled up and I could have covered the holes with my hand. I just dunno. The warthog was slated as leopard bait and I also gave it a .375 solid too far back, exactly in the center of the body as it was turned sideways to me. I thought it was a miss as the *ngulube* didn't even trot off. Lining up carefully at two hundred yards, I shot again and it dropped as if dynamited. Yet there was a hole that had drilled through on the first shot and just had not hit anything important, or at least nothing immediately so. Of course, you could not have expected much more from a soft-point. Solids aren't magic. Like any bullet, they must be placed in vital areas. Still, if you do your job, they'll do theirs.

Professionals tend to carry solids in their rifles not only for fleeing wounded game but also because they're responsible for the safety of the whole party at all times. Wandering around in cover, any one of a number of unseen, injured, mating or just plain cantankerous big game animals can come boiling out in a full charge with no warning. The logic, and it's valid, is that with solids in his rifle he can stop a buffalo, rhino or elephant as well as a lion or leopard. In fact, he should be able to stop *anything*. With soft-points in the pro's gun, he would be okay on lion or leopard, the thin-skinned stuff. He wouldn't have much of a hope on the really big boys.

Karamojo Bell, possibly the world's top ivory hunter earlier this century, who died in 1951 a wealthy man from the proceeds of his hunting, was an absolute devotee of the solid during his years in Africa (although he later expressed an affinity for killing British red deer stags with a soft-point, high-velocity neck shot). Bell had very nearly been killed by a lion he shot in the face with soft-point, copper-capped slugs in Kenya while a teenage guard and meathunter for the Uganda railway. Switching to solids, he never stopped using them. As he wrote in his autobiography, *Bell of Africa*, completed and compiled by the American gun author Col. Townsend Whelen, "I have always found the solid to be *very deadly for any kind of game* [my italics]. With an end-on shot with this bullet the vitals are sure to be raked if the holding is as it should be."

Obviously, Bell's experience taught him that game doesn't stand around looking like calendar paintings of the Hartford Insurance stag. Although light-skinned, moderately muscled creatures such as lions are generally taken with soft-points, Bell specifically commented that solids were equally good medicine for them: "Speaking personally, I have killed sixteen lions with .256 and .275 solid bullets as well as dozens with other calibers (using solids), and so far as I can recollect none of them required a second shot."

If you won't take Bell's word, how about Hemingway's? Writing the foreword of François Sommer's *Man and Beast in*

Africa (Herbert Jenkin, London, 1953) Papa as usual pulled no punches:

> If I may add one technical observation it is this: a very strong case can be made for using only solids on all African game. You can then take a shot from any angle if you know anatomy and the solid bullet will not break up, nor expand and slow up. It will continue straight on its course toward the vital organ you intend it to pierce. Shooting by anatomy from any angle with solids is the deadliest and most merciful way to hunt. But first the hunter must learn the anatomy of his animals properly. Then, until he is really "checked out" he should see each animal skinned and butchered and trace the paths and results of his shots. Eventually he will be like a surgeon except that he will be armed with the lightning rapier of the long-reaching solid instead of a scalpel. Then he should try to take his shots closer and closer: for the pleasure of the stalk and to be able to apply his surgery the better.

Ernest Hemingway may not have been a professional hunter, but he knew of what he spoke.

Today, solids are commercially available in .375 H&H, .458 Winchester Magnum, .378 Weatherby Magnum (which we haven't mentioned, as it's to the .375 H&H what the .460 is to the .458) and the .460, and many smaller calibers are handloaded with solids. More on that when we get to handloading your own ammo. Unfortunately, there are solids and good solids.

I started off in Africa with the old bluff-nosed Winchester 300-grain .375 H&H rounds, an old style developed when the firm started loading the caliber nearly sixty years ago. They're worse than useless; they can get you hammered. Unlike the classic British-designed solids, which have a lead core reinforced by a steel jacket covered with a cuprous alloy to take the rifling of the barrel, the "bluff" Winchester slugs have no reinforcement beyond a thinnish gilding metal or "Lubaloy" sheath wrapping the lead core of the slug. As such, they're just not up to the tough shoulder bones of buffalo and used to tear in half at the cannelure joint of the bullet, tumble, keyhole and completely rupture on heavy bone. I have a handful of them that still give me chills, having been dug out of wounded buffalo after I had sorted them out. Oddly, they worked just fine on elephant brain shots, but there's a good deal of difference between a buffalo's shoulder bone and the spongy, honeycomb structure of a jumbo's skull.

The best solids I have used are those typified by the current 300-grain load in .375 by Remington, which are round-nosed and properly reinforced. There's not much that gets in their way that they won't go through. The older Kynochs were also excellent, the difference being immediately obvious when I got my hands on a couple of boxes at the same time that I was still using the old bluff Winchesters. The .458 Winchester Magnum solids, as loaded by most manufacturers, are first-class, as are the Weatherbys. If in doubt when buying solid ammo, make sure that the bullet point is round-nosed and not the military pointed shape. These are not really meant for tissue penetration, as are the hunting rounds. And unless they're black-tipped, which indicates "armor-piercing," they're not reinforced in any case. Far better to leave any military loadings alone, as they're just not meant for the same job and don't perform very well in pointed conformation on game.

Some people not familiar with them have the impression that solids are good "brush-busters." I suspect that they're better than soft-points, which are manufactured to rupture their noses on meeting any resistance, but the simple fact of the matter is that there is *no* bullet design that will do a reliable job of penetrating any but the very lightest leaves without wild deviation in trajectory. In fact, this has been well proven by many authors' deflection tests, using various sizes of wooden dowels to imitate branches and sticks.

The problem is caused by the bullet's being stabilized by the rotation imparted by its spinning through the rifling as it goes down the barrel. This spin is delicate, as you will realize if you've tried to stabilize 100-grain .30-caliber bullets in a barrel that takes 220-grain slugs as well. The delicacy of this rotation, based on the per-inch twist of the barrel lands and grooves, really came home to me when I was still in college (technically, at least, as I spent most of my time hunting woodchucks near the University of Virginia). I had a custom hand-me-down wildcat varmint rifle in the old .219 Improved Zipper, a fire-formed version of the standard round, although now obsolete. One day, fooling around with some 60-grain bullets of .224 inches in diameter, I loaded up a batch and was astonished to find that every slug went through the paper target *sideways*. Actually, the groups weren't bad but the novelty of the idea of a bullet going through the air side-on and, at that, hitting the aimed point of impact, fascinated me. Of course, it was the rate of twist of the barrel that wouldn't "set up" the longer heavier bullets as it would the 53-grain slugs I had been using. I wish I'd framed those targets. They were sure a conversation piece. For antipersonnel use against the enemy, the military .223 (5.56mm) ammo used in the M-16 U.S. rifle is favored *because* it loses stability so terribly on impact, creating severe wounds.

So the problem with any bullet meeting an impediment before it arrives at the target is that the spin is impaired, which makes the round react just as a football pass does when tipped by a lineman. The only chance of getting a killing bullet into a target covered by brush is in direct proportional chance to the distance between the obstruction and the target. If an antelope is only a couple of feet behind the obstruction, you'll probably still get a good hit unless your bullet self-destructs through hyper-velocity or poor construction. If it's more than a few yards, you might as well save your ammo, because your bullet will be completely deflected or, worse, it will wound the animal.

Speaking of solids, one of the most fascinating tales I have ever heard was recently imparted by a famous ex-professional hunter from Kenya days, also a well-known animal "catcher" for zoos and circuses, Ken Stewart. Ken and I were having a couple with Ron Selley, a South African game ranger, when Ken asked if I knew that two bull elephants had been killed with one shot each from a .22 Long Rifle cartridge. I took a large swig and allowed that I, indeed, did not.

The story had to do with two other well-known pre-*Uhuru* types whom I haven't met and so won't use their names, although I do believe the proceedings.

The two men, related by marriage, were out to collect their annual personal elephants for which they were entitled to buy licenses in colonial days. One had an express rifle but, as the elephant was "bumped into" near camp without really having been spoored, the other was carrying only a lowly .22 with a standard 40-grain unjacketed lead load, used to collect the odd guinea fowl. The tusker in question was smack in the middle of an acre of bush, with only little patches of his battleship-gray anatomy in evidence. Darkness was falling and, after a whispered conference, it was concluded that the bull probably wouldn't move on his own and facilitate a heart or brain shot. The man with the rim-fire agreed to "sting" the jumbo into changing position with a shot, on the chance of enabling the hunter with the big rifle to get a shot in.

Doves cooed and hearts thumped as the man with the .22 moved into position. Raising the rifle, he squeezed off a shot where the creature looked biggest. Although not very sporting, this certainly brought results. With bellows and screams that blew leaves off the surrounding trees, the elephant ran directly away, offering no angle to the big gun. The two men looked at each other, shrugged and lit a smoke each. As one opened his mouth to speak, there was a god-awful gurgle and a crash some one hundred yards away. The hunters stared wide-eyed at each other.

Yup. The jumbo, a good tusker in the eighty-pound range, was down and gone. Dead. Struck by a .22 rim-fire.

As it chanced, the tiny slug had caught him facing left, just as his left leg was moving forward for a pace, exposing the thinnish skin of the "armpit," which covers the main arteries flowing into and out of the heart. The little lead solid had drilled straight through what I presume had been the aorta and the bull had piled up within ten seconds.

Once, I would question. Twice?

The story, of course, went around the area—despite the fact that the use of the .22 was illegal—and came to rest with a high game official. The social beat being small, he didn't swarm the hunter, whom he knew well as a responsible sort. He did, however, strongly question the veracity of the tale. One well-irrigated evening some weeks later, though, the matter came to a confrontation, leading to a £500 bet between the two that the shot couldn't be duplicated. It was accepted, not by the man who shot the original bull, but by his companion who carried the express rifle, and who thought quite a bit better of his rashness the next morning. Five hundred pounds was one healthy sockful of money.

He was nevertheless at the official's office with his own license in hand, ready to go kill another elephant with a .22 rifle. They hunted most of the day and, at about three o'clock, cut a good spoor that led up to the heels of a sixty-pounder.

The agreed-upon rules stated that it had to be an elephant whose size the official approved as being adult. This fitted the bill. For twenty minutes the hunter tried to remember exactly where his in-law had placed the tiny slug and, when in position, he gave a little noise. The loafing bull, not unduly alarmed, took a pace forward from right to left broadside and got 40-grains of lead for his trouble. He only went one hundred and ten paces.

I wouldn't have been too quick to accept the saga of the small bore had I not fooled around with the .22 for fun, testing on both elephant and buffalo carcasses to see how far it would penetrate. When things such as muscle tension and sinew location are just right, I would have to concur that it is possible to take an elephant with a .22! For my money, I'll buy it, although I wouldn't try to duplicate it.

Soft-points are not, by previous implication, to be thrown out into the snow and sleet as poor cousins. Given a good angle and a proper caliber, they'll do a grand job on most of the beasties they were meant to handle. In fact, one of my favorite leopard bullets is a 300-grain .375 H&H Winchester Silvertip with the alloy cap *carefully* prized off the nose of the bullet, giving instant expansion. Leopards are a set-up shot, so there's not really any reason to worry about intervening bushveld.

With lions, if you're not using a solid, the ordinary Silvertip or the other deep-digging soft-points are fine. Lions are much more ruggedly built than leopards, outweighing them three times or more. To get a frontal shot past those chest steaks and into the heart or lungs, you'll probably prefer a slug such as a round-nosed Corelokt by Remington, which has little lead exposed at the tip for slower expansion.

Whatever you decide to choose as your bullet and caliber, at least take this advice to heart: don't use different bullet weights for the same calibers. There just isn't a case, the example of the .375 H&H being typical, for using 270-grain soft-points for one class of game and 300-grain solids for the heavy stuff, particularly when the designs are available in the same

300-grain weights, which will have a closer bullet-strike point than you are capable of holding the rifle. To raise your rifle to fire at a longer shot and then to have to stop and think which weight ammo you have stoked is just a waste of time.

I and most of my colleagues believe in the heavier, slower choices rather than the lighter, faster bullets in a given caliber. If you're going to shoot a .30-06 or a .308 as your medium rifle, use at least 200-grain and preferably 220-grain slugs. A little extra lead goes a long way. The same rule would apply for any caliber.

An increasing proportion of my clients bring handloaded ammo. If you happen to be a reloading buff, there's no need to advise you to work up some loads for your favorite caliber to use on your safari. Even if you're not into the "sport" of reloading, you might well consider consulting a custom-loading service to work up a variety of different loads for your rifle, try them out and decide which "prints" the best groups.

One nice advantage of handloading is that you can not only hand-tailor a combination of powder and bullet for your specific needs, you can get a variety of bullet types for reloading not offered commercially. This is especially true of solids, which can be extremely effective in smaller-bore rifles as well as in the big magnums. You may have to order them, but excellent solid bullets are available from Hornady, Colorado Custom Bullets or Barnes.

Some inexperienced hunters worry about the reliability of home-loaded ammo. The quality of such cartridges is, in fact, considerably above that of factory-loaded ammo, as even the ammunition manufacturers will agree. Of course, any hand-loaded round is only as good as the care taken in its loading, and I suspect that if you were working up a batch of fodder for use on African lions, you'd be inclined to take a little bit of extra care! Incidentally, the World Practical Pistol Shooting Championship was lost a year or two back when a cartridge that was issued failed to fire. It had no powder. It was a factory load, not a hand load, either.

How much ammo to bring is a common question. Considering actual hunting as well as frequent zeroing in, one hundred and sixty cartridges for your rifle or rifles ought to be more than plenty for a safari of up to one month. Personally, I carry nearly all solids, but if you're not yet a believer or will be shooting in more open areas for smaller species, then you may wish to have a preponderance of soft-points. You certainly won't go wrong with three boxes of twenty solids and five boxes of softs. If buffalo are involved, you'd better switch that ratio around, as it can be unbelievable how much killing they take. Sometimes you imagine you'd use less ammo to repel kamikaze attacks.

It should be born in mind, however, that the number of trophies per day that may be taken by a hunter, even though properly licensed, may be limited to two or three. This can also be a government regulation in some areas. The basic reason for this, from the safari firm's point of view, is that the skinning staff can only prepare a limited number of animals properly per day and there is a risk of spoilage if they are overworked.

If you bring too many shells, don't forget that because of the import duties for the local people, ammo is often literally worth more than its weight in sterling silver, especially in the bigger bores. Right now, in South Africa, where it is cheaper than in many smaller countries in the interior, the cost of imported U.S. or European ammo is about double, although there is excellent locally produced fodder.

We'll cover a lot more on shotguns in the chapter on bird shooting, but this seems the proper place to comment on what you might consider bringing as a scattergun.

African bird shooting can be fabulous. It can also be lousy. Just like anywhere else, it depends on where you are. For the most part, but with some notable exceptions who will cheerfully shoot your blushing ears off, professional hunters aren't much on hunting birds. I've hunted with several operations that could have offered incredible scattergunning had they but recognized the resource. To most bush-bred types, hunting birds is largely confined to sniping the heads off a couple of francolin or guinea fowl for the pot. Some years ago, in the then-Rhodesia, I noticed a large area of corn and millet under cultivation at the edge of the concession. I actually only presumed that's what it was, as it was practically blanketed with doves. Man, I've seen doves in Mexico, Argentina, Colombia and the other great spots for them, but this looked like a positive migration. Unable to resist, I insisted that we hie our way back for the shotguns.

"What for?" asked Trevor Roark, who owned the place. Gibbering and drooling, I brought his attention to the doves. Had I declared that I wanted to hunt lizards he couldn't have been more astonished. Well, I went through the entire supply of shotshells for the whole safari in about two hours, but was wise enough to be sure that Trevor, who had never wing-shot before, used a couple of boxes. So excited was he that he drove for about four hours collecting borrowed shells from his distant neighbors. The next day, we *really* got stuck into those doves, which Trevor had never heard spoken of as a game bird. Wing shooting, especially if you've never tried it, is rather like Space Invaders. Addictive.

We spoke earlier of the problems of bringing autoloading firearms of any kind to Africa, so forget your Winchester 1400 or your Remington 1100 or any of their kin. If you don't happen to be a really keen bird shooter, then you may well be better off to rent a shotgun from your outfitter if you don't mind that it won't likely be a Diana Grade Browning over-under. If you're serious about your wing shooting, then by all means bring your own. On the assumption that you're bringing your own, there's no need to offer the slightest opinion on what it should be, provided it's a 12-gauge. To try to buy .410, 28-, 20-, or 16-bore ammo is a nightmare in Africa. Hell, 12-gauge is tough enough in many places.

If either previous clients or your outfitter advises that there is good bird shooting of a type you like, the answer is to have the safari company lay in a stock of shells for you before your arrival. Sure, bring as many boxes as you can stick into empty corners of your luggage, because to import the cases that would be required for a real bird safari would be cost-prohibitive.

I used to carry a fine over-under Beretta back and forth each season until I became aware of how much field wear it was collecting. Then, one day at the Winchester franchise trap and skeet club, I saw that they were selling used Model 1200 pump guns, 12-gauge with the detachable "Winchoke" system. At the prices they were asking, it was an offer I couldn't refuse and I bought two. One or the other of these is now my bush gun as it will do anything I need a shotgun to do. It will place large, unsightly holes in wounded leopards, sleet buckshot into hyenas in the dead of night and acquit itself magnificently on such exotic fauna as guinea fowl, rock pigeons, doves, ducks, geese, francolin, partridge and quail. A couple of snipe have also gotten in the way of it. I have also killed two buffalo with them, using rifled slugs, just to see what would happen. The choketube inserts give it all the flexibility one could ask for and, by taking the plug out of the magazine tube, I have only slightly less buckshot firepower than an SS Panzer division.

Since those original two 1200 Winchesters, I've bought four more, mostly as gifts left behind with friends. Costing me less than $200 each secondhand, they're reliable and as highly esteemed in Africa as pigeon-blood rubies. A couple of years ago my Beretta, along with my double .470 and a minor duke's ransom of other guns, were stolen from my old home in Florida. Since then, I haven't used anything but the old pumps, and although my elegance afield may be marred, my game bag surely isn't. So rather than risk a really fine shotgun to the naiad airs of chance and a sure thumping in the back of a safari car, perhaps you'd be better off to pick up a used, inexpensive—if there's such a thing anymore—unfrilled scattergun.

Speaking of thumping, all your guns should be transported in hard cases, *not* cloth or leather types. I'd reached the point, before I moved to Africa for good, where I completely broke down my guns and wrapped each component securely in plastic bubble wrap. In some areas, you'll have to leave your hard cases at headquarters because light aircraft flights to your hunting grounds don't permit the long, stiff ones. The safari company will supply soft cases.

When you're hunting, your rifles will either be in some sort of secured rack in the back of the safari car, carried by one of the gunbearers in the rear or even held in your own hands, which isn't a bad idea. You won't be shooting from or even near the car but when you hold your own rifle, it's one less thing to sort out. You'll also know exactly what you've got and not have the big surprise of being handed the wrong gun unnoticed in the excitement of glimpsing something that will go into Mr. Ward's book of implied derring-do.

Carrying your rifle afield is pretty much your own business, provided that safety is seen to. Not many professionals will permit anybody—including themselves—to wander about with a cocked and supposedly safetied rifle, for obvious reasons. Some don't agree with me, but I prefer to carry my rifle—magazine bolt-action—with a cartridge in the chamber and the hammer down. It is absolutely true that, given a tremendous blow exactly in the right spot, the round *could* fire, although I have diligently searched but never heard of a genuine case of this. The danger for the unfamiliar is in putting the hammer in the down position without letting it slip:

Hold your rifle in your left hand at the forestock balance, with the muzzle carefully raised in case of a slip. Work the action so the bolt picks a round off the top of the magazine and chambers it. *Do not lower the bolt to the closed locking position!* Bracing the buttstock against the top of your left thigh, and with the bolt handle still up, hold the trigger back with your left hand trigger finger and *slowly* lower the bolt handle down into the closed position. This will ease the firing pin forward into the uncocked position, which will leave the pin resting in many rifles against the primer of the shell. I know it sounds hairy, but since the visible and unshielded portion of the firing pin mechanism is now completely protected and recessed by the surrounding metal of the rear of the bolt, you'd have to insert the head of a spike into the recess and hit it with a hammer to get the shell to fire.

Why go to all this trouble? It's safer and quieter when hunting. Now, instead of having to carry a rifle whose safety may have been slipped off into the "fire" position by any contact with brush or with your clothing, all that is needed to arm the rifle is a deliberate lifting and lowering of the bolt handle, which will slip the firing mechanism back into the grip of the seat. This is almost completely silent, no small consideration when game is close.

Naturally, the safest position is to carry your rifle with the chamber empty of a cartridge, which it should be when you're not actually stalking. I and many professionals have a camp rule that all guns are *completely* unloaded at a certain landmark close to camp. Don't think you're being treated as some sort of Boy Scout. We've all seen "accidents" by otherwise experienced and reliable clients that could have only been engineered by my pal Murphy. One gentleman put a .375 H&H Magnum 300-grain soft-point through my collar. I was in the collar at the time and nobody's going to get a second chance if I can help it.

EIGHT

People, Politics and Safari

At this point, your trip should be squared away and Bristol fashion. We've covered everything I can think of except one of the most obvious: African politics and upheaval and how they may affect your safari, such as your being shot at dawn as a Yankee imperialist spy or perhaps, as a variation on the theme, an Enemy of the People.

This subject is a little tricky because I want to be objective yet not instill the latent panic that most press reports about African differences of opinion tend to breed.

I was hunting in Rhodesia during the bush war that culminated in the country becoming Zimbabwe. Certainly it was highly interesting, especially as I would have thought that any terrorist general worth his epaulets would have attacked the isolated safari camps crammed with Europeans and Americans in hope of shutting down one of the largest sources of foreign exchange besides chrome. After all, a blood bath of Texas tourists or Italian noblemen wouldn't have done much for the balance of payments of a nation already under United Nations sanctions. In fact, the guerrillas who came to power in Zimbabwe never did

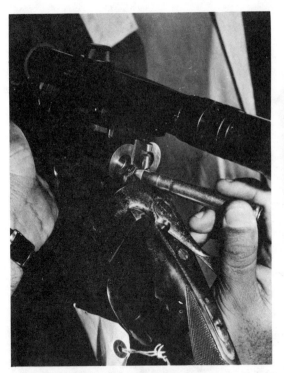

The business ends of the .375 H & H and the .458 Winchester. The size is obvious, the performance isn't. (Peter Hathaway Capstick)

Loading a fine, scoped .375 H & H double. (Peter Hathaway Capstick)

The author zeroing in his .375 H & H. (Peter Hathaway Capstick)

The sling position described in the text in detail. A single, smooth motion takes the reversed rifle from a point in front of the shoulder to the firing position in well under a second. (Peter Hathaway Capstick)

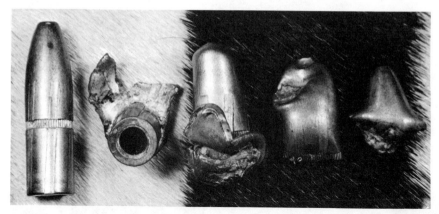

Perfect solid performance (note rifling marks) on extreme left bullet and damaged bullets recovered from buffalo when the author was a cropping officer. Heavy bone has tumbled and flattened them. (Peter Hathaway Capstick)

The author shooting from a bamboo monopod rest. The use of a rest is strongly advised. (Peter Hathaway Capstick)

LEFT: *Two .375 H & H cartridges against the background of the author's work permit as a professional hunter in Zambia. At left is the 270-grain soft-point; right, the 300-grain solid.* (Peter Hathaway Capstick)

BELOW: *Practice shooting from different positions you are likely to experience on safari. Not many outfitters carry bench rests around!* (Peter Hathaway Capstick)

Typical shooting conditions in the scrub bush, or miombo, *which so defeats the rifleman in passing a bullet cleanly through the intervening bush. The barely visible animal is a sable antelope.* (Peter Hathaway Capstick)

Low growth mopane *deflected a .375 bullet, and the shot was lost.* (Peter Hathaway Capstick)

hit a safari camp, as far as I know. Safari camps were, however, attacked in Angola in the 1960s by the MPLA and possibly by other guerrilla movements. My friend Richard Mason had his camp in Angola shot up and some of his black staff killed in just such an attack. Fortunately, neither he nor his clients were present at the time.

A fellow professional hunter pal of mine in the old Rhodesian days recently had the chance to ask a high-ranking former member of the black terrorist army why they never attempted to do this. The answer was that they also appreciated foreign exchange, so necessary to the economy of the country when they took over. Africa's turmoil today is a far cry from the old days of Congolese *Simbas* doing rather rude things, or even the bloody oathings of the Mau Mau back in Kenya.

When reading in the press about "turmoil" in Africa, take it, if you can, with some knowledge of African real estate. I have so often seen otherwise intelligent people cancel their safaris and lose their deposits because of a basic lack of understanding of the vastness of even small African countries. To decide to cancel a safari in Matetsi, Zimbabwe, because there's trouble in Bulawayo, Zimbabwe, is as stupid as calling off a trip to Philadelphia because there's a forest fire in California. The problem is, and I don't mean this as a complete indictment of the free press, that a certain sensationalism is apparently required to sell newspapers. I have read later accounts concerning the Rhodesian bush war and what was supposed to have gone on where I was at the time. I can assure you that Baron Münchhausen would have had a case of blushes, had he authored the accounts.

The thing to remember is that there is no safari operator who, even if he has no morality or fear of mortality whatsoever, will take you or his valuable equipment any place where he reckons he may get shot at. After all, he's local. He speaks the languages, knows the area as well as his last overdraft statement and also has an interest in remaining unperforated. Don't let the international press carry you off with their enthusiasm. If it isn't safe, your safari operator won't let you near the place.

As you will have gathered by this point, I'm not a social scientist of any description. I have, though, spent a lot of years in Africa and they have taught me a few things I think you should know and understand. When I am in the States, liberals tend to describe me as occupying a slot somewhere just right of Barry Goldwater, and conservatives see my views as those of Eleanor Roosevelt after three sherries. I don't know, I don't think labels for a place as diverse as Africa have much validity in the West. But I do have opinions based upon what I have seen and the places where I have been.

America and Europe perceive Africa as presumably homogeneous through the color black. Nothing could be further from the truth, as Idi Amin pointed out clearly by killing four hundred thousand Acholi tribesmen. Africa is divided more distinctly than a chess board by the lines of tribalism. Black Africans do not think of themselves essentially by any other label than their ethnic tribal definitions. Four years after independence, I had a Zambian ask me what a Zambian was. He thought of himself only in terms of his tribe, Awiza. This is hardly unusual, considering that if one American asks another in America "what" he is, the answer will never be "an American" but his ethnic or tribal background, Scotch-Irish, Jewish, English, Italian, Yugoslav, etc.

The point of this exercise isn't in any way to demean the structure of Africa and her peoples. These are simply facts that you should be aware of if you're going to Africa and will be dealing with Africans of every type, black, white, Indian, colored (the African designation for a person of mixed blood) and Bushman. If you're going to Botswana or other areas of Bushman/black cohabitation, it won't take you very long to see the different status of each, the black the conqueror and the Bushman the conquered. In fact, one of the greatest areas in modern Africa of nonviolent tribal conflict is South Africa, where both white groups are still mutually perceived as "tribal," the Afrikaners being of Dutch/French Huguenot stock and the English-speaking community largely of British origin. Each "tribe" is a separate yet cooperating entity, having different languages and customs.

I had a very interesting dinner with a black American doctor two years ago, upon his return from a safari in Zambia. He too was surprised that there was no affinity whatsoever beyond personal relationships developed on the hunting trip between the local blacks and himself, despite his race. As he said,

"Nobody seemed to know what to make of me. I suppose if I had to put it into a phrase, I was seen as a black white man." It's a good example of tribalism. None of the Zambians had any reason to relate to him, as he was not of the same tribe, did not speak their language or actually have anything more in common with them than any other foreigner would have had. The bush African you will meet on safari has a lifestyle and priorities quite different from all that is familiar to the European or American safari client, who often comes from a highly urbanized, sophisticated background where such things as ancestor worship and the *lobola* marriage custom are utterly alien. By keeping this in mind, you will perhaps be in a better position to appreciate the bush African safari staff and the very great role they play in a successful hunt.

One of the aspects of Africa that I find continually fascinating, and we're not talking of the darkest Ituri Forest, is the huge and persistent interest and belief in witchcraft. I know that this sounds sensational in this day and age, but just wait until you've finished your first week in the bush.

Essentially, witchcraft is light years ahead of modern concepts of medicine in the minds of most tribesmen. I'm not speaking of everybody, but the proportion even among university-educated people would give you a chill. Ritual murder for body parts—don't worry, the local product is preferred—is a major motive in many homicides and that's not just in the *bundu* but in large centers like Harare, Johannesburg and Cape Town.

The essence of the witchcraft concept is that nothing happens that is evil unless it has been caused by somebody "hexing" somebody else. Really! And it's no joke, now possibly a billion-dollar industry in southern Africa alone. If your goat drops dead, somebody put a spell on it. If you get gallstones or a social disease, guess why. Basically, the idea is that everybody has something against everybody else, a notion not overly played down by the practitioners of the faith, the witch doctors.

You think I'm kidding?

The sovereign state of Swaziland apparently believes in the powers of witchcraft for assassination. The September 10, 1983, edition of most southern African newspapers reported that the future king of Swaziland—a mountainous black nation independent since 1968—Prince Makhosetive, sixteen years old and at school in Britain, had been set up for witchcraft murder by an imported witch doctor (*Inyanga*), Nhlavana Dantshi Maseko, upon his arrival in London. The professional hexer Maseko was detained by British authorities following a "clandestine visit to England to administer unknown charms to Crown Prince Makhosetive." It was further charged that the former Minister of Home Affairs had conspired with the former queen regent to have the prince killed by witchcraft.

Should you question the popularity of some traditional *muti*, the local term for magic or "special" medicine, remember that the "Conqueror of the British Empire," Idi Amin Dada, was a confirmed cannibal, as was the deposed Emperor Bokassa I of the former Central African Empire.

Witchcraft is very interesting stuff, though, as the most casual perusal of any period of African history will point out. One true tale that has always appealed to me took place during that period in the early 1800s when Shaka, who founded the Zulu nation, was still in the midst of warfare with the other clans of the region. Before things got organized for the tribe that was to thump the British at Isandhlwana and nearly again at Rorke's Drift, Shaka was still a warrior for the Mtetwa, and Dingiswayo, his chief, was scrapping with Zwide, king of the Ndwandwe.

Zwide, who held all the aces in local witchcraft talent, sent Dingiswayo a young, beautiful and apparently savvy lady, who managed to collect a smear of what might tactfully be called Dingiswayo's impropriety. Of course, no more powerful *muti* could be imagined in a land where people even burned their fingernail parings for fear of their being used against them for hexing.

The Ndwandwes were delighted. They "doctored" the fords of the river, successfully keeping back the enemy—who were actually waiting for late reinforcements—or so they thought—and bewitched Dingiswayo into leaving his army, unarmed and in the company of only a few girlfriends. Wandering around the bush smelling the flowers, he was caught by one of Zwide's patrols, kept as a guest for a few days and then decapitated by Zwide's dear old mum, who collected the dried heads of her little boy's competition. It doesn't take many incidents like that to keep witchcraft alive and well in Africa.

Lest it be thought that my observations are somehow a slur

on the facts of life in much of Africa today, let's not forget that superstition is by no means the exclusive province of any racial or ethnic group. Even in the United States, the bastion of gadgeteerism and technology, practical witchcraft is hardly dead. If you doubt me, try to find a floor in an office building numbered thirteen. See what I mean? Let's not even bother getting involved in walking under ladders or throwing spilled salt over the shoulder.

It is common custom still to have one's rifles "blessed" by a witch doctor. I know several professional hunters with university degrees who would not dream of starting a season without such a ceremony. Ah, well, why not? The concept of "playing it safe" goes a long way in Africa. . . .

If I've digressed from the "hardware" of this book, you must excuse me and put it down to the fact that I want you to have as much insight as possible into every aspect of safari life. This, most of all, includes the way of life and some of the beliefs of the people with whom you'll be most closely associated, the rural Africans themselves, black and white.

NINE

Lingua Franca

Before I became a Professional Small Boy in Africa, I was first an amateur small boy in New Jersey, although not on purpose.

How well I recall my Tarzan comics, the language of which I memorized in uncounted drizzling days in the grapevine-and-evergreen huts I built in the depths of the wilderness—at least a hundred yards from the kitchen door—and my blood-curdling adventures with White-Skin (Tar-Zan), screeching my defiant yell of *Kreegah! Bundolo!* at any Girl Scout in range. Yes, sir, *Ungawa!*

You can imagine my unbounded rapture when I saw my first safari guidebook, featuring a KiSwahili appendix, more commonly known as merely Swahili. Hot Damn! Some of the stuff was full of unquestionably useful material such as "Don't put your thumb in the soup, you baboon," which perhaps reveals the racial sociology of the time. In most places you care to research, Arabic-based Swahili was considered the lingua franca of Africa in general, a strange idea if ever one was heard. In fact, while on the subject, it's positively amazing that Kenya ever got the reputation of being the "capital" of Africa, considering that it is only about a two-percent slice of the continent of 11,685,000-odd square miles.

In any case, having mastered Tarzan's tongue, I got stuck

into Swahili as far as I could because it wasn't especially popular in the neighborhood. When called to dinner by long-suffering mother, I would sagely nod my ten-year-old head and observe, "*Ndio. Chakula tayari.*" No wonder father used to look at me with that far-away stare, gently shaking his head.

By the time I was twelve, I honestly think I could have Swahilied my way out of a Mau Mau ambush with a small profit, but I was getting an odd reputation for talking to myself. As might be expected, trout poaching, archery and my new Marlin 39-A .22 rifle soon made inroads into my career in linguistics to the extent that by the time I was twenty-nine and could have used Swahili, I could hardly ask where the men's room might be.

Happily, since the demise of most East African hunting, Swahili is largely passé for the hunter, except in Tanzania, or unless you're going to run a tearoom in Nanyuki or shine shoes at Nairobi Airport. Today, considering the major zone of safari activity more to the south of Africa, the lingua franca is no longer KiSwahili but a simple dialect known variously as Fanagalo, Fanakalo or Chilapalapa.

As a catch-all language, Fanagalo has comparatively as many moving parts as an anvil. Essentially, it's a composite tongue, developed for commerce and trade reasons in South Africa, and has spread widely to the north. You can now get along in it not only in South Africa but in Swaziland, Zambia, Botswana, Mozambique, Angola, Malawi, Zimbabwe and practically everywhere else south of the Congo River. The mining industry, which has such a need for manpower, uses it as their working language and, as laborers come from nearly every imaginable country in the region, they carry Fanagalo back home.

One major labor-recruiting organization some years ago ran a brilliant advertising campaign. This was before my time but I can tell you the story as I heard it. When tribal Africa began wearing underwear and young bloods were dissuaded from either spearing lions or whacking each other's skulls off as qualifications for manhood, a culture gap was created. How would the young maidens know who was brave and worthy of their charms and who wasn't? A little applied capitalism provided the answer. A billboard campaign was run in the native tongues in the remote areas, proclaiming, YOU AREN'T A MAN IF YOU HAVEN'T WORKED IN THE MINES. Among the young men anxious to establish their machismo, recruitment soared. I'm told that so effective was this ploy on the young women that there was a time you could hardly buy a wife without doing your time in the mines.

I would not suggest that you need to learn a foreign language for your safari. Yet you might want to consider picking up just a few Fanagalo words for no other reason than the fact you'll have fun with them and the African staff. We're not speaking of Celtic, Cretan Linear B or Mayan, but of a tongue that is literally the most easily learned language in the world. The excellent little phrase book and dictionary by J. D. Bold called *Fanagalo* and published by Hugh Keartland (Pty) Limited of Johannesburg, is readily available. Since there are nine written and spoken languages just in South Africa, including Seswati, you can see that communication problems can arise. The answer has been Fanagalo, which translates itself as "like this" or "in this way." Fanagalo, the most common term for it, is a greatly simplified form of Nguni, a black group of languages incorporating Zulu, Xhosa and others. I suppose you wouldn't be completely amiss calling it pidgin Zulu, although it has developed into a viable means of communication with slight differences between, say, the Ndebele-speakers of Zimbabwe and the Zulu-speakers of South Africa.

The beauty of Fanagalo is its flexibility. It's a common sense approach to language, exemplified by such queries as this one, to inquire one's name: *"Bani lo gama gawena?"* It's not, *"What* is your name?" but *"Who* is your name?" Many words do yeoman duty, especially such terms as *lapa*. *Lapa* is a directional or locational term, usually accompanied by a hand wave to indicate degree. It means "here," "there," "way over there," or any place indicated.

One of the two more interesting words I had to learn as a professional hunter were *kashane*, meaning "far," and *duze*, meaning "near." Believe me, when you're cold and tired, with a stomach sounding like a pack of hyenas fighting over a bagpipe, there are great differences in one's opinion of *duze* and *kashane*. One problem, if you've asked a tribesman who may never have been in a car in his life, is that he will judge distance by how long it takes him to walk. *Kashane* can mean anything from just over the hill to a two-day tramp. Watch out for *"Kashaaaane"* as it's likely to be roughly the distance between the Bering Strait and Brooklyn Heights, so designated by a casual wave.

Fanagalo not only "pulls" from the Nguni tongues, but it's shot through with English and Afrikaans. As might be imagined, it's not very strong as a technical language. It was never meant to be. "Television" is *televishini* and "radio" is either *wayiles* or *wailisi*, from the British term "wireless." Many words are positively charming. "Push" is *shova* and "pulse" becomes *gazi shaya lapa lo mtambo*, meaning "blood strikes upon the vein." The point is that you don't need to know a complete vocabulary of Fanagalo to express yourself.

I have included this little chapter on Fanagalo in the hope that you just might get as much kick out of it as I have. In many cases, your professional hunter will speak the genuine language of the local people where you're hunting, if he was born in the area.

Today, in southern Africa, English is the premier language among blacks, although there are wide areas where black Africans will know only their own mother tongue and, for example, Afrikaans. The speaking of English has a status to it, though, and you will sometimes come across tribesmen chatting away in "*Singisi*," although they are of the same language group. Actually, black Africans are among the very best linguists on earth, commonly speaking five or six languages with ease, including English, Afrikaans, Portuguese and, in South-West Africa/Namibia, German.

TEN

Great White Hunter

He's six feet six under the stained, floppy, leopard-banded bush hat, his face a sculpture of rugged brows and dazzling teeth set in a tan darker than a Florida beach boy's. The expanse of his epauletted shoulders, studded across with the dull gleam of chest-looped double rifle cartridges, tapers deltalike down to sun-faded khaki shorts above a pair of neat-kneed legs bulging with calves an Alpine climbing guide would envy. At his battered belt hangs a skinning knife longer than a samurai *katana* and in his right fist is balanced the cool, Circassian walnut-and-blued-steel splendor of his .600 Jeffery's express rifle. In his faded sapphire eyes, there still lingers the sadness of the thing that drove him here to the wilderness; what could it have been but a woman? Shifting the rifle in mahogany forearms rippling with muscle and long, white scars under the tropic-bleached blond hair, he gives a shy smile and says, "Hullo, chaps! I'm Lance Sterling-Whipsnade, your professional hunter come to fetch you. Uh, I say," with a small blush, "sorry to be latish. Couple of man-eaters and a rogue elephant to sort out on the way to the airport. Pink gin before we *kwenda*? Anybody peckish?"

At this point, I would recommend that you get out of your seat and go buy a bag of popcorn, provided the theater offers

nothing more substantial in liquid form. Lance may pretty well
fit the Hollywood idea of the Great White Hunter but you'd
better not hold your breath while you're looking for a real one
who fits the mold.

Actually, despite the years of image-building on the silver
screen, not exactly damaged by Gable, Peck, Granger, Mature
and other people who were supposed to look like genuine professional hunters, the real-life pro still has one of the most difficult,
demanding, physically dangerous and stimulating existences on
earth. So if many look like unsuccessful shoe salesmen, errant
schoolboys, college professors or rogue British beefeaters, forgive them. Most still do a good job. As for me? I have not
recently been mistaken for Tom Selleck.

I remember in my first book, *Death in the Long Grass*, discussing a bit of the professional hunter's apparent mystique
when explaining how I had come into the business myself. Perhaps a short digression would be in order here.

Practitioners of the trade are known, with various degrees
of accuracy, as professional white hunters, white hunters,
PWHs, PHs (the latter two mostly in safari brochures) and
Great White Hunters. "Professional hunter" is the most common and correct today, considering that in some areas the pros
are black men. If the term *white* once had significance, it no
longer does. One of the bigger old firms dropped that descriptive appellation from its company name, White Hunters Ltd., to
become Hunters Africa Ltd. True, *most* pros are white, but the
term has bent considerably with the winds of change. This business of "*great* white hunter" is probably, as I observed, an
Americanism, where "black" may be "beautiful" and "white,"
for some reason, "great." It works for sharks, Moby Dick,
hopes and Broadway, so why not hunters?

Reading through the old books, so many still deliciously
reeking of the smoke of ancient wood and peat fires from British
hearths near which they perched for scores of years, you can get
an idea, though, of where the original image of the classic professional bwana was spawned. Certainly, it was East Africa, especially Kenya.

In the early days of safari, as we've touched upon, the professional was a different sort of person, at least as far as his
background was concerned. There are still fine pros who have

titles before their names, but one really wonders if we'll see the likes of the Danish Baron Bror von Blixen-Finecke, husband of the author of *Out of Africa*, penned under the name Isak Dinesen, or their good friend, the Honorable Denys Finch-Hatton, killed in a plane crash in the thirties. I believe that there are professionals operating today who are the equal in talent of such greats as John Hunter, Philip Percival, R. J. Cuninghame and the cousins Hill. Perhaps, though, bright as these gems are, their setting has faded with the disappearance of the truly wild tribes and with the barbed wire that has constricted much of what was the old Africa.

It won't be all that long before the last of the final East African crop of professionals, hung out to dry when Kenya stopped hunting in 1973 and when Uganda went mad under Idi Amin, have retired. Now, they are still operating in places like Sudan, Botswana, Zambia, South Africa and Zimbabwe. Of the mixed group who have either changed to photographic or game viewing trips in East Africa or who are still hunting elsewhere— some even having just plain thrown in the towel—are names like Glenn Cottar, Reggie Destro, Dave Ommanney, Tony Dyer (for years president of the East African Professional Hunters Association), Tony Archer, Harry Selby, Andrew Holmberg, Donald Ker, Sid Downey, Bill Jenvey, Brian Coleman, John Kingsley-Heath and quite a few more who would have to work very hard to be forgotten, although not being mentioned here for lack of space and personal acquaintance.

I think the East African professionals were the most highly trained of their profession because of the stringent licensing laws of the old Kenya, Uganda and Tanganyika government game departments. This takes away nothing from the professionals who earned their licenses elsewhere, most of whom are absolutely first class. But many didn't have the long period of apprenticeship and the varied experiences in different departments of their safari firms, such as provisioning, as did the East Africans up until the early 1970s. To the professional, his license is everything. To lose it would be the same thing to him as a medical doctor having his ticket lifted. In fact, in the old days, it took just about as long to be educated in each profession, less the physician's residency.

The professional hunter today is considered an endangered

species but, in actuality, that doesn't seem to be true. Writing in 1958, my good pal and companion, Col. Charles Askins, made an educated guess that there were about thirty-five full-time pros in East Africa, not including the occasional farmer or other bush-wise soul who might fill in as a licensed "second" hunter from time to time on safaris for one of the established companies. Today, I would guess that throughout Africa there are about two hundred licensed professional hunters who, to one degree or another, are employed in a far greater safari area than existed in 1958 on a commercial basis. Many are part-time, and it's very difficult to come up with a hard-core full-time figure, but I would estimate this figure to be about eighty men (and, at one time, at least one woman) whose livelihood comes entirely from safari.

I partially base this on the membership of the IPHA, the International Professional Hunter's Association, of which I am honored to hold a full professional life membership. Of two hundred and twelve entries for "full professionals," not easy to obtain, worldwide, eighty-three have African addresses. Of course, there are more whom I recognize as having given their off-season addresses outside Africa. Another thing, not every pro is a member, for whatever reason he may choose. Still, I'm satisfied this is reasonably valid. Many listed are no longer fully professionally active.

Being a successful professional hunter largely depends on a single personality factor: flexibility. It's the original jack-of-all-trades position, which takes a fairly unusual temperament to fill. This further amazes me in that the personalities of most pros I know are obviously different, yet somehow they're held together by common sinews.

I've never seen an advertisement for a pro hunter but I think the job description might read something like this:

WANTED: Young, active man interested in low and infrequent pay to play bwana in remote bushveld. Must be proven raconteur and socialite without liver trouble, expert card player, bartender, caterer, barbecuer, philosopher, African historian. Experience in sanitary engineering, local architecture, labor relations, navigation, medicine and pharmacology, botany, zoology, ichthyology, mineralogy, entomology, butchery, taxidermy, dietetics, optics, photography and radio operation essential. Applicant should speak at least two black African languages fluently as well as English and one other modern European tongue. A solid knowledge of mechanics, driving, gunsmithing, toxicology, ballistics, tracking, marksmanship, hand-loading and experience as a professional bodyguard are required.

Benefits are twenty-four-hour day, unlimited fresh air, including rain, sun and dust; no medical, dental or life insurance and no retirement benefits. Applicant should supply his own rifles. Vehicles on a per diem basis.

The duties of the professional hunter on safari are essentially the same as those of a ship's captain, and with the same responsibilities. He's everything from the social director to the ship's surgeon, if needed. He's the author of the strategy of your hunting plan but also the tactician as to how you make each stalk. He keeps the peace among the staff, oversees the food and drink, translates and interprets, sees that your trophies are properly handled and is shooting coach, gunsmith, stand-up comedian and diplomat any time he is called on to be so. Your relationship with your professional hunter is perhaps best summed up in the observation that he is the social equal of anybody while on safari, up to and including a duke.

You'll probably get on well with your pro, as he wouldn't be very successful in his business of living in his clients' pockets were he essentially unlikeable. Most clients form very close bonds of friendship with their professionals, barring some or another social or personality disaster. Still, it's crucial for you to understand, at least within the parameters of my own interpretation, what he is expected to do and what isn't his bailiwick.

The toughest part of hunting professionally is the impossible lack of sleep. Normally, a pro gets to bed around 11:00 P.M. If dawn is at 6:00 A.M., your hunter will usually be wandering about shooing off jackals and owls by about 4:30 A.M. as he double-checks that the hunting car is in proper shape, with fuel, oil, water, proper tire pressure, plenty of spares and tool kit, and sees to the rest of the precautions that will postpone as long as possible your having to walk back to camp. That done, and the person who physically sees to these things dismissed after his all-night work, it will now be about 5:00 A.M. and time to send the waiter to wake you with a pot of tea or coffee the way you like it while the hunter checks out the day's menu and the *skafu* box with your portable bush food. I promise you faithfully, no matter how often it is packed by the same person, there is always something missing, whether the jar of milk for the tea or coffee, or maybe the sugar, butter, sandwiches, biltong or Cokes. Unless the box is physically put in the vehicle now, it may well be forgotten.

The cook will suggest what he thinks best for lunch and supper and the pro will possibly decide that rice, potatoes and corn meal mush all in one venison meal is maybe just too much starch. African cooks are usually very good but unless they are old-timers, they don't necessarily understand the mixture of different foods the whites prefer. By like token, I'd like to see a white cook, for that matter, who could do well in a black African restaurant without a good deal of experience.

While you are shaving, the stores will be checked. It is an essential difference in philosophy that kitchen and skinning staff consider only what is on hand, without anticipating the obvious running out of a critical item such as salt or flour. It is possibly because of the basic inability of the bush African to preserve perishables without freezing or proper refrigeration that creates this logic gap. But you will be told that the camp is out of eggs, cooking oil, butter, tea or—God forbid—beer, only when the last bit of any of these items has been used. Anticipation of shortages is not an automatic part of African philosophy in the bush.

A general walk around the camp will probably bring the professional to the breakfast table about the same time as you arrive, just soon enough to be on your way before dawn breaks yet with enough light to track and recognize spoor that has crossed the trail during darkness. (Of course, if you're hunting elephant or buff in a special area some distance from camp or checking a lion bait, you may be leaving some time before dawn.) When everything's ready, you'll assemble the guns and personal kits and push off with the field staff, trackers, and gunbearers as well as carriers for your camera rig, water, food and personal equipment.

We can investigate hunting techniques for different species in appropriate chapters later on. For now, let's just say that you'll usually stop for tea, a soft drink or a cold beer with a sandwich at about ten o'clock, after several hours of hard driving or walking, depending on what area you're in. This is usually about a thirty-minute break, after which, if you haven't collected anything that will take a great deal of time to skin or prepare, you'll move on again. Since game will have become noticeably less active and less evident after the cool dawn hours, this is the time to spook around for signs of lion and leopard as well as to hang baits and erect blinds.

In Zambia and Botswana, where hunting is really fairly close to camp in comparison with some eastern or northern African areas, we would normally be back in camp at about quarter past one for as light or as heavy a lunch as you wished.

From two until nearly four o'clock, not much moves among African wildlife. While you snooze or read away the hot hours in your tent or hut, the pro will be checking over the skinning operation, as the light is insufficient near dawn for close inspection of hides and horns. If salting or folding is improperly done, the hair will slip and the cape or skin will be ruined. Borer beetles, which lay larvae or eggs on horn surfaces, can destroy a set of unprotected buffalo horns in hours. Fortunately, the skinners are among the very best of the staff and it is rare for their work to be anything but perfect.

As the shadows get a bit lazy, you'll head out again, usually in a different direction, to hunt until falling murk makes it impossible and, finally, darkness makes it illegal. Back in camp as late after dusk as it takes to drive there, it's usually time for sundowners while you anticipate your shower, the kitchen *toto* drawing the water. Probably after a noggins with you, the pro will see to the off-loading and treatment of trophies while you shower, and then spruce up a bit himself before dinner, which is normally at eight. Actually, it's whenever you want it, as it is, logically, your safari.

The above are merely a few of the pro's standard duties, allowing little for the frequent visits of Mr. Murphy. Were the very nature of safari not such that some bloody thing is always breaking down, going wrong or getting sick, it would be a princely life, worthy of barons and the second sons of peers. But so effective is Murphy that the majority of the effort must be spent just on preventive maintenance.

As a very complex subgroup of people, professional hunters are particularly adept at avoiding legitimate labels that might be hung on them as types. For each one you'll meet parboiled to the eyeballs and with some highly interesting examples of mammalian pulchritude clinging to each arm of their leased formal wear at a safari conference in Las Vegas, there's an equal number of professorial types who will be in the darkest corners, discussing Ethiopian fungi or the reverse adiabatic rate of the Zambezi Valley. The only observation that can be validly made, in my opinion, is that, beyond being people of great personal flexibility and resilience, they are also absolute individuals as well as being poetically sensitive, even if they themselves would laugh at the term for how little it conveys my meaning.

One wouldn't tend to call seasoned guerrilla warfare fighters especially sensitive, at least not according to the label the world has given them. Not so. They're good at this sort of thing, the ex-Mau Mau fighters, the ex-Rhodesian veterans, the current South African "Recces" and the rest of the people who meld so well with not only the best but the most savage of nature. Pro hunters are tough, no question about that. Many of them have been seasoned in African bush warfare and, were it not for their toughness, they'd shortly be dead. *But* they're only in a position to be tough and use their knowledge if they have that special sensitivity to the bush or mountains or swamp around them. Even getting the chance to be tough means being able to recognize, weigh and evaluate the tiniest muffled sound, the thinnest tendril of odor, the slightest glimmer of steel or horn, from feet to miles away.

The physical danger of professional hunting is obviously real, particularly when you consider that, as an educated guess concerning the pros I know, about seventy-five percent get nailed at one time or another by dangerous game. Some are well and truly killed, as Hemingway might have observed, and others have multiple encounters any one of which should have got them obituarized but, for some fluke, didn't. I know three men who have been mauled at least four times at last count, and who are still hunting. You have to be fairly fond of the bush to do that!

Most pros start young, and it's a young man's game. This, of course, takes nothing from the real legends of the occupation who have hunted for decades stacked upon decades. Wally Johnson, who, as I write, is still active full-time with Safari-South, is roughly seventy! John Hunter, Philip Percival and others have been pros well into their sixties, and for sure you never heard a client complain about them!

Looking through my files, I note that I get about a letter a week from people, mostly Americans, who would like to become professional hunters. Boy, do I know how they feel! Most would literally be willing to work for no pay for the opportunity to land a professional hunter's license and probably experience the same desire I did when I pitched up a Wall Street career to play Rover Boys. This seems a reasonable time to discuss the matter. Let's start off with the negatives.

The essential problem for a non-African becoming a bwana is that he's not really familiar with the terrain, not only physically but linguistically. I don't know if hunters are born or made but those who are born with the talent have to go through a lot of polishing before they can successfully conduct safaris without somebody getting hurt. A really talented American hunter must still face the fact that he's not been raised on the land he may be hunting, and although local guides can get him about with no problem, he hasn't had the advantage of being familiar from the cradle with African game. It takes considerable time to be able to judge horn length or width of unfamiliar species at a distance, yet that's as much what a hunter gets paid for as for anything else. A knowledge of the local dialects is essential and not easily learned in the United States. Yet these things can be overcome if you're really determined and have the great advantage of some cash or impressive credit.

The odds of a non-African applying for a job as a professional and being accepted are about those of my winning the Victoria Cross. Besides the factors mentioned above, there is also the competition from people who *are* Africans, who don't need work permits or visas, who do speak Zulu, Tswana or KiSwahili, and who did plug their first elephant at age nine. Whom would you hire?

I got into professional hunting through the wildest chance and a tidal wave of good luck. But at least I was in one side of the business as a booking agent and I knew safari operators, one of whom was willing to take a chance on me because I had some experience in South America. Actually, I first went to Africa not as a professional safari hunter but as an elephant-cropping officer for the Zambian Government. As things turned out when I got there, I decided to join the safari firm instead because I didn't feel I could commit myself to a three-year government contract. Today, the chances of a non-national in most parts of Africa being accepted for game department employment are almost nonexistent. Such organizations are being "Africanized," the meaning of which I'm not entirely sure, except that if you're a white foreigner, you need not apply. In one African safari country, most white professional hunters in fact "work for" their black gunbearers as far as the laws of the country are concerned. Of course, this isn't the case in practice, but restrictions are such that this is officially required.

About the only way for a foreigner to become active in the safari business in Africa would be to buy into one of the smaller organizations. This would not rule out the possibility of applying in person for a job and of the owner taking a sufficient liking to the cut of your jib to give you a try, but I wouldn't spend the airfare having counted on it. Your best bet is to hock the farm and go in person, wander about speaking to people while learning what's where. You might also consider a divorce.

I was going to ask Harold Robbins to write the next couple of paragraphs on "Safari and Sex" but he wasn't in the phone book. Of course, it being a custom-made triangle, much is made of the supposed amorous aspects of safari life through that most reliable of all media, the Hollywood screen. Oh, yes, it sure does happen and I know professionals—ah, ex-pros—now living outside Africa with wives they met on safari who were the clients' wives at the time. But it's unusual. Most professionals are absolutely hands-off types for the simple reason that they have to be. They rely on word-of-mouth to promote their business if they're private operators, and it wouldn't take long for a complaint to get back to their superiors if they work for a large company.

I might mention that, some years ago, a safari of a group of successful American bachelor-girl models into East Africa didn't do much to dispel the lurking speculations of the public. Nor did the press reports that the professional hunters were working in relays. . . . After all, hunting's hard work.

As your chief of staff, your pro will have more to do with the success of your safari than any other factor. He, in turn, can only perform through his staff of black African gunbearers, skinners, cooks, trackers, waiters and other personnel.

During colonial times, and even today in some areas, the black race was called by their own general term, *bantu*, the plural of *ntu* meaning "a person." Like so many words considered to have some kind of racial prejudice attached, such as *native*, it has largely given over to the use of simply *black*, although the expression *abantsundu* or "brown-skinned people" in Fanagalo seems to be gaining some popularity. The term *muntu* is technically correct for a black person, especially a male, but is definitely now seen as derogatory. After all, it's my impression that the use of *Negro* in America is now socio-linguistically passé and, in some quarters, rude. It will take some years to see if the same fate awaits *black*.

At the top of the black staff is usually the professional hunter's gunbearer and general assistant. He is seen as senior to everybody but the cook, who works in a different world anyway. Today, since the demise of sixteen-pound rifles, most gunbearers are essentially trackers, although there may be a man or two hired who will do nothing else but spoor.

All of the field staff, meaning those who actually go out hunting as opposed to the men who keep and run the campsite, wear several hats. I always try to bring along the head skinner when hunting game difficult to prepare for taxidermy and he, in turn, supervises the simpler skinning tasks, which are largely done by the rest of the men. So gunbearers will track, skinners will carry load and trackers will skin. Of course, in areas that were new, I would often hire a local guide to show us around the place, or I would take on a specialist in finding one or another kind of game. Silent, my old gunbearer, was originally put on as a kudu specialist in the area of Chabunkwa in Zambia's Luangwa River Valley before I realized how good he really was. Actually, he was phenomenal with the big, chalk-striped, spiral-horned ghosts of the *miombo* but no less so with elephant. Another chap had a gift for finding lions where there weren't any. The fact that old Silent twice saved my life, once by feeding his arm to a man-eating lion until I could pick myself up and kill him, and the next time by throwing a flax water bag into the face of an elephant that I am positive would have had me after a bad cartridge misperformed, seems in retrospect to prove that he wasn't a bad investment.

Meanwhile, back in camp, you'll find the cook baking fresh bread daily and generally cranking out three squares a day, provided he hasn't gotten into the vanilla extract. Most safari cooks are first-class, but the best I ever had was Isaac Manyemba, a Tswana, who had been head chef for a well-known Johannesburg hotel before having to return to Botswana through some or another difficulty with his papers. Thank heavens for bureaucracy! Manyemba could call the cherubs down with the smell of his cooking, and we got on famously. He and his wife offered to work for me privately for a lot less than he was making, and I have always regretted that my lifestyle at the time prevented my accepting his services, although it was just as well for my expanding waistline.

The waiter and camp boss sees to the making of beds and the general supervision of the state of affairs in your temporary bush home. He'll see that your wine is properly chilled, the linen and silverware correctly laid and that there are plenty of mixers and booze of your choice. As I think of it now, it's odd that the waiter was never called upon to mix drinks but just brought and opened beers for those with a taste for the suds. Certainly, all my waiters were competent to make anything from a Singapore Sling to a Tequila Sunrise but, like so many things about safari, it for some reason just wasn't traditionally done. Either the pro or the client mixes the drinks, much as two good pals would in visiting each other's homes or when out on a camping trip in the Adirondacks.

If there was another headwaiter and camp major-domo such as the likes of my man Martin, I haven't seen him in action, although they are generally truly talented men, considering the unsophisticated rural background of most. Martin was a fine-looking, very black gentleman somewhere in his fifties when he worked for me in Zambia. I don't recall his tribe, a small one from East Africa, that somehow led to his being enlisted in the King's African Rifles, a colonial British outfit considered about the most crack native contingent on the continent. Of course, with his natural suaveness, Martin became the batman or personal servant of the ranking colonel, who must have sorely missed him when he went back to Britain and Martin headed south for Zambia, for reasons never made clear to me. Who knows? Many men have dark secrets in their pasts. Perhaps Martin was one of them.

Martin invariably pulled the largest tips, and his sense of innovation earned them. He would never think of handing a client a frosty mug of beer without a crisp, open-palmed British salute and a smart crash of well-polished shoes on the hard camp earth. If there were women in camp, he would search far and wide for a few wild flowers, which were always presented on their bare plates at mealtimes. Where he picked up that charming little trick I can't imagine, unless his old colonel was something of a ladies' man. To keep even a good grass hut clean in dusty midwinter is a nightmare. Martin must have swept and dusted six times daily but everything was always neat and clean. The kitchen *toto*, who helped him set the table, risked his life if he left a fingerprint on a glass. And heaven help the little chap if the shower water wasn't just right.

The interesting thing is that Martin, except for a very few words like "beer," "please" and "water," spoke not a word of English as such.

Except where absolutely necessary, in the old days I normally did not employ bush hands who spoke English, as it was frankly often true that a man who had reached that degree of sophistication might have had a bit more of "civilization" rub off on him than was desirable. The only time I have run across out-and-out theft on safari was in the old Rhodesia. The culprit was a mission-trained, English-speaking young man who had, in the course of his education, learned all about how to fence stolen goods. In the same area, one could leave a Land Rover full of goodies completely in the open for days and never miss a thing. Admittedly, this is not necessarily the case everywhere in Africa. The tribesmen in that particular region simply didn't steal unless they had learned the notion in the cities.

Having spent years living in the bush with them, I must say

that I am very fond of the rural Africans. In my experience, they are loyal to a fault, absolutely hard-working, reliable and honest. I have seen nothing but friendship and comradeship from them, provided they were shown the same courtesy. That so many of the early hunting books regarded these people as stupid, lazy or treacherous is a classic example of a real, uninformed prejudice against primitive peoples who just didn't fit the mold of another culture. Typical is the notion in some quarters that the more primitive blacks have no concept of appreciation or thanks. This just couldn't be farther from the fact. Nearly a year after I had given some first aid to a man for an infected leg in central Africa, he walked more than fifty miles to bring me a gift of several young bushbabies (*Galago senegalensis*) after he had heard through the local grapevine that I wanted them for pets. His gesture was by no means exceptional.

Incidentally, in southern and central Africa, the black people have a particularly charming way of accepting even the smallest gift, with the hands lightly clapped in appreciation from a sort of clamshell position. Black African body language and customs are good examples of the cultural difference in people from different backgrounds and parts of the world. I suspect that many of the original misunderstandings between the races may have come from these misinterpretations. Where a European would rise, if seated, to indicate attention and respect to someone addressing him, the custom of most blacks demands the common courtesy of remaining seated, as they would when spoken to by their chief. The custom of walking ahead of you as a courtesy probably derives from the fact that the first man in a file was in the most danger from ambush or a hidden trap.

After years of living closely with them, I have noticed other characteristics about rural black Africans that, at least to me, are of ethnological interest. Whereas most whites will wear their shoes out on the soles or heels first, blacks who have been raised traditionally have their shoes fall apart along the outside seams first. The reason for this, I can only surmise, is the slight degree of bowleggedness caused by their being carried on their mothers' backs or hips with their legs splayed. Another thing that would be quickly misinterpreted by a European or an American who has a notion that such things indicate deviousness, is the reluctance of many Africans to look you in the eye when speaking with you. They will usually stare slightly past your face. Direct eye contact is often considered rude.

One potentially big problem in the bush for a person who speaks a black language as imperfectly as I do is, again, directly attributable to the deeply ingrained cultural courtesy patterns of the blacks. If you issue an order and it is not understood, the normal reaction would be for the employee to say "yes," as if he had gotten the message correctly when, in fact, he has no idea what you are talking about. This is also coupled with the fact that most rural black Africans have a definite tendency to try to tell you whatever it is they think you want to hear. If you put out a reward for information leading to the killing of a good elephant, for instance, you'll get a good example and quite a few blisters realizing that what I say is true. These people aren't really lying; they just want you to be pleased, and if shifting a few facts around will do it, all the better! That's just good manners.

One of my most revealing insights into how differently each side sees things came when I managed the famous Khwai River Lodge in Botswana for a short time, the lodge being a game-viewing camp on the Okavango Swamp. A youngish Tswana with quite a good education asked me for work in grounds maintenance. He had a game leg, so I hired him, as he would not have had many other options. Despite his handicap, he pitched in and did a good job, which led me to quickly promote him to lodge staff, where he worked at the bar and was generally responsible for the large terrace surrounding the spreading *Ngamo* fig tree growing through it.

One morning, as I was having tea on the terrace, I noticed that it was time the bar area had a thorough cleaning. I called him over—his name was Massapukhwa—and explained that he was to take down all the bottles from their shelves, wipe the shelves and the bottles as well as the bar itself, and put everything back. Noticing the hinged section at the end of the bar where it swung and latched up to permit the bartender to enter behind the bar, I also told him to clean behind it.

As I had my tea and a smoke, I saw he was doing a good job, carefully cleaning and replacing everything. Finally, he came to the hinged section, which was latched with an eye and hook against the wall, where it had been for some time. As I watched, he lowered it, revealing a very large rhinoceros beetle, a gleaming black beast a couple of inches long with a pair of harmless but impressive head protuberances much like a tiny rhino, clinging to the wall. He looked at the beetle, looked at me and back at the giant bug. Whistling softly, he plucked the creature off the wall, carefully wiped it down with a soft cloth and, with equal care, replaced it. He polished the hinge section and swung it back up.

I had, of course, told him to clean and replace everything. He did.

To the rural black African, the ability to speak English is often considered a social grace. Thus many servants will hang on to and parrot every word they overhear in a household where that language is spoken. Sometimes it leads to interesting results. There was the famous and undoubtedly true tale of a colonial couple having the governor to tea in the then-Nyasaland. As the governor and his lady were settled among the guests, a man-servant came in carrying a sterling tea set. He paused in front of the hostess and, in a deep and loud voice, announced, "Tea is ready, darling."

ELEVEN

Everything Bites

The potential confrontation between the hunter and dangerous game under the sporting ethic is really the essence of safari. So far as I can tell, the interglacial collection of ranking man-killers, as found in Africa, exists nowhere else on earth. Generally known as the "Big Five," the group we're talking about comprises lion, leopard, elephant, Cape buffalo and rhino, although not necessarily in that order. Some exclude the leopard on the simple basis of weight, although a higher percentage of professional hunters and gunbearers, in my experience, go to their graves with leopard autographs than any other.

Africa, of course, offers many other game animals at least equal in mayhem. Hippos kill as many if not considerably more humans each year in Africa than do the buff and the jumbo put together. Crocodiles undoubtedly take as many souls awinging as do both lions and leopards these days. Never mind the snakes in the rainy season. They're usually protected.

There's hardly a game animal in Africa not capable of killing a hunter. As I have said in an earlier work, they all bite. A pal of mine in Botswana some years ago nearly died after being severely gored by a steenbuck ram he kept as a pet in his garden. We both agreed that it was some sort of mating season aberration for the little thirty-pound antelope, but his leg sported damage worse than I've seen from some lions. Bush-buck and bushpigs are both pure, undiluted, industrial-strength mean, especially when wounded. Leave them strictly alone unless you are looking for some new dimples, or worry lines on your jugular.

There are a couple of antelope, though, that don't seem to have any built-in genetic resistance to becoming T-bones for either the normal predators or man, notably the greater kudu and the biggest of all, the eland. I've never heard of anyone being injured by either, even when wounded and bayed, which makes them nearly unique. Perhaps speed and deception are their sole defense, despite their impressive horns, which are mostly used in rituals of courtship. Eland, although famous for their untiring ten-miles-per-hour trot, have often been reported to have been run down and speared without any fight, especially in wet weather and gummy mud. Karamojo Bell noted this in particular. While on this, I have seen cheetah run down by Somalis and Gallas in Ethiopia on dry ground. The cats go like hell for some distance, but have no staying power at all, at least not like that of the desert nomads.

The first thing you will notice is the incredible tenacity of life, to put it mildly, of all African game. I have spoken over the years with sportsmen and clients who have hunted extensively in other parts of the world and I've compared their observations with my own in North America, South America and Europe. This is one tenet of African hunting not much contested. African animals die harder, given the same shot, body weight and circumstances, than do those animals of other regions.

My late brother, Tom, considered by some of his peers as one of America's most distinguished and accomplished fly fishermen and angling historians, had a theory on this that makes some sense to me. Couched in terms of his experience of fishing, he compared African game, in the relatively high density of one animal to another, to salt-water fish in relation to fresh-water fish. For sure, there are some magnificent fighters among the small-mouth bass and the cold-water rainbow trout and Atlantic salmon, but most fresh-water species just don't fight as hard as do the salt-water types when hooked. Tom felt it had something to do with the degree of fitness and competition required to stay alive, and I think he had a good point.

The frenetic activity of salt-water fish, with so many predators always in evidence to gobble up the weak, sick and slow individuals, must be a practical application of the elements of Darwinism and natural selection. Only the fittest, fastest and most enduring survive, and their descendants get better at surviving through better genes. I don't think there's a trout that ever lived that could outfight a bluefish of the same weight on a line, or a Northern pike that could hold a dim glow to a barracuda of the same size on identical tackle. The same, I believe, applies to a comparison of the white-tail deer of North America and, just as a casual choice, the impala.

It's been nearly a century since the last deer in Pennsylvania or New York State had to worry about pumas or wolves. Today, all he has to do is stay out of the way of the deer hunters for a couple of weeks and take his natural chances the rest of the time. Should you doubt me, remember that there are far more white-tails alone in America today than was the case at the turn of the twentieth century, not to mention the increase in virtually all species of big game, except predators, besides man. Deer don't have to work nearly so hard to stay in business, man cultivating much of the forage they used to have to obtain naturally. I can't believe that these conditions make for a creature with more rather than less natural resistance, as would be apparent upon receiving a bullet. Sure, deer are still tough and probably quite a bit smarter than they were years ago, but they don't have the sheer vitality of most African game.

The contemporary impala, for comparative purposes, is a potential veal chop from the instant he hits the ground from his mother's womb. A baboon (oh yes, they're carnivores too) may rush in, grab, dismember and eat him in a twinkling if a cheetah or a leopard doesn't see him first. Failing this, there are plenty of hyenas, jackals, wild dogs, lions, lynxes or caracals, honey badgers, crocs and God-only-knows-what-have-you, including massive eagles, that will make his entire existence like that of a chicken in Colonel Sander's pens. Obviously, only the most durable survive to breed. Weak impala, or those of any other species for that matter, just don't cut the mustard in Africa. No wonder they can take a pummeling that non-African animals can't.

Since African game is generally so difficult to down for the count, and since so much of it is dangerous, accurate shooting on your part, chum, is triply important. We'll start wading through individual species in a few minutes, but first how about a solid look at the rules that apply to all?

It is unlikely that your professional hunter will start you off on wounded buffalo or leopard in the long grass. The first thing you'll do is drive to an area sufficiently distant from your hunting grounds so the noise of your shots won't frighten off game. You must zero your rifles after your flight out to make sure they're still "on" at what is most probably a different altitude and in different humidity. I'm not writing the weather report here but such things are *very* important. Most of Africa is considerably drier in the hunting season than most of America and certainly more so than nearly all of Europe. Thus, because of the change in tension through shrinkage between your wood stock and the screws and the barrel of your rifle, you'll almost surely have a different point of impact than at home. I can't emphasize enough that you must pay particular attention to the degree of tightness of the screws that hold the barrel and action to the stock, as they can very easily, through wood shrinkage, loosen as much as a turn or more on the first day. This will throw your rifle completely "out of zero." You must check this every day, especially if coming from a moist climate to a dry one like Southern Africa in the winter. I've seen rifles, either through rough handling in shipping or because of differences in humidity and altitude, shoot as far as three feet off zero.

Your hunting of dangerous game begins well before you even buy your air ticket. You simply *must* shoot your rifle! Go to a 200-yard range several times and bring at least twenty rounds each time. Optimally, you should go back four more times, totaling one hundred rounds at least. Shoot at 100 yards and try to fix in your mind just how far that is. Do the same at 150 and 200 yards. Get the rifle zeroed, as I have advised earlier in the chapter on guns, and then get the hell away from the bench rest! Shoot off-hand, sitting, prone or with a monopod rest. Try to practice for bush conditions. Your staff will not be carrying a bench rest along with them.

In shooting at different ranges initially, hold dead on, not allowing for increases or decreases in elevation through distance allowance. In this way, you can see perfectly how high or how low to hold your sights to print the bullet on the center of your aiming point when under field conditions. During the second or third trip, start trying hold-over or under and see if it fits with your previous calculations. Make sure some of that zeroing includes a few shots at five to ten yards. At that range, you'll have to aim a bit higher because of the rising curve of the bullet's path. Do it! It might save your life.

Unless you back over a record-book lion or have a head-on with a hundred-pounder elephant on the way back from the airport, you won't start your safari with the really mean stuff. You'll be on probation for a couple of days, the professional sizing you up in such a manner as to decide how much of his own epidermis he can reasonably risk with you, and under what circumstances. First, you'll wander off into the dawn to collect a bit of camp meat (after rezeroing, naturally), maybe an impala or a wildebeest for the staff rations, gradually getting into the heavy work. Your hunter will want to know if you can cross a tennis court with the net down without falling or whether you are given to fits of nervous sneezing. The first halfway serious game you will collect will be your zebra because, although it can bite back with enormous enthusiasm, it's unlikely to. Zebra hides take a long time to field-prepare and your skinning staff likes to get them out of the way early.

To paraphrase a famous comment by a grand old bwana, when things get hairy, what interests the pro is not how good you are on antelope at four hundred yards but what you can do with a buffalo at five feet. Let's hope you never have a chance to show him the second half of the proposition. But since we're speaking of hunting dangerous game generally, there are some pointers that I have accumulated through the years that may well be of help to you.

The first would be for you to keep your eyes open and your mouth disengaged while on the spoor of any kind of game. And I'm not being flippant. The human voice is the most disruptive sound to game of all kinds you'll experience in the bush. I never permit my staff to speak when we are hunting, as one never really knows just where game will be. If you have an important comment or question, motion your hunter aside and whisper in his ear. Almost all African hunting is done with hand signs and nods in any case.

Getting clients to see game in the first place, coupled with finding it in their scopes, is the most difficult problem I have come across, and I really don't know the answer to the dilemma. You can't expect a person fresh off Wall Street or Chicago's Loop to have the eyes of a WaNdErobo tracker. But then you can't shoot it if you can't see it! Much of the difficulty is allied to the same problem inexperienced hunters have in handling both their binoculars and their telescopic sights. Turn back a bit and have a look at standard procedure for finding an object in your scope; it will work the same way for binoculars, only more easily, as binoculars allow for stereoscopic vision. To reiterate, *don't* take your eyes off the place where the animal is reported, just slip the glasses up and into place without changing your eye position. Rest them securely against the bones under your eyebrows, cant your head slightly forward and you're in business with a solid anchor point. Your head and eyes should be in an attitude as if you were looking over the tops of half-lensed reading glasses.

Another difficulty in the first few days until you get used to it will be that of recognizing what you're looking at even though you see it. You will rarely see entire animals standing about as if on a pool table, waiting to get swatted, but you must learn to recognize mere parts of them. Try not to look for a complete outline but for more obvious things, such as legs beneath bush cover, the twitch of an ear or a tail tip. Motion, not only by game but by the hunter, is the big give-away

Not knowing a better place to interject this, let me mention that another very difficult hang-up with clients' shooting is that of getting their timing right. I'm not speaking of how quickly you squeeze the trigger but how smoothly and efficiently you can get your shot *off!* Because it's so important an aspect of success in hunting, let me try to explain. . . .

As many professionals have confirmed, clients tend to shoot either too fast or damned near never upon seeing a trophy animal. I had a Texan, and a grander one you never knew, who literally fired the instant his rifle touched his shoulder, rather in the manner advised by some British shotgun-shooting coaches. Well, a waterbuck at two hundred yards is not a partridge or snipe underfoot. His companions, registering some consternation when he had fired on six animals without a touch, also began to wonder what the matter was, since the gentleman in question was considered one of the top "falling plate" or metallic silhouette marksmen in the area; not easy shooting for sure. We checked his zero point twice. Perfect.

Now, any professional knows from the first half-second when a man picks up a rifle whether he knows what he's doing or not. This one did, although he was shooting wildly. It took more than a week to get him calmed down; so excited was he at real hunting that he was rushing his shot badly. Metallic silhouettes are a great long-range test of shooting skill without field duress. Hunting, at least to this gentleman, gave plenty of psychological pressure. He had no idea he was shooting so quickly. Eventually, he did very well.

His was not the normal problem.

I suppose that the simple mechanical action of firing a shot at game can have three possible results. First, you kill cleanly. Next, you miss cleanly. The last possibility is that you wound the animal to one degree or another. Following the last possibility, the conclusions are that you either catch up and kill him or he escapes. If he's one of the big boys and gets away, you've broken the law and it must be reported. Further, if you're a safari client, you'll have to pay the same game license fee as if you had got him and, as in the case of most big game, you won't be permitted to take another.

One of the most common causes of this is slow shooting, as opposed to cranking a round off the instant something is seen and identified as shootable, as with my Texan friend. Holy Saint Swithin, give me the wild ones! At least they seem to miss cleanly. Some people, though, shoot like they're waiting for the maple sap to run in February.

Most game offers a shot—if at all—when it has already become aware of the presence of the hunter, which makes it alert as hell and all poised to push off posthaste nonstop to the southern Gobi Desert. The big stuff worth collecting often seems to have an eighth sense. A typical example would be the following. . . .

"*Tsssst!* Kudu bull! About two hundred at eleven o'clock, under that lone tree on the hillside." I lock the binoculars on him and decide he's a good one. He's looking at us as a discerning circus-goer would a bad dog and pony act. Seen us? Hell, he can tell the brand of my buttons.

"What hill?" asks my client with a vigorous wave of his hands. I line him up and suggest he try his binoculars. After perhaps a minute, he finds them hanging around his neck and, reversing them twice, eventually gets them proper-end-to. "What tree?" asks the gentleman. Silent has lain down and is starting to doze. Invisible, my number two, is counting his toes just to make sure. I am earning my fat fees.

"See him?" I ask more hopefully than expectantly.

"Mmmm," says the client, looking forty degrees too far to the right. "Mmmmm."

"No, not that one. The big one under the tree. The only one, in fact. He's about fifty-five inches. Incidentally, he won't be there for the spring rains so you'd better take him."

"Mmmmm."

My gentleman takes his rifle, removes the scope caps, which he insists on keeping in place, and shoulders the gun. Raising it at forty-five degrees, he fits it to his shoulder and starts to take a rest against a thick piece of scrub in front of our position, the while staring into the sky through the scope. It takes literally another forty-five seconds to even have him locate the tree through the sights, let alone the bull. When he is ready to fire, or so I presume, the kudu is still miraculously there. He most likely can't believe it either, probably having watched quite a few hunters to have been able to grow a hatrack like he's got.

"Take him," say I almost mute with astonishment that the big bull with the ivory-tipped nutmeg-colored corkscrews is still in the same province. After several shooting breaths, three shifts of position and the elaborate blowing off of a real or imaginary speck of dust from the rear lens, my client's .300 Magnum bellows over the hill; precisely one thousandth of a second after the bull has begun to spin away and disappear past the ridge line. There is a brittle whack, rather like a baseball bat being broken, and a tip of the bull's right horn flips and arches away, neatly shot off. I muffle a groan. My client does not muffle a highly original and descriptive oath. Snake's eyes! Not only has he not wounded the grand bull fatally, he must also pay for it as well, since he has ruined the horns for any other trophy hunter. In some places such a hit would be overlooked, but I'm not about to take a chance, seeing that game department spies are in my camp.

Another incident of this type happened with a big tom leopard. The client had not brought an express rifle and so was using my extra .375 H&H Magnum. He had fired the piece about twenty times and we had carefully zeroed the scope for his eye, so I thought that there would certainly be no problem with a stationary leopard at about thirty yards.

To avoid movement when the cat arrived, I had the rifle perfectly aligned in a pair of sturdy forked sticks, each contact point with the sticks carefully insulated with foam rubber to prevent kick-up and the high shot that you'll always get when resting on a hard, unyielding surface like wood, which changes the natural vibrations and oscillation of the bullet up the barrel. Everything went like clockwork, the hulking big cat appearing in the tree by the bait like black magic. I nudged the client, seated on a camp stool, to take him once he'd begun to feed. Instead of just slowly leaning forward, snuggling up to the rifle and putting an easy hole in the leopard, he somehow decided he just didn't "feel" right.

To my growing horror, he then got off his canvas stool and tried to shoot kneeling. After perhaps forty seconds of this, he didn't like it either and got back on the stool. I was dying! The leopard was only about thirty yards away, a bit closer than I prefer, but there was a dead tree that made such a perfect base for a blind I had decided to use it.

Leopards are no more stupid than they are deaf or blind. I saw the big bastard tense up and stare hard at our blind, sure he had caught some sound or movement. In fact, I'll never forget those incredible golden-green eyes boring into us. I knew he was just about to jump and disappear. Of course, now was when the client had decided he would shoot, after all. I still had my binoculars in place and could see the rippling of the cat's muscles as he bunched for his spring—at thirty yards with binoculars you could hardly miss it. I was just about to knock the hunter's hand away when, as might be expected under the influence of old

Murphy, the shot crashed exactly as the leopard began his spring.

I saw him knocked off balance by some sort of a hit as he leapt into the dusk but knew it wasn't a death wound. He disappeared from my sight into the surrounding bush even before he hit the ground, one hell of a growl of rage and pain still ringing in our ears. Uh-oh. Here we go. This was the first situation I had been in during my budding career as a bwana that involved a wounded leopard, but I'd had plenty of audio-visual prompting from other pros as to what to expect. Trouble.

That a nasty bite from a wounded jaguar in my left foot the year before in Brazil had been sufficient to drive the metal grommets of my bootlace holes down between my footbones was also hint that maybe I should have stayed on Wall Street. Jaguars were bigger but, by reputation, not as thoroughly vindictive as leopards over such minor social infractions as a hot bullet in the guts. Ah, well, I knew I had to go in after him. And I won't tell you I wasn't scared. I was purely motherless terrified but I was even more afraid of washing out as a professional. So I checked the shotgun and smoked a cigarette to wait until the cat had either hopefully died or at least stiffened up from the wound, which, from the blood, looked muscular. In those days before I acquired Silent and Invisible, I had a so-called gun-bearer named Misteke or, more commonly and correctly, Mistake. He would have been drummed out of any respectable elderly ladies' crocheting club for lack of moral fiber. Being reasonably intelligent, he was aware that wounded leopards had pronounced tendencies to bite people and he wasn't about to be one of them. Smart chap. I was lucky that this leopard had come unusually early to the bait, probably because it was in very thick cover, whereas in more open stuff they will often not show until nearly dark. After the cigarette—I wished I had smoked magnum panatellas—I started on the blood trail into the thick crud.

The first few yards are very intimidating. The visibility is a maximum of about four paces but normally about two and a half. I can't resist thinking to myself: What on earth am I doing here? The odds are at best even that I'm about to get one hundred and fifty pounds of teeth and claws all over myself. What for? So some stranger I'm not even very pleased with can have a nice rug? You know I really am crazy! I agree with my own logic and trundle carefully on into the dusk, which is starting to swirl around the thicker stuff like a dark fog. My dripping palms are wrapped tightly around my shotgun, stuffed with No.1 buckshot, in this case the old Beretta I had then. After ten minutes, I've only covered as many yards, the currant-jelly gleam of blood now fading with the light.

Each step is an adventure. Turn slowly completely around, duck down and look under the bush as best I can, always aware that I'll get the charge from whatever direction I'm not looking at. Ears thumping and ringing, I hear a flight of ibis squawking and calling overhead in the copper, crimson, cobalt of the sunset. Guinea fowl near the river sound like a taxi fleet or Model A Fords with bad starters. An elephant shrew, not noticing me in my caution, scurries across my shoe, sending an icicle of genuine terror up my spine. And then he's there. No, not over there, right here. Lying right in my path stretches the big male leopard, his eyes still as bright as life, facing straight down toward me. His belly lying in a drying puddle of gore, he has been courteous enough to have bled to death, but had that bullet been a quarter of an inch off and not caught the femoral artery, just about now I would have been trying to peel him off as an unauthorized boarder, a big spotted sable stole that would probably have shredded me as finely as vermicelli if I hadn't been able to get a swarm of buckshot into his waterline.

Well, we'll never know. The same thing has happened since, once so close that the dead cat, falling out of the tree where he had been waiting for Silent and me to pass under, nearly hit me. He too had caught a very lucky slug in an artery and drained dry just before we came along.

But that's not the point. If my client had got his shot off properly instead of screwing around with different positions, there wouldn't have been a problem in the first place.

You should, from the time you raise your rifle to fire, be able to either decide not to shoot or get the shot away in fewer than five seconds. Five seconds is quite a long time, as you notice if you either check your watch or put your hand in a candle flame for that period of time. In fact, an experienced game shot would be dragging his feet if it took him three seconds.

The natural rhythm of shooting means that you shouldn't

have to rush but you shouldn't dawdle either. You'll never be absolutely perfectly steady, but if you feel you will miss, better not shoot because of the financial and time penalties associated with wounded game. Still, if you're going to shoot, line up as best you can, squeeze steadily but don't waste time. Game just doesn't hang around. Shoot or cut bait, if you like custom-blended metaphors.

Probably the first thing you ought to get straight with your professional hunter is the matter of wounded game. Like mechanical breakdowns, this is one very tender point of safari about which there needs to be mutual understanding before you fire your first shot.

Let me begin by explaining precisely what the pro's responsibility is to the game laws and also to you if something is wounded. He's not there to shoot your game for you. Most pros will refuse if asked to do so. Not all. Money *does* talk. But most will not think much of you for such a request. For starters, it's illegal. The only time your hunter will fire his rifle under field conditions is if, in his judgment, an animal you have hit is not fatally wounded and may get off into thick stuff where it will have to be followed up. During this process, it may well kill somebody, and he's an odds-on favorite for the honor. He will also shoot if, in his opinion, it may escape entirely to die in lingering agony in some lonely spot. This is your hunter's responsibility to his license and one of the main reasons why most people can't hunt dangerous game without a professional; at least foreigners in most African countries can't.

Some clients don't like this at all. I actually had one man run from a wounded buffalo that charged us instantly on being hit. When I killed it and he climbed back down, he refused to accept the trophy or even have it skinned. I had "spoiled" it for him. Well, there's no doubt in my mind that if I hadn't put a hole in the damned thing it would have put a hole in me, definitely spoiling my plans for the future. In fact, I wonder what the man would have done had there not been a tree so handy for him. . . . Another gentleman, and he was, too, just couldn't stand it when he wounded a fine kudu bull through a flesh wound in the leg. I dumped the *mbalabala* with a very fortunate shot from a long way off as it was about to disappear. Yeeeh! He was furious! But he calmed down when he saw where his shot had hit, realizing that if I hadn't fired, he would have been out of kudu on his license, the one thing he had come so far to collect. He finally calmed down and thanked me for being able to kill the bull.

Wounding, as we've touched on, directly affects two things that should be of interest to you: *your* time and *your* money. When you wound nonfatally, no matter what the species, you run the risk of losing the trophy as well as the time required to track and follow it up, in addition to the license fees if it is not found. Further, if you have to spend two days trying to sort out a wounded zebra—and remember how much it's costing you per day—that's time you can't use to be on the trail of some other animal, a big elephant, a lion or whatever. Once you squeeze the trigger and hit meat without killing, the considerations now are twofold: either you or your professional gets off another shot and finishes the deed, or you are committed legally and certainly morally to what may be a very long follow-up. If your wounded animal is a lion, leopard or other dangerous species, you could be responsible for creating a man-eater, should it escape.

My advice, then, is to ask your professional to back you up if you don't kill cleanly. Far from being unsportsmanlike, it is cheaper, safer and unquestionably more humane.

The matter of the second shot in this context is of immense importance. Your rule should be that if whatever you fire at does not drop with the bullet, for heaven's sake stick it again as rapidly as possible. It's while game is in range that this can be done, not after it has started to run and has put some distance between you and it. You may have to walk for days for the same chance of a follow-up shot that you might pass up immediately after your first round. Extra holes are easy to patch up, provided they're not in your hide.

The "insurance" shot is an inviolable principle of mine, simply because the odds are that one fine day you will be mistaken in believing that something capable of biting scalloped-edged holes in you is dead when it isn't. Remember the old East Africa dictum from the boys who really knew what they were doing: "It's the dead ones that get up and kill you."

Karamojo Bell, possibly the grandest off-hand game shot in the world, noted in *Karamojo Safari*, that time and again "brain-shot" elephant did not show the characteristic death quiver they should have. Considering that one of his standard maneuvers was to instantly run up onto the carcass of a brain-shot jumbo for better visibility in killing the others of a group, he took special care in "paying the insurance." If the typical spasms weren't present, he either shot the bull again or had it speared by Pyjalé, one of his close friends in the Karamojo region of Uganda where he gained his sobriquet.

Even Bell wasn't always right, as he has recounted. One of the best tuskers he ever shot got up, after his tail had been cut off in the customary manner to establish ownership of the carcass, and was never found. This by no means applies only to brained elephants. Buffalo will pull this stunt every time you let them, through negligence and a glancing spine or head shot. It was not a close thing but might have been one morning in Botswana with a waterbuck I presumed was dead. I had sat down near the head and was smoking a cigarette when the animal lurched, whipping his horns in an icepick scything motion about six inches past my chest. As a panic reflex, I stuck a .375 solid in his ear while trying to avoid his stepping on my toes as he raced past. Not dramatic but sure plenty enough to kill you. I very much hope you never have occasion to recall anything like the next few paragraphs as a participant, but since you are hunting dangerous game and there is always a possibility of getting caught, I believe a few words on what to do next might be in order.

It is definitely rare for a client to be savaged or killed by an animal on safari, but don't think it doesn't happen, chum. There's always the chance. Such items are hardly well advertised, though.

There was an especially chilling instance of this that took place in my old stamping grounds of Zambia's Luangwa Valley on October 19, 1982. An American hunter and safari client, whose identity will remain anonymous, was caught minding his own business and was horribly castrated by a hippo.

To quote a South African newspaper report of the incident:

> I was walking along when all of a sudden this thing charged me. I did not know what the hell was happening.

I was knocked down before I even realised that an animal was attacking me.

I was petrified and screamed like hell. Pain shot through my whole body and I thought I was going to die. It bit me in the lower part of my body and I passed out from pain.

It was only later that I learnt that a hippo had attacked me.

This man was only twenty-five years old.

Another horrendous example of what can go wrong on safari is the case of Dr. W. Brandon Macomber, no relation to Hemingway's famous subject in "The Short Happy Life of Francis Macomber," although I suppose it might be thought of as a more modern "Macomber Affair." Dr. Macomber, a well-known and skilled American hunter, along with Ian Henderson, an old friend of Rhodesia days, his professional hunter, were both badly mauled by an unwounded lion in northern Botswana a few years ago. Dr. Macomber was bitten through the chest and back and had crushed ribs threatening to pierce his lungs at any moment during a tortuous six-hour ride to medical aid across the Botswana border to Victoria Falls, now in Zimbabwe. Ian's father, if I recall correctly, was the first Rhodesian winner of the Victoria Cross. I won't try to retell the tale as Dr. Macomber has done it beautifully in *Sports Afield Magazine*, as well as in James Mellon's excellent book, *African Hunter*. Despite the licks both took, each survived. It is, nonetheless, a lesson to be considered. No matter how careful you are, very unpleasant things can happen.

If a decent elephant is one of your priorities, you're probably going to have to do a bit of running from stroppy cows and unshootable bulls. Obviously no man could outrun an elephant on a direct basis, but because their eyesight is quite poor (don't count on it, some see unnervingly well), the trick with avoiding jumbos is to "cut the wind" on them. This means that you must run cross-wind so as to keep your scent from reaching them. When the breeze is shifty, this is more than a little delicate, yet it's the only sure way to escape. A determined and thoroughly aroused herd will actually hunt you, as I have had happen on a couple of occasions after taking a good tusker from their midst. It ain't funny.

With buffalo, you'd better think about climbing rather than trying to run, although it is very rare to be chased by buffalo except in a direct charge by an individual. In the chapter on buffalo hunting, we'll explore herd behavior more closely.

The big problem is the cats. What should you do if everything goes wrong and you find yourself in the jaws of a lion? Well, I think the best advice would be to start feeding him the most unimportant parts of your body available until somebody can settle his hash. Start with your arms and move along to your legs when they're gone. You might also consider poking your fingers into his eyes with great enthusiasm. What you must avoid is the big body bite, if possible. Dr. Macomber was very, very lucky that he didn't get snuffed by that chomp that crushed his ribs. You might not be so fortunate.

It is far and away more likely that, if you do have some bad luck of the bloody kind, it will be such that your professional hunter gets hammered, a much more common circumstance than the client's being bitten, gored or stomped. Comforting, right?

Many professionals I know owe their lives to either their clients or their gunbearers and trackers. Others have all too frequently been accidentally killed by rifle fire meant to help them.

Look, if somebody is under a lion or buffalo that's trying with great dedication to kill him, don't forget that no lion or buffalo as deadly as an express bullet has ever been spawned. Obviously you will do all you can to try to kill whatever it is that's savaging your hunter, but just remember that your bullet will easily pass through the animal and may well kill the pro. Try to get in close and shoot from a very low angle to prevent the slug hitting the man you're trying to save. Sounds pretty academic in print, but some good men would be alive today if this had been realized in the heat of combat.

This isn't a first-aid manual, but just file away in the back of your brain that stopping the bleeding is the first thing you should try to do. After that, make sure the victim is kept warm. If odd parts of his insides are hanging out, do not try to suture them, even after application of a good antiseptic. Doctors advise me that this is conducive to septicemia, one of the greatest problems in the bush. Use tape or "butterfly" sutures, made by snipping U-shaped notches out of the middle of a piece of adhesive tape so the middle is much thinner than the ends but the ends retain their width to permit adhesive purchase on either side of the wound. Pinch the lips of the wound together with the fingers of one hand and attach one end of the butterfly firmly across the cut. With the wound held closed, stick the other end in place. It works very well and will hold things in place until the arrival of professional medical aid. Use several butterflies if needed. And while we're on this topic, it's a good idea to familiarize yourself with the first-aid kit kept in camp and in the hunting vehicle. You literally never know.

Antiseptics are, of course, essential. In the old days hunters used to carry a cartridge case full of potassium permanganate crystals, but we now know that that did damn near as much harm as good. I carry sulfathiozol powder and one or another good brand of liquid. In case of a mauling, remember that a good deal of the real trauma will be inside the wound, even though the wounds look simple enough on the surface. This is especially true of lion bites. Before dropping this rather depressing aspect of big game hunting, let me also advise that you should most carefully inspect the whole body for wounds that you may have missed and that the victim may not even feel. The teeth and claws of carnivores are all coated with rotting films of meat from their kills, and infection will kill you as dead as would a Polaris missile.

The odds are very, very slim that you will be hurt by an animal. The possibility is, however, the main factor that makes hunting dangerous game the challenge it is. It can and does happen.

With such a possibility existing, one of the first things you might consider upon arriving in camp would be to ask your pro to show you how and on what frequencies his radio works. Not all camps have radios, depending on the need and the area, but if such is the case, you might conceivably be required to work it in case of emergency. I don't know about you, but I'd sleep better with the knowledge in hand.

An excellent black-maned lion. (M. Philip Kahl)

A good reason to stay out of the way of lions. (Peter Hathaway Capstick)

A piece of bait (zebra haunch) after having been ravaged by lions. (Peter Hathaway Capstick)

The African Lion—Vital Points (Petersen's Hunting magazine)

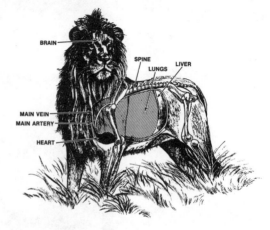

BELOW: *P.H. Geoff Broom, Daney Hull and P.H. Russ Broom with a magnificent lion taken by Daney at Matetsi. (Geoff Broom)*

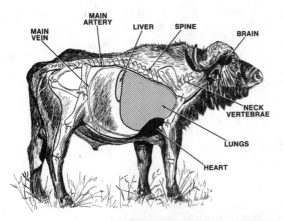

The Cape buffalo—Vital Points (*Petersen's Hunting* magazine)

Forty-six-inch spread Cape buffalo taken by seventy-four-year-old C.F. Mann of Houston with Russ Broom in the Luangwa Valley. (Geoff Broom)

Herd of Cape buffalo in mopane *scrub; Luangwa Valley, Zambia.* (Geoff Broom)

A specter from the past: an elephant in Tanzania with tusks well over a hundred pounds each. (Peter Hathaway Capstick)

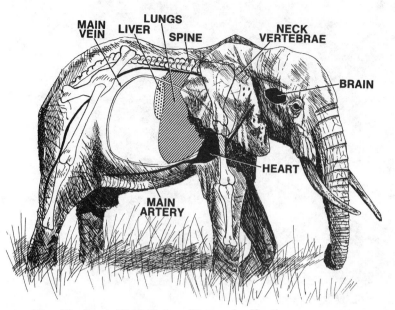

The Elephant—Vital Points (*Petersen's Hunting* magazine)

The elephants' tail hair makes handsome and interesting bracelets. (Peter Hathaway Capstick)

Study of a fine male leopard. (M. Philip Kahl)

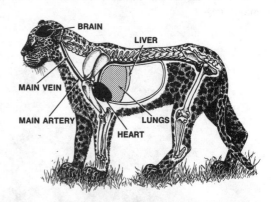

The Leopard—Vital Points (Petersen's Hunting *magazine*)

BRAIN
LIVER
MAIN VEIN
MAIN ARTERY
LUNGS
HEART

Hanging leopard bait. (Peter Hathaway Capstick)

The leopard is shy, but rarely afraid. While the author was checking the bait, the leopard was checking on him, as this pug-mark over the tire track shows. After a four-day wait, the cat was finally taken. (Peter Hathaway Capstick)

Gary Ingersoll and Russ Broom with a whopper of a leopard. (Geoff Broom)

Time for drumbeating and handclapping, while camp staff celebrate the killing of a fine trophy with the "leopard dance." (Geoff Broom)

A black rhino, now virtually extinct because of commercial poaching of his horn. (M. Philip Kahl)

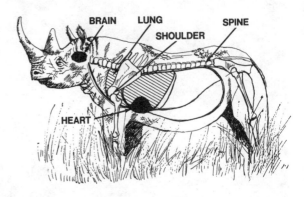

The Rhino—Vital Points (Petersen's Hunting maga-zine)

Howard Pollack, current president of the National Rifle Association, with a fine crocodile taken in the Luangwa Valley with Geoff and Russ Broom. (Geoff Broom)

Zebra at Chirisa in Zimbabwe. (Courtesy of HUNTERS TRACKS (PVT) Ltd., Chisipite, Zimbabwe)

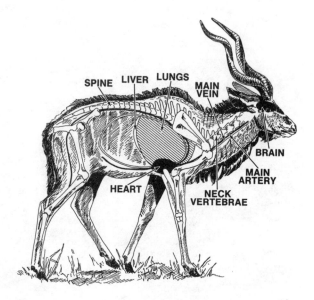

The Kudu—Vital Points (*Petersen's Hunting* magazine)

Waterbuck and impala at a water hole, Matetsi. (Beth Morian)

The authors' clients passed up this otherwise record book sable bull because of the odd flare of his horns. Sometimes being different is not unlucky. He would place well up in the book. (Peter Hathaway Capstick)

Gladstone, a Rhodesian gunbearer, with a brace of Swainson's francolin. (Peter Hathaway Capstick)

Brian Marsh with a fine tiger fish and an elephant looking on. (Brian Marsh)

TWELVE

Lion

There are probably more interesting things to do in your spare time than hunt lions but I don't think I have her telephone number anymore. I'd undoubtedly get some argument, but to me the lion is *the* classic African big game animal, not to take away anything from leopard, elephant or buffalo. It's just that he's so damned *African*. In strict terms of natural history this is of course not so, as lions *do* occur in Asia, especially in the Gir forest of India, whereas Cape buffalo, African elephant and both black and white rhino are entirely limited to the Dark Continent. Leopard is found throughout Asia as well as on the fringes of Europe and in most of Africa. Still, that's my private opinion.

The great charm of hunting the African lion is the sure knowledge that, if you give him a decent chance, he will cheerfully bite large, painful, raggedy-edged chunks out of you at every opportunity he gets. He's big-league in terms of hunting species and is surely one of the most prized trophies of safari, if not the most prized of all. Safaris generally sink or swim on their success with lion, so he'll probably be the first dangerous game that you will be seriously hunting.

Besides being damned hard work, lion hunting also requires wholesale, economy-sized doses of luck. Like gold and tax collectors, *Simba* is largely where you find him, which makes his pursuit a sport of opportunity, unless you're baiting in a static position.

Certainly lions are territorial, but depending on how easy the pickings are in a particular area, these territories or "beats" may be very extensive. A black-maned lion may look very big indeed when he's hurtling down on you through long grass at a speed approaching forty miles per hour, but he's also a mighty little creature to find in a couple of hundred square miles of African bush.

The roar of the lion, if you haven't heard it in the wild, is practically worth the trip to Africa. The power and sheer volume of the sound is almost unbelievable, and the distances a roar will carry equally so. I have had clients sitting around the safari campfire at night hear a concert that I knew to be near a water hole more than two miles away, yet all three of the clients agreed that the sound could not possibly be coming from farther than five hundred yards! When I lived in Florida, I could hear them at a commercial safari park four miles down the road, clearly roaring at dawn. Here, in Pretoria, the zoo lions are also audible at least four miles away.

The classic full-blown roar of the male lions is, for fairly obvious reasons, not given when they're hunting prey, although lower grunts may be murmured by both sexes, sort of a method of keeping in touch. The actual roar, most authorities agree, is a territorial warning to other lions that might be infringing on another pride's back yard. Females often roar after making a kill, perhaps as a dinner bell to more distant members of the same pride or their half-grown young.

That it's better to keep your mouth shut if you want to stay out of trouble is good advice for lions. Probably more are taken by sportsmen after being located by their roaring than by any other way, but don't get the idea this is any simple operation. Most mammal carnivores are nocturnal in Africa, and the lion is typical. During daylight, lions loaf in well-watered areas of heavy cover and emerge only to hunt at night. Occasionally, you'll catch them in daytime moving off from a kill or bait, but this is less than common. So, if you want your lion, most of the time you have to go into the very thick stuff after them, which is a highly attention-getting pastime.

Frankly, it's just as well that you can't legally hunt lions at night. With the possible exception of the leopard, no animal pulls such an impressive Jekyll and Hyde act as does old *Simba* when the sun goes down. Big, lazy puddy-tats in the heat of the day, lions revert to what they're really all about in the blackness of the African bush: first-rate carnivores. That their prey may include you is not an idle conjecture.

Having written in great detail on lion man-eaters in previous books, a discussion of the same matter here seems, excuse the phrase, overkill. Just remember that you can never be completely at ease in lion country unless you're mentally deficient. Don't take chances. Man-eaters occur with lethal frequency in any area where lions exist. Maybe it doesn't fit into a Disney script, but it is certainly true. Why you don't hear a great deal about it is obvious from a commercial, touristic angle. Lions still eat a helluva lot of people.

Despite the facts of man-eating that I and many other contemporary hunters have written, the subject is nonetheless looked on with a rather jaundiced eye in corners of the world such as America or England, where, outside commercial parks, the matter is academic at best. If I am overemphatic, please ascribe it to the fact that I have come considerably Nearer My God to Thee on three instances from genuine man-eaters. Two of these occasions took place in safari camps where *you* might have been staying and it might well have been *your* hut that was invaded instead of mine. Sure, the odds are immensely slim that you'll have problems with man-eaters, but just don't forget they're out there.

Bear in mind that I see this as a book on hunting, not really natural history. The latter aspects of game animals may be found far better represented in books specifically geared to such considerations. Two I would recommend to you are C. A. W. Guggisberg's *Simba*, (Chilton, Philadelphia and New York, 1963) and a newer tome by G. L. Smuts, *Lion* (Macmillan, South Africa, 1982). Both are classic, well-researched studies of the beastie.

In the days when my KiSwahili was fairly polished, I used to remember a dictum of some black tribes that there were three times when a man felt the gut chill of fear from a lion. I won't try to quote it precisely, but the drift was that the first instance that gave a hunter the cold goose was when he heard the lion roaring. The next was when he saw the tracks and the last when he actually saw the lion. If you're sitting near a lovely leadwood or *mopane* fire one fine evening on your safari and you hear a big male tuning up a couple of miles away, I think you will agree with the east African blacks. Anticipation is such a part of lion hunting. You may first hear him—or them—near midnight, and realize that before dawn you, yes, you, will be padding through the boonies in the insane declared mission of actually trying to catch up with the animals. Not only that, you'll be paying big bucks to do it. Some would have you believe it is an exciting prospect, and in a very rarefied sense of the word it is. Essentially, I find it intimidating as hell, rather like going to your doctor for a cancer checkup.

It will still be as black as the tunnel of love when the hunting car grinds to a dusty halt and you, your pro and a couple of gunbearer/trackers pile out and start into the slimy dew-slicked wetness of the tall grass. You've been theoretically awake since about four, but the dazzle of the lancing headlights and the swirl of gnarled bush whisking past have seemed part of some weird, surrealistic dream. The chill of the dew soaking through your clothing brings you alert, though, just as the first molten copper of false dawn bleeds all over the eastern sky. It's almost as if you haven't noticed that the inky sable of the bush is now a sickly mamba gray as you feel your way along, ducking limbs and being held up by the everpresent wait-a-bit thorns snagging into your legs and the backs of your hands.

After nearly a mile, your hunter signals a halt. Lighting a smoke, you listen to him explain in a whisper that he's waiting for another roar, as is so often the case at dawn. Sitting in the grass, the fireflies of cigarette ends glow like flares and you wipe off a sheet of moisture from your face, which you realize is as much sweat as dew mixed with spiderwebs and powdered bark fragments.

The seconds flicker and twitch by like crippled minnows in dark water as you listen to the throb of your pulse in your ears and jaw hinges. Far away, down at the river, a fish eagle keens a flinty shard of wild sound and a late jackal answers like a tortured child. The whispery flutter of a giant fruit bat past your face makes you flinch involuntarily as you notice the primeval blend of dust, sweat, tobacco and gun oil on the still air. A cigarette gives a swift death hiss as the live coal is pulled off by the calloused fingers of the gunbearer and dropped into the dew, the reeking butt of the smoke stuck into his wild thicket of hair for later. Then it comes.

It is everywhere at once. And nowhere. It begins as a sliding moan on a down scale, crescendoing to pack the air as solidly as putty. It erects the hairs on your forearms, elevates your sopping hackles and rolls through the pit of your stomach as if you were leaning against a bass drum. *UUUrrrunghhh!* Again and again. At last a series of deep, threatening grunts, like a giant with the dry heaves. But from where? The sound has filled your grassy world like a cloud of noise. Then the gunbearer is nodding and pointing with a slender, ebony arm. Thataway. The pro agrees.

Waiting a few more minutes, the professional whispers his constant amazement that no matter what the circumstance or place, lions always seem to roar out of the rising sun, in the one position where they will be so hard to see before the bloodshot orb gets higher. Not only must the hunter's eyes be shaded by a hat or hand, but that direct assault of low light also blinds binoculars and telescopic sights as well as glancing with a dazzle on all but the darkest metal sights. Finally, he rises, glancing around at the horizon, and checks his rifle. With your handkerchief, you wipe off some drops of condensation from the scope and reclose the bolt on the bright brass shell.

"Now, listen up, bwana," hisses the hunter as you are ready to push off. "This is gonna be a mite tricky. The cover's thick, which means you won't see him unless he's close enough to bite. It's not bright enough to follow spoor yet, and in this stuff, that would take forever anyway. We're going to go in straight, slowly but steadily. Rely on surprise." He takes a last, somehow regretful drag at his cigarette. "Just don't shoot this bastard in the guts, hey! They don't like that. If you're not sure, really sure you can nail him in the boiler room, for chrissake don't shoot. Okay? Got it?" You nod, feeling a tingling in your shins spreading up to your lower stomach. Somewhere close by in heavy cover there is a big, live, wild lion. With teeth. And claws. Maybe several big, live, wild lions. And you are going into that migraine of vegetation after him, accompanied by a social drop-out and two aborigines. Now, aren't you a clever chap?

After an hour you regret that you didn't think of asking just how close "close" is. The sun is lancing laser beams that seem to pass through your eyes and bounce off the inside of the back of your skull as you pick your way in the professional's footsteps through a horror show of bush that looks like your backyard before you hired the lawn service. It's all very African, as advertised, with razor grass in the wet places, anthills or termite heaps (you have noted that African termites eat anything less resistant than chrome steel bars, which, by reputation, they merely dent), and some marvelously snaky haunts that have proved astoundingly poor for not harboring at least a pair of Gaboon vipers. Still no lions. No roars, not even a purr. Maybe they've pushed off to more verdant pastures? You stifle a reflex of relief.

Everything seems in order, as you check for the fourteenth time. Scope screwed down to three-power, rifle loaded, chambered with a round, sling snug in your pocket and the swivels also off so they don't clatter. Sheesh! It's hot now. The wind, which you have learned doesn't make a hell of a lot of difference with lions unless you bathe in bay rum, is extinct, permitting the dew-soaked grass to have developed into a steam bath that would make an Olympic-grade Finnish sauna fan stagger with the humidity. Lots of fun, lion hunting.

Another forty minutes creep by as you inch along, the now-visible spoor leading toward the really thick stuff along the river, cover that must have provided the backdrop for some of the earlier Tarzan movies. Lord! Why so much walking when the damned thing sounded as if it were in your back pocket a century or so ago, at dawn? Twice, you've tried to whisper something but have been squashed by the pro's gesture to hush your fuss, no matter what it is. And, in another step, you realize why.

It looks like a well-tailored hessian gunny sack lumping out from under a hollow of some bush twenty-five yards away. It also draws as many flies as you do. A hard fist grips your shoulder as the pro steps behind you, easing his hand up to point. Like a thunderstroke, you realize that it must be a lion! But what part of a lion? Or is it a lioness? Slipping the rifle up, you check it out through the scope despite your heartpounding. Well, it *is* a lion, or at least a mighty fine imitation thereof. But the dappled blending of shadow, leaves and grass makes it impossible to tell what you're looking at, his front, back or side. In fact, there is only about a square foot in view. You remember the pro's warning and lower the rifle.

Slowly, you turn to gesture to the professional. In that instant, there is a whoof of surprise and a scamper of movement as something tawny-gold races through the right side of your peripheral vision. "Take him!" shouts the hunter and you scramble to get the rifle back into position. A flash of motion as the scope sweeps past and then empty bush.

"Come on," says the pro in a hard voice. Instantly, you're running like a madman to keep up, bulling through branches and grass, tearing free of the snagging snare of thorns as you crash on in the wake of the disappearing pro. What's he trying to do? Take the damned thing prisoner? A full thirty seconds of mad activity brings you up to a huge grassy *vlei* snaggled over with the deep green of *conbretum* shrub. Still running, you follow down a natural corridor of the bush, halting only as you nearly run over the hunter, who has stopped. "There! Stick him!" says the pro, pointing to a very large dog that is watching you from behind one of the *conbretums*. He is lying flat and has a very active tail and has obviously escaped from a local circus, as he still has a big black paper ruff around his neck. Interesting, there are two more very big dogs with this one, all having quite extraordinary dentition, and obvious vocal ability.

"Thump him, man," says your hunter. "That sucker's gonna come for us." Up go the crosshairs to bounce, wiggle and squirm as you try to catch a shooting breath. They hold for a second just below the chin and you squeeze.

Nothing happens.

The safety catch is still on. Nice going, nitwit. It comes off smoothly under your sweaty thumb and you pull back down on the cat, getting the shot off just as he starts to move. The 300-grain slug blows a tiny explosion of hairs from his throat where it meets his chest, hanging there in a column of sunlight gleaming through the scope as they drift downward. Without a thought, you have operated the bolt, jacking in a fresh round.

"Again," says the pro and you do. There is a shiver of impact from the big golden body, then stillness. To the side race the other two dogs, instantly disappearing down another natural corridor. You have gotten your lion.

The four of you carefully walk a forty-yard detour to come up behind the cat, both you and the pro ready every second for a sign of life. Every few moments the hunter checks that the lionesses are not coming back, as they so often do. At last, the professional reaches over and taps the inert body in the eye with the muzzle of his cocked, unsafetied rifle. It is well and truly dead. Hemingway dead. Almost anticlimactically, the gun-bearers break into shouts and dances of joy and excitement, alternately pounding your shirt through the skin of your back. Africans purely love dead lions, it would seem.

The first shot would have been enough, but why take a chance? It had angled down from its neat little blue-and-white-edged hole, almost lost in the front of the mane, and did some very rude things to the big artery over the heart. Actually, the pro is surprised, upon following the path of the slug when the skin is off, that the big chap died so quickly. At close range, lions can be terrors before a heart shot takes effect. But then each case is different. Even the two accompanying lady lions were not inclined to give trouble. Essentially, an easy lion. Next one, who knows?

If you really want to know what you're up against when you take on a lion, stick around while he's skinned. I can't think of another animal in his weight category with such incredible musculature. The massiveness of the chest and what in man would be the pectorals as well as the forelegs are among the more unbelievable things in nature, so unusual as to defy real description here. But if you want to talk about muscle tissue, here's a grand place to start! One sees so easily how light, expanding, high-velocity bullets have gotten so many men killed by lion. I'd as soon try to shoot through a brine-full pork barrel as a lion's chest and, as I have mentioned elsewhere, the 510-grain .458 Winchester Magnum has never, in my own experience, gone through the chest of an adult male lion, even with an easy, straight side-shoulder angle.

Lions are highly individual in how much it takes to kill them. A proper first shot will usually settle their problems very nicely, but some are astonishingly tough. Mind you, I don't think the lion has been whelped that could take the punishment a zebra or a wildebeest or for that matter, even a big boar wart-hog can handle. Carnivores seem to be, by my observation, easier to kill than the herbivores, but there are exceptions. One very big but nearly maneless lion of my acquaintance in Rhodesia took nine chest shots from as many angles from .375s and .458s before he cashed in. One for each cat's life, I expect. Still, unless it was mere theoretics, in the old Kenya one required at least a caliber .400 for elephant, buff and rhino, but could take lion and eland with not less than a .375 H&H Magnum. Sounds rather like the opinion of one or another clerk, but being under-gunned in a nasty situation is no joke. Of course, as I've said, most nasty situations wouldn't come along in the first place if hunters weren't toting more gun than they could handle.

Before I forget, while your lion is being skinned out, be aware that one of the most prized trophies of the animal is the pair of "floating" collarbones found in the fronts of the shoulders. Any reputable safari firm or professional hunter will be sure you receive these crescent-shaped, highly charged black magic bones, but sometimes they do disappear, as they are so greatly prized for witchcraft. You had also better make it known, if in any doubt, that you have counted the whiskers and expect them all to be there when the skin is shipped. Whiskers are variously used in a chopped-up form for poison or in incantations. The floating collarbones are lovely things when mounted in gold and used as ladies' brooches or as tie clasps. The claws are also valuable, but if you're planning on a rug, leave them in place for the skinning process. The same collarbones and whiskers are of equal value in leopards.

In my experience and continued belief, the central shoulder shot placement is the safest and the most generally effective for all the big cats. Naturally, a perfect brain shot will do the job instantly, but it has its drawbacks. The brain is shielded by the skull and, in many species, by horn bases. The head is more in motion than other parts of the body, and so this shot is generally unreliable without a good deal of practice, as I picked up cropping elephant. The skull is also one of the most important trophy parts of the body, and bullet damage does this aspect little good.

When I speak of the central shoulder shot, it is important to understand that I am really referring to the middle chest region.

It's just that the shoulder is often the most accessible route to the goodies therein. Reasonably, if an animal is facing you, a shot on the point of the shoulder will do no more good than to crease the skin as it parallels the body. With an animal standing three-quarters away from you at an angle, the shoulder shot may have to be placed nearer the rear near hip than the actual shoulder.

If you happen to be relatively inexperienced, let me just pass along one of the basic rules most professionals adhere to, and also one of the reasons they use deep-penetrating solids. The idea is to shoot for the "away" or *farthest* shoulder joint or bone, no matter the animal's attitude or stance. If an animal is facing to your left, just try to imagine where his far shoulder lies and pay more attention to trying to get a bullet there than the near one. Of course, if the creature is at a close broadside angle, then, naturally, the nearest shoulder should be your target.

The advantages, by my lights, of the shoulder or central chest shot are several. Most of them are simply a matter of putting the odds in your favor. It is here that the lungs lie, as well as the heart and the main bone support system for the animal's front end. The spine is also resident in this region as are a wonderful collection of arteries and major veins, any of which, if cut, will shortly result in your getting a season pass for the pound seats.

The heart is always a nice thing to put a large hole through, but the lungs are far bigger and equally deadly, although not quite so dramatic. A cat's spine is too small to fool around with and too dicey a shot when hunting lion or leopard. Sure, if you smash it, you'll get him, but far better to play the odds.

The brain shot on cats should only be taken in self-defense, and not even then unless a good chest opening is impossible. To make an effective brain shot on a lion that's coming at you in a hurry, you'll have to hit him no higher than the bridge of the nose or muzzle. Most attempted brain shots on lion are far too high, passing through the fatty tissue above the skull proper. Part of the reason for this is that lions are built low to the ground and they charge in a very low sweep or rush. Let's hope you never have the opportunity to test the shot, but if you do remember, try to get your body down to his level to improve the angle and, if your slug passes too low, you should have good raking effects as it passes on into the body.

The neck shot is very popular with many Americans and, if properly executed, certainly kills better than a hyperactive thunderbolt. Personally, I don't like it, for the simple reason that I have seen it fail quite a few times. Maybe that's not completely fair, though, as I've also seen many chest shots bungled too. The problem is that it's a relatively small target that must be hit squarely in most larger species. True, there are loads of vital blood vessels and arteries as well as concentrations of nerves in the neck. Still, I prefer the chest. One drawback of the neck shot is the damage a high-velocity light caliber will do to the cape when mounted. Use it if you are a real believer, but I suggest you give preference to the central chest.

Baiting for lion doesn't need much of an explanation. It's really the supplying of an artificial kill to keep the lion in the area, where he can then be stalked and tracked. Many lions are killed near or on the carcasses of elephants that have been collected earlier in the safari. Hippo are also very effective for this if they can be shot on land.

Although lions are well distributed in Africa today, some areas, judging by safari results, seem to produce more and bigger lions than do others. If I were trying to decide *at this date* where to arrange an encounter with a trophy *Simba*, I think I would be inclined to pick Botswana or Zambia. To second-guess myself, plenty of whoppers come out of both Zimbabwe and Sudan and a few well-maned types from South Africa, although I wouldn't especially suggest South Africa if lion is high on your list. It's a shame that the old Mucusso *coutada* or concession in Angola isn't still in operation, as many of the best in the *Rowland Ward's Records of Big Game* came from there. Kenya and Uganda in East Africa in the old days had some exemplary lions, but they're closed too. Tanzania, still in business, is another first-class choice. There were certainly plenty of lions in Ethiopia when I was there, and they assuredly weren't the shy type either! I have not been back recently, but there are safari arrangements in that country, so perhaps things are still good in the lion department.

Although best known as *Simba* from the KiSwahili, you'll

find, if you are hunting in Botswana, he'll usually be called *Tau*. In more southerly areas, it'll be *iNgonyama* or *uBubesi*. Naturally, there are lashings of other tribal language names, but if you stick with *Simba* up north and with the Fanagalo terms of either *Bubesi* or *Ngonyama*, nobody will wonder what you're talking about.

As relative trophies, it's mighty tough to find a lion that will slip into the record book with a minimum measurement requirement of nine feet three inches "between the pegs." Just so you know that nobody will "con" you that you may have a bigger lion than it looks, the accepted measurement is taken *only* in the following manner: the lion is laid out on one side and straightened out as best one can by holding the head and pulling on the tail. When it is properly in line, on level ground, two stakes are driven in exactly perpendicular to the tip of the nose and the end of the tail, but *not* including the hair tail-tuft. The lion is then removed and the steel tape run between the inside surfaces of the pegs. This gives the true length in the acceptable manner. Incidentally, I would highly recommend that the lion be dead before you do this.

The other method of measuring lion trophies has to do with the dimensions of the skull by length and width, the same method applied to leopard trophies. This is also measured between upright slabs of wood from the front of the jaw to the back of the skull and also between the zygomatic arches, which are the widest parts of the skull after the head has been skinned and cleaned. Personally, I don't see a great deal to this type of measurement, although many trophy systems are based on it, For my money, a big lion is a big-bodied lion, not a hydrocephaloid that just may happen to have exceptional zygomatic arches.

Just for the record, the largest listing I have for a lion as measured between the pegs is one of eleven feet even (338.28 centimeters) from Mucusso in Angola in October 1973, and is listed by *Rowland Ward's* as belonging to one G. Gladney. That's an awful lot of lion! Not in the same breath, but lion length measurements are not subject to the same verification by official measurers as are "hard" horned trophies. In fact, *Ward's* prints the following disclaimer before the lion section: "These are owners [*sic*] measurements only and cannot be verified by the editors." This old and venerated firm, now taken over by Game Conservation International in the records department, requires that lion trophies in terms of body length be taken in the field before the animal is skinned and merely certified by the professional hunter and the client who killed the beast.

The weight of lions, as an aside, is generally overestimated. For example, during South African tests in which 344 lions of all ages were weighed after being darted, the biggest was just 495 pounds (225 kilograms.) Of course, this was a sampling from a limited area where the local races might have been a touch smaller than some other animals other localities or countries might have produced. Still, they were heavier than an East African selection. There are reliable records of lions that weighed as much as 660 pounds or more, but anything you manage to take better than 450 pounds would be a very large and probably full-bellied lion.

My own safari career has averaged out pretty well on lions, probably because most of the places I hunted were good lion areas. I have had some very invigorating times with them, both wounded and unprovoked, not counting game department days with man-eaters. They're a grand game animal, but the only thing you must engrave on your brain is that they're not to be fooled with, no matter what Joy Adamson or Walt Disney tells you. You foul up with lions in dense cover, pal, and you'll use your return ticket home at air-freight rates.

Logically, the best thing to keep you out of the cargo hold with a big blue tab on your toe is your rifle-cartridge combination. Look, a .30-06 in the right place will slay any lion, and probably more have been killed by the old British service cartridge, the .303, than any other round. Still, even where it's legal, don't go poking old *Simba* in the butt with anything less than a .375 H&H or, at the least, a .338 Winchester Magnum. Nowadays lion hunting in cover, as opposed to the wide open spaces of Kenya where they used to be chased on horseback, is rather the big game equivalent of hunting ruffed grouse. It's a sport of glimpses in most cases, and getting an unrushed but rapid shot off is the key to success. Use open sights or, if your scope is not removable, keep it at the lowest setting. Be certain not to forget to remove your sling and darken your open sights in a flame before setting out.

The trick is to try to stay calm (easier said than done). If you tend toward buck fever on seeing a white-tail deer with a decent rack, you'll probably go into convulsions on bearding your first lion. I wrote in *Death in the Long Grass* of a client who ran a whole magazine through his chamber on seeing a very fine black-maned chap, doing everything right except that pulling the trigger slipped his mind. Another I have mentioned got himself into the same frame of mind that wins medals of honor on battlefields, throwing his rifle aside and chasing the lion bare-handed. Fortunately, the lion was slightly faster, and probably as astonished as I was. I'm serious when I say this sort of thing goes on with some regularity, as most professional hunters will confirm.

Lion stories can fill books. There is one, though, an old classic that has probably found its way to us unchanged from the campfire grunts and groans of earliest man in Africa. It was first told to me by the late professional hunter Chris Pollet, who specialized in recounting it at cocktail parties before bright-eyed and presumably available young ladies.

Chris had a European nobleman on safari back in Congo days, a duke, in fact. Early one morning, hunting on elephant trails through such thick bush that it formed tunnels near a river, he and his client turned a corner and came eyeball-to-jowl with a magnificent black-maned lion. Chris pulled the duke forward and told him to shoot as quickly as he could. The half-petrified man pulled off both barrels of his Holland Royal, missing cleanly despite the range. Instantly, the lion gave a tremendous roar and leaped straight at the hunters, also missing and sailing right over their heads. Hitting the ground beyond, it was immediately out of sight.

After they had gotten their hearts restarted, Chris decided that a bit of target practice would be in order for the duke, as there was just no excuse for having missed the lion at point-blank. Walking off some distance, they came to a clearing and Chris whacked a blaze off a big tree as a target. Explaining as gently as he could, Chris suggested that the client practice his "snap" shooting, emphasising that he bring up the rifle quickly and get his shot off accurately at a very short range. His Grace backed off a couple of steps and was getting ready to shoot when Chris heard a small, odd noise in the thick bush off to one side. Not knowing what it might be, he hushed the duke to silence and the two of them began crawling off into the vegetation to investigate. Some twenty-five yards along, they found another small clearing. In it was the same lion. Practicing short leaps.

THIRTEEN

Cape Buffalo

That the African Cape buffalo is one of the toughest big game animals on earth wouldn't be disputed with much vehemence by the majority of people who have hunted him. Up to two thousand pounds of five-o'clock-shadowed muscle with the temperament of a hung-over linebacker, the buff is a clear example of the sort of critter that keeps people like Roy Weatherby in business.

Buffalo don't just look mean either. Maybe not pound for pound, but considering the aggregate he's working with, you'd have to go back to the age of the dinosaurs to find another animal so resistant to dying and, if necessary, so dedicated to taking you along with him. Some hunters, veterans of one or perhaps two safaris on which they took a couple of buff, have advised me that I speak with forked tongue, that the buff is no harder to kill than anything else. And, under normal circumstances, this would be true. The problem with buff is that there aren't all that many normal circumstances.

True, when you find an unsuspecting bull, lying down and chewing his cud in the privacy of a shady thorn tree, and place a reasonably big bullet in precisely the right spot, he will curl up like a spider in a campfire. Yet, under what seem to you to be identical conditions with the same shot, the bloody thing may be on its feet in an eye-blink and either coming your way with obvious earnestness to make your acquaintance or disappearing into thorn that would snare a bulldozer. You just never know with buffalo.

When I was shooting, on control, what piled up to be considerably more than a thousand buffalo, including meat rations for government staff and such, it really came home to me that you can't count on anything with buff. One day everything would go perfectly, each shoulder or spine shot dropping the *iNyati* like a big black bag of sand. The next day, with seemingly the identical bullet placement, half ran off wounded and had to be sorted out on their home turf. Well, maybe not half, but certainly enough to qualify me for hazardous-duty pay.

I've never really looked into the veterinary aspects of this, but have a couple of theories of my own. Surely nobody would argue with the fact that the meat of a wounded buffalo tastes more strongly than that of one which has had its spine broken and which had died instantly. Even a heart-shot buff that goes forty yards is not "toughened up" by the experience as would be the steaks of a bull that has been gut shot and lives some hours. It almost seems to me that buff that have been aroused or are nervous have so much adrenaline and other emergency chemicals flowing as to change the tension of their muscle structure to the point that it can affect bullet performance. There's no doubt that the bullet deformation I have had on wounded buffalo— although granted that some of it was undoubtedly from bone— is the worst I have seen on any species, especially with the old, unreinforced Winchester bluff-nosed 300-grain .375 H&H solids.

The Cape buffalo or, if you want to be technical, *Syncerus caffer caffer* (often seen in the old form, *Bos caffer*) is probably your surest bet of all the Big Five. He's not more widely distributed than, say, leopard or elephant, in fact less so, but he's in immensely greater numbers, being found in herds as well as in bachelor groups and alone. Starting from the bottom of Africa, you'll find him roughly from Zululand and the South African Lowveld right on up through Zimbabwe, Botswana, Angola, Mozambique, Zambia, Tanzania, Uganda, Kenya and eastern Zaire. The Tana River in Kenya is roughly his northernmost range. To the northwest and west lies the range of the North-Eastern and North-Western buffalo, *Syncerus aequinoctialis*, a much smaller relative that I have never seen but am assured is quite as cantankerous as his big southern cousin, if not more so. Both are wild oxen. A closely related form is the *Syncerus nanus*, the definition of which seems to be purely one of location. This is most commonly called the "dwarf buffalo" or "bush cow." Since the lesser species of the African buffalo are fairly rare items in most hunters' safari agendas, I suggest we stick to the big Cape race of the south, central and eastern regions, not that there certainly aren't family variations among them too.

In my experience, it seems unreasonable to rank a Cape buff from South Africa with one from Zambia or East Africa, although this is the same classification in *Rowland Ward's* system. Before I ever hunted in South Africa, I used to wonder at the illustrations in the books of men like Selous, Baldwin and earlier African hunting writers, showing quite different buffalo than I was used to seeing on the safaris I was running in Zambia, Botswana and Rhodesia, where the horn conformation was generally wide and sweeping, a really good helmet of boss being, if not rare, at least unusual. When I had a chance to hunt the Letaba region of the northeastern Transvaal, near the Kruger Park, I immediately noticed that these buff looked different, in fact right out of the old books. Despite the fact that there are huge differences in individual buffalo horns, the South African variety seems clearly to favor a massive boss, which is split in the center like the part of an old-fashioned barbershop quartet singer's hair, and with a much shorter or narrower spread. My impression is also of less droop to the horns compared with up north, where they may loop down well past the face. A glance at the record books will also seem to correlate what I have seen, as most of the really big chaps have come from the old East Africa, Zambia and such.

I believe this is merely a good example of local race differences in the animal, but if record-book trophies are your bag, don't waste your time in South Africa where, incidentally, buff are also very expensive because of their relative scarcity.

Of the places I have hunted, I would suggest that the Zambian stuff was the best. In Botswana, although there were slathers of *iNyati* in herds, I never saw the occasional real monsters that I used to see near the Luangwa. Every year with my old safari company in Zambia, we used to get a few in the very

high forties in breadth of spread, and every now and then, one
that would break fifty inches, which is to buffalo what Raquel
Welch is to girls.

This is not to say that the very rare exceptional specimen
does not come out of South Africa or anywhere else that the
animal is found, but don't bet on it being a very frequent happening. If I were looking for a whopper buffalo, you'd find me
in Tanzania or Zambia, take your choice.

Your hunter will judge the quality of your buff first off by
the apparent width of his horns from the widest point of each
outside loop. This is the measurement that really counts. Next
would be the thickness of the horns and their general conformation. The boss is also extremely important because, when
the head is cleaned, the closer the "seem" between the horn
bases, the more desirable. In general, the southernmost buff
have more oak-burl bosses, the others being rather smoother.
The main measurement is between perpendicular planks at the
widest point, but another way of making the record book is by
measuring along the length of the front curve, which is reasonable to me. Many buffalo horns turn well back on themselves
like the first stages of a bow knot and actually measure longer
along the curve than they would between their widest points. To
give an idea of the practical aspects of this: in Zambia we usually wouldn't take a buff unless he would tape nearly forty-four
inches across the "wide," but in Rhodesia, a forty-one or forty-
two-incher was pretty decent. In South Africa, anything over
thirty-eight inches is lovely, the difference in width usually being
made up for by the massive bosses. The minimum for the record
book, incidentally, is forty-seven inches in width or forty inches
along the front curve of the spread on the longest horn.

The temperament of the buff varies as much as do his looks
across much of Africa. Rather like the reputations of crocodiles
in different although nearby rivers, some of which are notorious
for man-eating while those practically next door are not, the
buffs seems to be more cantankerous and stroppy in some places
than in others. Personally, it seems to me that this sort of thing
is largely a matter of one's own adventures. I knew some hunters in the Luangwa Valley who were almost contemptuous of
buffalo, yet the statistics for charges there were quite as high as

elsewhere, so far as my experience and research could determine. As we said before, you never know with buffalo.

Buffalo hunting is largely a matter of stalking and, in some cases, ambushing a group that's moving across your position. The best horns are unquestionably found among the herds of old bachelors. Logically, these crusty old boys are among the most interesting to take on, as their collective sense of humor is less than jolly.

Most buffalo hunts start with the picking up of spoor from dawn or the night before where the animals have crossed a hunting track. It's fairly easy to figure out from the dung when they passed, and their logical direction (buffalo normally water twice a day), and you can possibly interpolate an approach that results in a collision course. As we've said, the big boys tend to be on their own or in small groups, but sometimes you'll find a shootable head in a herd with cows and calves. One of the problems with the headgear of the old-timers is that when they get to the age of independence, they start to wear down the fine horns they have until, although massive as baobabs at the bases, the tips are smooth nubs, not ranking very well as trophies.

Actually, of all the Big Five, only the buff is horned in the true sense, and it must be remembered that horns are a one-shot deal. They are not shed like antlers, but grow around a bone core for the life of the animal. Both cows and bulls have horns, although cows normally sport nothing like the massive structures of the bull. Some, however, can develop extraordinary spreads. In fact, in thick cover even at close range, it can be extremely difficult to tell the two apart without some visibility.

The Cape buffalo is an amazingly adaptable critter. When the great rinderpest epidemic of the late 1890s came down the African continent, it was reliably estimated that but one buffalo out of every ten thousand survived the disease, which is one hell of a lot of dead buffalo. Yet by 1912 the consensus of the game departments was that they had bred back to about their former numbers. In their ranges, they also live happily from sea level to well above twelve thousand feet, which is more than I can say for myself!

When you take your buffalo I would suggest that you take the advice of the old-timers: break him down. The "far shoulder theory" applies, in my mind, particularly to buffalo, but the important thing is to break bone. This way, even if you don't scramble the vitals, you'll slow him up a bit. Retrospectively, this isn't necessarily always so. A buff with a broken shoulder is as mobile on three legs as you are on two, even more so. Yet, if you can break the shoulder, you're ahead of the game because, in doing so, you will likely have done a hell of a lot of other damage too.

I can recall one outstanding exception to this idea, though, with Geoff Broom back in Matetsi days in the then-Rhodesia. I didn't have a client at the time and, as we took off a few head for commercial meat, Geoff suggested that I collect a big cow (we didn't waste the shootable bulls for meat) for the larder. I took Amos, my gunbearer, Gladstone and Rota, an apprentice of Amos', and wandered down near the Bembe River, where we soon cut the spoor of quite a large herd. As I was in fear of having my bullet pass through my target animal and hit another in the group, I was using the Winchester 300-grain Silvertip controlled-expansion bullet, a very fine one by my lights.

We "smoked" into the edge of the herd of about eighty buff, none of which noticed us. Using a small sapling for support, I stuck the crosshairs right on the money on the shoulder of a big, calfless cow and swatted her. She swung around with the rest of the crew and raced off in typical fashion for a buffalo with a slug in the arteries over the heart. Only she didn't fall down. I was so sure that the bullet had been in the right place that I decided to save the solid bullets that lay below in the magazine of the Winchester and just have a cigarette until she crashed.

After twenty minutes, we took up the trail and were rounding the edge of a big thicket when I saw the old cow, forlorn but still very much on her feet. Surprised, I belted her again, seeing her fall this time, but she was back up and off in a blink. Just as she flashed through a gap in the bush, I was able to give her a solid raking shot that flipped her upside down, heels over nose, in a really spectacular fashion.

When I had a chance to look over the carcass, I was surprised to see that my first two shots were right where I wanted them, in the center of the shoulder, and by luck nearly touching each other. Since they looked fine to me, I wrote out a note to Geoff, asking him to please have a look when she was butchered as I could see no reason why the cow hadn't died immediately. The next day he sent me back the three slugs—which had acted properly—and a return note saying that somehow those first two rounds had just missed everything important in the buff's chest. Well, I'm glad it wasn't a bull coming my way. . . .

It's the bulletproof aspect of *iNyati* that makes most professional hunters choose a magazine rifle for this game, even if they own a good double. When a buff gets a head of steam up, it becomes absolutely unbelievable how many times you may have to thump him before he goes down for good. I have many times had cases with clients where ten or more doses of persuasion were required, and these from guns as heavy as the .458 and the .460. Now, I know that sounds like very sloppy hunting and even worse shooting, but you can't often pick your shot in heavy bush and, to check or prevent a charge, I believe the best exercise is to smack him in the chest as often and as hard as you can until he's down.

The second shot is very important in buffalo hunting. If you are spooring a single old bull, okay, stick with solid bullets. But if sorting one out of a herd or in company with a couple of other old boys, your best bet is to have a big soft-point in the chamber and as many solids stacked below it as your rifle's magazine can handle. This way, you'll cut down the odds on having *two* wounded buffalo at the same time by overpenetration. At the shot, if he doesn't go down in a heap, most buffalo will spin away and rush off in that odd, rocking horse gait of theirs. It's at this point that you can save yourself a huge deal of trouble if you can get off another round or two up his bum, letting the solids rake forward hopefully into the vitals. My maxim is "If you can see him, you ought to be firing at him," provided he's wounded. The first shot, of course, should never be let off unless you're positive you can place it properly. Even if the follow-up shot doesn't bring him down, he's going to be a lot sicker than he would be from one slug alone and he will be less able to sort you out if Murphy takes a hand in the proceedings.

Magazine capacity is really something to think about when selecting a rifle for work with buffalo. Most .458s hold three rounds, .375s normally four, including one "up the spout." My first .375, a custom design with buffalo very much in mind, by Continental Arms of New York City, was a Mauser action and I had the magazine well extended to hold five cartridges plus one in the chamber. There have been plenty of times I have used the first five, and once I had to spend the sixth, which indicates a very hirsute happening indeed. It was, predictably, with a buffalo bull that had developed a most disconcerting habit of getting up every time I shot him dead. He dropped about nine or ten yards from me, which isn't really close, but then I wonder what might have happened had I not had that big fat stack of cartridges.

While we're on it, always try to preserve the last round in your magazine for a life-and-death possibility. I always try to pick a clear spot to reload in a wounded-game situation, even if I've only fired one shot. You never know when you'll need all you have. One aspect of this, though, requires caution, although it's not of absolute importance in a potential charge situation. As your cartridges lie in the magazine, they take some very substantial thumping from the recoil of the bigger calibers. In some cases, this may tend to drive the bullet down in the cartridge-case neck, which will affect performance by "compressing" the load to higher pressures. At longer ranges, this can make a noticeable difference, but for emergencies, don't worry about it. Don't, however, let the same cartridge or two in the bottom of the magazine stay in that position for long with others being fired above them. Change their position upwards.

The old double rifle habit of carrying a pair of extra cartridges between the fingers of the left hand dies hard, particularly if you are used to handling a double. I sort of feel naked without them and so continue the practice, even with a bolt-action rifle. It saves digging around in your pockets or a belt for a couple of rounds if you need them in a hurry.

Like much big game, buffalo have a reputation that is well-earned but often exaggerated. The great majority of wounded buffalo don't charge, and a high percentage of these, depending on where they've been hit and with what, show no inclination at all towards aggression. Naturally, if your pro is doing his job, a large portion are killed before they get a chance to even consider attacking. Buffalo *are* tough. But so are express bullets. Still, the point that can't be avoided or denied is that every buffalo is a potential individual wave of destruction, particularly if you put an off-center hole in him. Once he puts a close-quarter charge into gear, your options have been wonderfully simplified: you kill him or he'll kill you. With that pig-iron resolve and nearly a ton of muscle to go with it, he can make it stick, too. I've heard it said that a buffalo, once he's decided to charge, will never ever veer off or be turned by a bullet. It's nearly true, too, although like most so-called rules with big game, there are exceptions. I have twice had them turn from a bullet, one a .470 Nitro in the face and the other a .375 in the chest. Still, twice in eleven years and after more than a thousand buffalo isn't much, so I recommend against making book on it.

You'll find some countries with restrictions on minimum caliber rifles that may legally be used for buffalo. It is my impression, though, that since Kenya closed, the .375 H&H Magnum is acceptable everywhere. As we have seen, however, these rules are always changing and you should check with your outfitter. Personally, I go along with Karamojo Bell's theory, which he converted to a practicality, namely that a small bullet in the right place is effective while a big one in a poor spot is worthless. You will notice, however, that I don't shoot my buffalo with 7mm or .256 Mannlichers, nor am I very likely to commence the practice. Speaking of Bell and buffalo, there is a passage in *Karamojo Safari* that I have always found enticing:

> Although buffalo can be easily killed with soft-nosed bullets planted in the soft parts behind the shoulder— indeed, I have killed in recent times many buffalo with the .22 high-velocity soft-nosed bullets—by far the best bullets for all-round shots at buffalo are the solid variety. . . .

My interest lies not so much in his endorsement of the solid but in his reference to the .22 caliber. Surely he can't mean the .22 Long Rifle rim-fire cartridge, which is how I have sometimes seen this comment interpreted. I believe he must have been speaking generically of the .22 caliber in center-fire, such as the .220 Swift or the .22 Hornet of his day, which did have *jacketed* bullets with a soft nose, rather than the solid lead bullet of the rim-fire, which is technically not a soft-nose. Perhaps the key is his designation of "high-velocity" to refer to the .22 center-fires. In any case, no mean feat!

I have killed quite a few buffalo with the .30-06 with 220-grain solids in more open cover and must say that I never had any cause for complaint. But the .22 is a touch light for my taste. I think it was this bit by Bell that caused a friendly argument between another professional and myself in Zambia some time ago. He said that he believed a buff could be brain-shot with a .22 Long Rifle and I figured it impossible. So we took the fresh skull of a ration buff and shot it from just about every angle. None of the little slugs reached the brain.

It seems a happy prospect that, despite the unquestionable decline in habitat generally, the Cape buffalo is doing very well over wide portions of his African range. Fortunately, he's essentially a group animal of considerable demographic vigor as opposed to, for example, the declining rhino and the poacher-harassed elephant. The lion and the leopard are, as carnivores, naturally much less populous. Hopefully, we will never get another catastrophe such as the rinderpest epidemic to let the buff prove his tenacity to life as a species. The Cape buffalo threatened with extinction? I don't think so. He's just too mean to die.

FOURTEEN

Elephant

Very possibly it was the late Major W. Robert Foran who summed it up most succinctly when he described elephant hunting as "The Classic of Big Game Hunting." Or another way of looking at it would be to observe that if one plays at it, it's sport; if you have to work at it, it's either golf or elephant hunting.

That the realities of elephant hunting are either widely misunderstood or simply unknown seemed obvious to me nearly every time I would meet a new safari. If it was the client's first trip, over our initial drink he would invariably advise me that he under no circumstances wanted to shoot an elephant. Yet, and absolutely without exception, after being in the field and seeing elephants under wild conditions, not one of them failed to completely change his mind.

I think the impression most non-Africans hold of the world's biggest land animal must be based on childhood association through circuses, zoos and peanuts. Certainly the domesticated Asian elephant, mostly found in such displays, has little in common with the wild African variety, as you will find out in short order on safari in elephant country. Elephant hunting under the sporting ethic is one of the toughest and most dangerous pastimes on earth, and if you pooh-pooh this, I would be respectfully inclined to suggest you haven't tried it.

Probably because elephants are so big and seemingly familiar through Jumbo and Dumbo, emotion has blended freely with reality in terms of most people's understanding of the African elephant's ecological status in the middle of the Great Age of the Endangered Species. Normally perceived as practically over the biological hill, the species itself is in no more trouble than other game considered reasonably unthreatened in modern Africa, although it is for sure true that *some* groups of elephants in *some* areas are under great pressure from man for commercial reasons. As usual, the big problem is casual as well as mass-organized poaching, the latter frequently now done with automatic weapons, aircraft and explosives. In the case of the elephant especially, here once more is the seemingly classic illogicality of man, the *sport* hunter being the main supplier of funds to protect elephants from poachers through his license fees; fees paid to hunt a small number of selected elephants so that the rest can live and multiply in habitat preserved from agricultural or urban encroachment. The interesting thing is that where hunting is permitted, this works!

African political and military upheaval has been the main recent factor affecting elephant poaching. Former game reserves and wild areas are now packed with troops who don't exactly look at game through the eyes of a budding Audubon but merely as rations and ready cash on the hoof. Look at Uganda after Amin's fall. Or areas of the Sudan. Armies and elephants don't mix too well, at least from the elephants' viewpoint.

To further confuse the issue, though, consider other areas of Africa where the elephant is actually overbreeding and destroying its own habitat even faster than man does! Here, the situation is the reverse. Just as a single example, as I type this, the Zimbabwe government has recently reached the figure of 1,500 elephants cropped from 4,000 scheduled to be culled in the Hwange (formerly Wankie) National Park alone! In fact, I first came to Africa as an assistant cropping officer in Zambia, where we were culling 1,800 per year in just the Luangwa Valley. The point is that elephant status is highly localized and what may be valid for one group could be totally inapplicable to the next.

Because of the increase in poaching, dictated by the rise in the price of ivory, it is true that there are far fewer areas for jumbo hunting than even a few years ago. Elephant, however, may still be taken in a variety of countries and others are anticipated as coming back to offer elephant after temporary bans. At the moment, Tanzania, Sudan and Zaire are the prime ivory grounds, Zimbabwe offering a few decent tuskers.

A jumbo with tusks of which one is at least one hundred pounds in weight is the dream of all elephant hunters, a goal that has long been difficult to realize and which is far tougher now than ever before. Today, given that some areas just don't have a reputation for big ivory, any jumbo with tusks over about fifty pounds each is shootable and still a fine trophy. Some places it will be less than this. Having written in considerable detail in previous books about the many aspects of elephants' tusks and ivory, records and such, I see little need to cover the same ground here but for a few basics. Ivory is dentine covered in some areas with enamel. The tusk itself seems to grow and wear down through the life of the elephant, which rarely exceeds fifty-five to sixty years as an extreme, and is nurtured through a carrot-shaped conical nerve pulp in the hollow bases as thick as your arm. The size of these nerve channels greatly influences the weight of the tusk as large hollows of course displace ivory. As a rule, the older the bull, the smaller the cavities, but this is not always so.

You'll rarely see a reference to them, but at times the pulp cavity will yield what are called "pearls." Greatly prized, especially in the Orient, these are produced by an infection of the nerve area that causes single or a series of globules of secondary dentine to form. These globules or pearls are especially valuable in Sri Lanka, where they also form in Indian elephants. I've never seen them actually in an elephant's nerve cavity but have had other hunters show them to me. They are seemingly sufficiently rare as to be nearly unknown in Africa, as I could find no reference to them even in rather detailed books in my library on the species. But keep your eyes open. You may be lucky.

Some hunters have their trophy tusks polished smooth and white but I opine that they're prettier just cleaned up and not polished. To my eye, they're a far more attractive display with their darker natural color, and showing their peculiar nicks and dents, one of which is always the deep groove across the tusk tip where the animal draws grass and branches to knock the dirt off.

Since import regulations are always changing for bringing trophies into the United States or Europe as the status of different species shifts, there's no point in exploring whatever may be the status of elephant by-products such as skin, ivory or tail hair now. Just make sure you check carefully with your outfitter or taxidermist.

As a rule, elephant hunting will be the most strenuous part of your safari. Hunting jumbo is eighty-five percent walking, with the rest of your time spent running for your life, praying and rarely, very rarely, shooting. The reason for all this activity is based on the lifestyle of the elephant, which, depending on whose estimate you believe, requires around six hundred pounds of forage a day to keep the seven tons of a big bull rolling. I suppose it's what you might call the original high-fiber diet.

Not wishing to turn this chapter into a natural history of the elephant, let's look at him in terms of your hunting him. A shootable elephant is getting to be a rare item, as we've noted. The reason is simple pocket-calculator mathematics. *Perhaps* in a good area one bull in every sixty elephants of both sexes and all ages carries ivory of better than fifty pounds a "side," as elephant jargon runs. Of this lot, many will be broken, depending on the terrain hunted. The point is that you can't tell if he has either big or broken tusks from the size of his track. In the old days—which isn't all that long ago—it used to be a pretty fair bet that big feet equaled big teeth. When enough time had passed that those unfortunate tuskers with manhole-cover tracks had been tracked down and taken, mostly by the professional ivory hunters earlier in this century and before such as Bell, Stigand and Sutherland, it was the bulls with big tusks and *small* feet that prospered, as most hunters wouldn't follow a small track for fifty miles when the probable result would be "toothpick" ivory. So, when you come across any bull's spoor, today, you tend to follow it, unless it's just too old to promise any chance of success.

Elephants cover amazing chunks of territory in their daily feeding and, in many parts of Africa, they migrate to one degree or another. It is this movement that makes hunting them so tough. If not disturbed, and depending on the richness of their pickings, elephant may in fact stick pretty close to one spot, but even this means a good deal of walking on the track. Jumbo water any time of day or night, but they seem far more active after dark. Thus, tracks are normally encountered in proximity to water near dawn and are followed back into the heavier cover where the animals spend their time, if they don't feel threatened loafing in the thick stuff during the heat of day. Ideally, you want to catch up with them in the hot hours when they are at ease but, as with lions, that's when they're in the densest cover imaginable. A fifteen-mile hike to accomplish this is really a fairly easy day in terms of elephant hunting, although you may be much luckier.

Personally, I hate it when we happen to bump into a good tusker as it takes most of the real fun of tracking out of the game. If you happen to see him by accident, gone is all the suspense of what his tusks might weigh, how he is moving, whether or not he'll stop and the rest of the real elements of hunting elephant. Of course, the stalk for the possible kill is hardly a minor part of the African *corrida*. There is still the maneuvering, the heart-thumping terror of moving up to within fifteen or twenty paces—which will suddenly get a lot closer if he winds you. Elephant are taken up close. You don't snipe a jumbo, you go in and take him on his own terms. Just not done at long range, old boy.

Probably no shot in hunting dangerous game has been so discussed or is considered such an art form as the brain shot on elephant. Personally, I would observe that it's not so tough as generally advertised, but only if one has done one's homework and knows where the brain in fact lies. It's in the center of the skull, on a direct line or axis between the ear holes. It's also the size of a loaf of pumpernickel, which is a fair target at twenty yards, despite the skull. Although some will tell you that there is a particular wrinkle at the top of the trunk to aim at, the slightest thought will show how misleading this is. When an elephant is agitated, a state in which they spend considerable portions of their lives in my experience, they will throw their heads around to the extent that the entrance point of the shot from a mere frontal angle would vary as much as three or four feet!

This, naturally, is a guess as I have never measured the fore-heads of any agitated elephants. Some elephants have been killed by the brain shot actually up through the roof of the mouth and others, with heads very low, well above the middle of the forehead. I have written it many times before, but just remember that the brain is reached with no particular attention to the *outside* of the animal's head, just a clear mental picture of where the brain lies *inside*, no matter what the position. Ka-ramojo Bell even mastered the rear brain shot, at an oblique angle through the neck muscles, on this principle. And that with the 7mm, even the .256. You do your part, and your rifle with a good solid will do the rest.

Well, nearly always.

As many of the ivory hunters have noted, some jumbos simply appear immune to the brain shot, although it would not seem reasonable that their gray matter is located elsewhere. What may have been the best bull that Bell ever killed was a huge old boy very near death from natural causes when Ka-ramojo found him. Bell took two perfect side brain shots at him from a few yards and got absolutely no reaction at all! Another round in the heart put the patriarch into a slow walk and he finally dropped to a frontal shot when Bell ran around him. The behemoth's teeth weighed 145 and 148 pounds.

Although I have always hugely enjoyed his writings, I can see little practical merit to the contention of the late ivory hunter John "Pondoro" Taylor that the value of a particular cal-iber consisted in major part in how long it would keep an ele-phant unconscious from a near miss to the brain. He referred to his system as "Knock-Out values," as we discussed earlier, and typified his contentions by a comparison between the grand .416 Rigby and the .470 Nitro Express: "If you take a frontal head shot at an elephant with a .416 and miss the brain by a small amount, you will probably not knock him out. . . ." wrote Tay-lor. "But if you had taken the shot with the .470, and missed the brain by the same amount, that elephant would have been knocked out entirely, unconscious, and would have remained down for anything up to about five minutes—yet the theoretical energies of the rifles are the same."

I just don't believe this and have not experienced it in the taking of something around seven hundred elephant, mostly cropping and on control in three countries. Quite probably, Pondoro Taylor killed a great many more elephant than I have, and, considering when he hunted, on both sides of World War II, there were a lot more big bulls around. I nonetheless think his conclusion that the heaviest rifle—he gives the .600 Nitro the numero uno position, although this was before the advent of the .460 Weatherby—is the best by definition, is simply not empirical. Every shot is different, and "miss the brain by a small amount" not very precise. By exactly how much? From exactly what angle? From how far? On how big a bull? Obviously, it's a very tough point to prove as there is no reliable sampling.

I suspect it is partially Taylor's thinking that has a lot of safari hunters toting much more rifle than they can handle well. We've been through this routine earlier but let me reinforce my experience by recalling just one afternoon in the Okavango of Botswana with a client who carried a .460 Weatherby Magnum. We waded about two miles through knee-deep water to catch up with a huge-bodied bull carrying about sixty-five pounds a side and sneaked onto a five-acre island where he was relaxing. My client, a Californian, was a fine shot and we were within about twelve paces in very heavy, leafy cover. We had agreed that, since the big bull was only about twenty yards from the water's edge, where a fairly deep channel ran, I would back him up as he tried the side brain shot, right in front of the earhole, in case he blew it and the bull escaped to die in the water, where he would be an interesting problem to retrieve. He took the shot and, to my astonishment, as I saw that it had hit the right spot, the bull just shifted into overdrive.

My man was fast and hit the jumbo again where I would have called spot-on, with the same result—nothing. And this was a 500-grain solid blowing along at not much less than 2,700 foot-seconds and about 8,000 foot-pounds of energy. Consider that this is some aggregated 1,400 foot-pounds *more* than Taylor's .600 Nitro Express and you'll get the relativity of things. Realizing that the tusker would be in the water in a blink, I stuck him in the head at an angle with the first barrel of my Evans .470 at about ten yards from the bank, and then had to hip him or lose him. I did and he went down just short of the swamp. A quick reload finished him.

Okay. He'd taken at least 21,000 foot-pounds of impact

from best-quality solid bullets in what could only be called *very* close to the brain, but never even staggered. Don't ask me, but it happens. Draw your own conclusions, so long as you don't decide that rifle power is more important than bullet placement.

I find it interesting that Bell recorded frequent instances of having to shoot a brain-stunned jumbo a second time. In fact, I would estimate that, from his writing, this was the case about twenty percent of the time. How fascinating, given other reports, that rifles between the .256 and the .318, far less than the .600 and the big nitros, gave this result so often. Bell had the rather suicidal habit as I have earlier related, of immediately running up onto the body of a newly killed jumbo in grass to see the others, so you can bet he paid attention to whether or not his perch was dead. If the death tremor was not seen to occur along with the other indications of brain death, Bell always gave another shot. Even at that, he was lucky he didn't get caught.

One important piece of advice: If you try a brain shot and miss, *don't* try it again with your second shot. Go for the heart or lungs.

I have had some people criticise me for advising brain shots, but I've had many clients take their tuskers with them. Actually, I have rarely had a problem with brain shots, the rate of success having been, according to a compilation of my journals, about eighty percent. Again, the trick is to know the technique, and to spend a little time near a few unsuspecting jumbos with someone to point out the vulnerable areas. It has been worth textbooks.

The brain shot, from whatever angle, should, however, only be taken when conditions are just right. Otherwise, count on the heart or lung shot. Actually, the heart shot seems to me more reliable than the brain shot, and what's the difference under most conditions—other than on an island as I commented—if the bull runs up to a hundred or so yards? At least you'll get him. Just remember that the heart and, far more vulnerable, the big arteries, are low in the body and partially obscured from the side by the edge of the foreleg.

Over the years I have heard a lot about the .375 H&H being a bit light for elephant but I just can't see where this is so. With its excellent penetration, it sometimes shoots completely through a bull's skull and out the far side. I can't imagine what more anybody would want. So long as strict attention is given to placement, it's plenty of gun for sporting circumstances, although I would agree that in control work with jumbo, a man needs all the gun he can handle. Even then, it's sometimes not enough.

Despite my years of safari work, I always first think of the elephant in terms of my experiences in either cropping or control of agricultural raiders. I have described cropping rather thoroughly in *Death in the Long Grass* and will leave it there, as it has little in common with the sporting ethic. Control hunting is quite different, as it largely involves raiding bulls rather than breeding herds and cows, and was really the closest thing that existed at the time I did it to being an old-time ivory hunter. If I may recall with you with some pain one episode of a few years ago, perhaps you'll see that it was true, pure hunting, the only essential difference being that it was by government order.

His name was Katwindi. He told me this in Fanagalo while throwing a crisp, open-palmed British salute, which I returned. For just having covered more than two hundred miles of heavy bush country on his bicycle, he looked very crisp and fresh for a replacement, his puttees nicely wound, his rifle properly slung and his drab uniform, if not starched, at least clean. I have often wondered what I might have said to him had I known that he would be dead in less than three days.

He was of the Ila People, from upcountry Zambia, an area I had not hunted. When I asked his age, he replied that he was born "the year the bridge was built." Since neither he nor I knew what bridge that was, the matter became somewhat academic. I pegged him for about twenty, very tender for a corporal attached to an elephant control unit. But when I tried him out the next day, I found that he was one of the rare bush Africans who did not believe that the harder the trigger was pulled on his issue Cogswell & Harrison .404 magazine rifle, the faster the bullet would fly. He was a cool one, absolutely nerveless as he put four rounds into the fist-sized blaze cut into the bark of an *umkukubuyu* tree at seventy yards within six seconds. That feat even raised the eyebrows of Charlie, my veteran sergeant, and Silent, my personal gunbearer from the old safari days, before I'd gone to work year-round with the game department on control.

Corporal Katwindi looked as if he'd do just fine.

I have never decided in my own mind just which few weeks in Central Africa I dislike most. It was now December, and thoroughly awful. But a few weeks earlier, before the rains had started, the parched, scorched red earth had been equally unpleasant. An airborne assault of dust constantly clogged nostrils, sandpapered eyes and seeped into the most unlikely places, including my waterproof watch and other areas of hopefully less interest. Then, as soon as the sun was up, the heat seemed to strike like a live thing. It left a physical impact that was like a blow to the stomach and at the same time a gritty, tightening rawhide band that gripped your skull like some exotic Apache torture at the scene of which the cavalry *never* seemed to arrive. Tempers had been short before the rains had broken, but on this elephant control unit, we knew that our troubles were only about to start with the first, fat drops.

The dry season from May through October was the easiest, with just the odd jumbo or small herd of village grainary raiders to sort out along with some man-eating lions and an occasional leopard that had developed some culinary bad habits. In the dry Southern Hemisphere winter, I could normally make do with just old Silent to track and his brother, Invisible, who was now back at his village with a bout of fever, to keep camp. Because of his age, I had to pay Silent out of my own pocket, but he was more than a man to whom I owed my life several times over. He was a friend and fellow hunter with whom I could spend two weeks in the loneliest bush, running down poachers or whatever, without ever the need for a spoken word between us. Privately, we called each other *Baba*, meaning Father, the highest respect one man can show another, regardless of age.

But then there were the rains. Not a steady, monsoon downpour as many imagine, just enough to keep things nice and soggy, muddy, mildewed, rusty and infected. It was the season of tropical ulcers that defied and even thrived on the most sophisticated drugs, likely because it was almost impossible to keep them dry. They were terrible, seemingly causeless sores that formed on your legs and ankles until—if you had an empty stomach—you could remove the bandage and watch the smooth white tendons slide back and forth as you wiggled your bleached, crinkled toes. I got all this paradise for the equivalent of $19 a day, plus food and uniform allowance, ammo and an issue rifle.

I used my personal Evans .470 double rifle in preference to the .458 Magnums issued to the white officers or the .404s given to the more slightly built Africans, who couldn't take the pounding of the bigger rifle. The boys up at supply would scream bloody murder at the cost and trouble it took to supply the .470 Kynochs, but they always seemed to scrounge a supply from somewhere.

Besides the increase of very nasty snakes and the tendency of your bush jacket to rot off your back, the rains meant the start of the planting season for the villages; and the planting season meant elephants; and the elephants meant trouble. It was enough that they would regularly raid the new corn and millet or sorghum, but they would also run afoul of one or another wild fruit, usually *marula* or the related *mobola*. Both produce a plumlike fruit that, when ripe, ferments in the elephants' stomachs, producing a rip-roaring, falling-down state of inebriation. Some of these animals' antics can be really funny as they stagger and stumble with obviously injured dignity, while others turn nasty and tear up trees with pure belligerence. But they are all potential multi-ton lumps of murder when they start to sober up and experience hangovers that must *really* be something. If there is one object on this earth you want positively nothing at all to do with, let me open the bidding with a hung-over bull elephant, let alone one with a few pals in tow suffering the same horrors. Nonetheless, that's what we got. Just lucky, I guess.

We found out in the usual manner, by human runner, that four big bulls had taken a village apart the night before, not twelve miles from my camp. One old man had been too slow and was stamped and tusked into nonexistence. Several huts had been destroyed and much of the corn crop flattened. Within an hour, we were at the village, more a small collection of grass *kaias*, name of which I don't recall. I had brought Silent and, on a quick decision, as there were only four bulls, decided to include Katwindi, so I could keep an eye on him. Charlie, my experienced sergeant, remained at camp. At a bend in a small river that flowed dark, its waters oozing along like rancid, liquid grease, we came to the field. It was brown and green like an ancient tartan, much of it torn and trampled. We stared wordlessly at the shattered village and at the gouges where the old man's life had been ground out.

Katwindi gestured to the tracks of the elephants, great garbage-can-lid impressions in the wet soil, the rear ones more oval than the fronts. I placed both feet into one of the largest, toe to heel, and still had inches left over. I gave a low whistle of awe. Silent placed his hand over his mouth and said, "Ow!" Katwindi just shook his head. At least one was a real whopper, probably better than twelve feet at the shoulder and weighing seven tons, a lot of elephant for one package. Silent took off at a slow trot on the spoor, which was as plain as if somebody had driven a regiment of self-propelled guns through the field. I didn't hurry, knowing he would find what he was looking for not far ahead. After two hundred yards, I saw him stop and squat. He was examining the huge pile of dung as I came up with Katwindi. I nudged it apart with a toe-tip, a fibrous mass of tree bark studded with roundish fruit pits. I took a sniff at it and passed it to Silent.

"*Yebo, Bwana,*" he agreed, "*marula.*"

The stuff still reeked of the smell of alcohol. These boys had really been on a bash!

"Silent," I told him in Fanagalo, "I'll bet your next tobacco ration these elephants are not five miles away. Nobody likes to travel with a sore head. I think they will be up this river, in the deep shade. If we hurry, we may catch them today and not have to sleep on the spoor."

He grinned and shook his head. "I will not throw the stones [gamble] with you, Bwana," he said with a laugh. "If I had drunk that much *tshwala,* I would be asleep in the shade too."

We walked fast for an hour and a half, dark perspiration forming wide, sopping stains under our armpits and on our jacket fronts. Those thick salt-edged patches were washed out as we caught the edge of a short but heavy storm. The tsetse were bad but we did not risk the sound of a slap, catching the saber-toothed little monsters in our fingers as they settled down to bite, then pulling their heads off and dropping them. Fine swarms of *mopane* flies mobbed us in nostril-clogging clouds.

The sun was out again, the great heat of the direct rays forcing us to stop and change cartridges, switching the hot ones in the chambers for cooler, fresher loads in our pockets. Cordite, the standard propellant for the big, British elephant guns, was temperamental in extreme heat and the metal of the rifle barrels had grown too hot to touch.

We found where the bulls had watered about four miles up-river and, by the sign, their heads must have still ached enough for them to spend at least two hours wallowing in the soothing mud. That was time enough, by our guess, to be their undoing. The spoor turned abruptly, as I thought it would, into the densest bush. We followed, noticing the ever-freshening dung spoor. After another hour of slower pace, in a deep, green stand of brachystegia trees, Silent held back his hand and stopped, hunkering on his heels at a fresh stack of droppings that had not even lost their glaze. He inserted his index finger into the middle of it, feeling for remaining body heat, pulled it out and shook it at me as if burned. He held up the fingers of both hands twice. It was about twenty minutes old.

Silent stuck out his lower lip, sucking in the upper in deep thought. I glanced at my watch, looked at the gathering sky and lit a cigarette, watching the tendril of blue smoke waft straight up through the dead air. It was as still as a mausoleum. I broke the action of the Evans again and examined the twin cartridges, shaking them to hear the soft rattle of cordite stalks in their clean, brass cocoons, then replacing the slightly tapered 500-grain solids in the chambers. I flipped up the larger bead of the night sight, blackened the rear express Vee with a tip of flame from the Zippo and removed the sling and its swivels. A last drag on the butt, and I passed it to Silent, who gave what was left to Katwindi. He took a drag and, with calloused fingers, plucked the glowing coal free, dropping the end into his pocket. Elbow to elbow, every nerve quivering, we started into the heavy cover until it swallowed us like a thick fog.

We stalked slowly, silently through the strangling thickness of undergrowth, the white-hot lash of nettles welting our legs, the low, fish-hook thorns snagging our flesh. Katwindi covered the left of our badly limited field of vision; I the right. In the nightmare of tangled, dead and elephant-maimed trees, we would not be able to spot the marauders at any distance, so effectively did the vegetation mask their silhouettes. Oddly, elephant were sometimes too big to be seen in cover, the eye unable to decipher the outline of the giant animals. There were true tales of old-time ivory hunters actually bumping into elephants, much to their immediate regret.

With each exaggerated step we took on the edges of our feet, the tension grew with the gloom. Although it was not so warm now, in the shade of the forest, we were visibly sweating more, the walnut and steel of my rifle as slippery as a freshly skinned sapling in my hands. I can remember thinking that I would have to take even more care than usual cleaning it tonight before the salt of my perspiration began to eat the metal.

It came from a thicket ahead, an almost impenetrable mass of *mopane* as closely set together, it seemed, as bamboo. We all froze at the sound, our eyes locked on the grove as we listened. The tiny, dry scrape of a branch on thick, heavy hide. A snap and a rustle came from the left of the first noise. I glanced at unarmed Silent, signaling him to edge away from the area to where he would not get mixed up with either an elephant or a bullet. My thumb noiselessly slid off the safety catch, and I could feel the extra pair of cartridges between my left fingers slick and slimy with acrid sweat. Katwindi raised his chin in the direction of the sounds, and I gave a small nod. We began to crawl into the thicket on hands and knees.

A few yards into its denseness I had the feeling of being in another world. It was much cooler, damper, the heavy smell of elephant mixed with the rot of spongy humus, what I imagined it would be like to open the tomb of some long-dead king. We edged forward toward the sounds of rumbling, the low noise that elephants use to keep track of one another in the thick stuff. We scoured the tangles for movement with aching, sweat-stinging eyes.

"*Hsssst!*" It was an almost inaudible sound from Katwindi. I shifted my eyes to follow his stare, pulsing with strain, but I could make out nothing, save the eternal ranks of trees and the trunk of a single larger one twenty feet away. As I watched, a flash of cold panic ran over me like a scurrying scorpion and settled in a hard knot in my stomach. My heart slammed in my ears and I felt an overwhelming suffocation, a claustrophobic need to draw great, gasping lungfuls of air into my chest. The larger tree took another step directly at me, the shifting of the immense weight absolutely soundless despite the bulk of the tremendous bull. I followed the column of leg upward, just able to see the lower edge of the chest as it disappeared into the dark green tangles of leaves.

My mind raced, forcing myself to think it out. No possible brain shot. We could stick a slug through the heart or the big ropes of arteries above it, but heart-shot jumbo always thunder off in the direction they happen to be pointing, and this one was aimed smack at us. We could kill him, sure, but he'd probably run right over one or both of us before his brain ran out of oxygen and he toppled dead. I felt Katwindi's body jerk as if from physical impact at the sound of a branch being torn away from almost over our heads. There was no wind, but our scent had to be building up and the bull would catch it the instant he lowered his trunk. I shifted my stare over to Katwindi, who met it. The man's jaw muscles were tight but he showed no sign of panic. He watched my hand as if staring at a snake as I signaled to him to shoot the bull in the chest, then immediately break to the left while I scrambled to the right. I had considered taking the shot myself but the difference between the .470 and the .404 didn't matter under these circumstances. He could, in any case, fire five times without reloading and I might need my two shots any instant. If we handle it right, just right, the dying bull should pass between us. What the hell? Was there any choice? And what about the other three? First things first, my boy.

I was on my feet, running wildly, zagging through the bush on rubber legs, the hot muzzle blast of Katwindi's shot still stinging my face like a slap, my ears ringing. Even half-deafened, I could hear the ear-splitting trumpets and screams of the enraged elephants and the crash of trees as they tore up the thicket trying to find us. I saw the desperate death rush of the stricken bull smash past five yards away, the reddish gray eye unseeing. A fine mist of hot blood droplets blown from the waving trunk drizzled across my face in a sticky sleet. A sapling, whipped over by the elephant's passing, clubbed me across a shoulder and knocked me down, but I was up and running after the bull into the clearer forest where I would have more room to shoot. In full stride, I could feel the earthquake stampings of the other elephants, the same sensation I remember as a boy on the concrete apron of the railway station as a highballing locomotive came past.

I turned my head and saw that one of the other bulls had seen me and was bearing down, tearing through the bush like it wasn't there, straight at me but still too protected by bush for a safe, clear shot. I measured the distance to the clearing, showing paler through the thicket. Too far. Frantically, I searched for a dodge, anything to shield me from that 14,000 pounds of screeching murder avalanching down on me. Then I saw the first bull, the one Katwindi had chest-shot, standing, head drooping, twenty yards away. As I watched, not wanting to waste a round with a side brain shot, it suddenly collapsed and fell on its side, the hind legs stretching and relaxing in death as I instinctively ran to it, ignoring the pounding behind me. There was the awful sensation of not being able to run, the bush holding me back like invisible fingers as it clutched at my clothes and tore my flesh. Then I was at the carcass, dashing around the far side and raising the rifle over the animal's rounded flank.

The big bull was almost on me, coming like a landslide, a mountain of roaring meat and tusks, tattered ears as wide as billboards. It hauled up for the second I needed, confused by the body of its pal. Then it saw me and resumed the charge straight at the carcass. The rifle fired an instant after the big tusker began to swing his head slightly, the bullet smashing up a big wallop of dust a few inches left of center for the frontal brain shot. The 5000-foot-pound punch of the solid swung the head—bigger than the cab of a pickup truck—further to the side but the poorly placed bullet merely staggered the monster. He lurched, and in a blink was coming again, his feet stirring a churning storm of dirt. I let him keep coming until he was within three yards of the carcass, then picked my shot, from this angle right through the base of the trunk, below and between the eyes. The bullet passed through the brain and completely out the back of the head where I could hear it rattle through the trees. Blood burst from both ears as the bull piled into the middle of his dead companion. I ran out of the way as both bodies slid eight feet across the forest floor.

Instantly, the smoking empty cases were ejected, and I dropped in the two fresh rounds from my left hand, replacing them with two more from my bullet loops. I ran around the tangle of dead meat, blood, dung and seminal fluid, hearing off to the side the trumpeting of the two remaining bulls, which had clearly taken after Katwindi. A heavy shot echoed through the muffling vegetation, then another closely spaced behind it. The meaty, unmistakable thud of a falling elephant sounded fifty yards away, then the insane, vocal hysteria of the other bull dropped to a chilling, throaty, rattling *BRRRRRRR*. A single human wail of pain was cut short by a grating, scraping noise. I knew what had happened. Katwindi was a dead man.

I tore through the brush horrified, my breath ragged in my chest, guided by the sound of the goring elephant. Nearly running smack into the rump of a kneeling bull, I instantly shot him twice up through the spine, which the bull ignored except to change the pitch of his sound. Reloading as I ran around the bull, an ice-water shock jolted through me as I saw Katwindi on the right tusk, impaled like some strange green and brown insect specimen on a long, ivory pin, nailed to the ground. I shot the elephant carefully, the muzzle blast scorching the temple skin. He never blinked, just stopped *BRRRRR*ing as if a phonograph needle had been lifted. The head remained upright, held in position by the thick, ivory tusk driven through Katwindi and deep into the dirt. Less than ten yards away, the last bull lay dead, a thin trickle of blood oozing from a perfect frontal brain shot.

Katwindi was, to my amazement, still alive. How, I couldn't imagine, with the eighteen-inch-thick tusk completely through just above his navel. I screamed for Silent, and he came running up with the water and my emergency equipment in the shooting bag, although the combined staffs of three major hospitals weren't going to do Katwindi any good. His eyes were bright with shock and his face was slick with sheeting sweat. He asked, I thought, for water, and even though I knew water was forbidden in cases of stomach wounds, it was clear this would make no difference. In fact, he died just as I was about to hold the sack to his lips.

I do not believe you would enjoy my thoughts as I sat with the body for three hours while Silent ran back to the village and brought enough men with torches to begin the grisly work of freeing that brave man's remains. We buried him the next day under a magnificent fig on the slope of a hill near camp, marking the site with a cairn of rocks, which would be replaced with an official marker. It would simply state his name, rank, date of death and the fact that he had been killed by an elephant in the line of duty. Not much. But what more was there?

It was several years before I could stop blaming myself that I had in some way been responsible for the incident. Perhaps there was something I might have done that would have changed things. But there just wasn't, and that, finally, was that. If a man will live his life in the pursuit of dangerous game, for whatever reason, be it sport or game control, there will always be that little spot waiting for him on some hillside, hopefully under a great fig, that will be the price he will pay. And there will always be some of us who find the price not only fair but downright cheap.

Fifteen

Leopard

After years of safari hunting, I suppose every professional has a favorite animal. For me, it's the leopard, the toughest, slickest and most dangerous of a rather nasty lot of big game, all of which are capable of rearranging your profile to the extent that the FBI couldn't identify you.

To me, the beauty of leopard hunting is that it's the pure essence of the chase, predator against predator, brain against brain and instinct. You don't spoor or track leopard, and only very rarely do you happen into one that will offer a shot. Even if you do—as in the case of that big bull elephant found by accident—you really cheat yourself out of a pure leopard hunt, the success of which depends entirely on outwitting the shiftiest of the big cats on his own terms. Other animals are chased and followed. The leopard must come to you. Not easy.

It's pretty well known that the leopard is the most widely distributed of the major cats, existing from below sea level to great mountain heights and in literally all terrain. Illustrating his secrecy and adaptability, several breeding pairs have shown up there recently long after the Sinai leopard was considered extinct. Obviously they weren't extinct but doing just what they do best: appearing not to be where they in fact are. And if I may add a personal comment, if two or three pairs are known to exist, you can bet the welfare money that there are twice as many in actuality.

In hunting terms, I've always noticed a similarity between leopards and ducks. When you pick up a shot grouse, woodcock or pheasant, they're always a little disheveled and tattered, somehow much less neat and attractive than they were in life. But a big mallard or a black duck looks as if he has just been dry-cleaned. If you're a bird shooter, you'll instantly know what I mean. In comparison, lions are always somehow verminous (while we're at it, did you know that there is a particular flea that lives only on the testicles of a lion?) and rather shabby. When dead, they really *look* dead, mane tangled and filthy, with dried blood and dirt and a layer of dust thicker than a clay tennis court.

Not the leopard. He always gleams, a perfect shimmering sheath, a mantle of magnificence over steel muscles as smoothly swirling as the tail of a trout pool. The sight of a big male leopard above the bait in the stark silhouette of a tree against a sunset that would require a license to perform anywhere else but Africa, is the high point of my safaris. Yet although he will be the simplest shot you'll ever get on safari, usually less than forty yards, stationary and perfectly outlined, while your rifle is supported on a rest, my clients have missed it more often than any other animal.

If life is a waiting game—as well as a contact sport—then leopard hunting is pure, undiluted expectation. If you love the whistle of wings just out of range in the chill of a Connecticut December dawn and feel the flutter of guts that I do at the gabble of incoming geese; if you feel your pulse in your ear and the lousy coffee on the back of your tongue and are always surprised how golden the grass of the blind is in the early light, you will like leopard hunting. If, however, your heart thumps through the front of your L. L. Bean chamois cloth shirt and you can't remember if you've put a shell into the chamber or, as the squeak of primaries draws closer, how to spell your last name, you'd better stay away from leopard hunting. It's a thousand percent more exciting than the grandest duck or goose shooting, and a coronary thrombosis is a great inconvenience on safari.

Trying to take your leopard is the only time you will spend in a blind or, as the British prefer, "hide." This is not simply because I'm lazy. I love blind hunting, whether for waterfowl or leopards, because it's the only real chance you have to see nature around you in an undisturbed state. You'll see more of Africa while waiting in a leopard blind than you will in days of tramping after elephant or tracking kudu. Fifteen minutes after you've moved in and settled down, the bushveld will start to come alive around you, lizards, beetles, weird insects and especially birds. As most hunters know, motion, or rather the lack of it, is the key to camouflage. Gorgeous bee-eaters will perch a foot or two from your head, never noticing you. I've had lions walk by and once, as I've written in *Death in the Dark Continent*, kill a few yards away. Even baboon troops have unknowingly completely surrounded the blind, which is just fine as they'll let you know in no uncertain terms when your leopard is on his way. Still, this kind of hunting builds a tremendous anxiety and this is the reason so many leopards are missed, or worse, far worse, wounded.

When the sky starts to turn into a kaleidoscope of blood, gold and malachite, there will be something you notice but you won't know what it is. There's a charge in the air like static electricity on a cold wool rug, rather the same aura of a dirty joke at a bishop's conference. Somewhere in the gathering gloom, a francolin may *churrrr* or a vervet monkey shriek in shock. Still, you know. You can absolutely feel the presence of the big cat, padding his careful lean-loined way to the bait. Were your blood pressure to be taken now, it would read like a bowling score. You'll be sweating despite the lowering cool of the evening but your guts will feel like icy steel cables. All the old senses come into play now, sensations you don't even recognize unless you've been in combat, because they have been buried for the generations, since we were as likely to be eaten as not.

He's there. How he could cross your whole, though limited, field of view is incredible, yet with a dry whisper of talons he is in the tree. It's as if he were conjured out of the smoky, shadowy whirlpool of dusk by *tagati*, black magic. But he's there, right there, hulking like a dappled lion in the crotch, as clear in your scope as through a magnifying glass. Every hair is crisp and even the green motes in his golden eyes show. There's a notch missing from the tip of his right ear and a big, bloated tick just below his eye. My, and doesn't he have big teeth!

The cross hairs twitch and throb across the mottled expanse of shoulder as you draw your shooting breath, refusing to settle down. Hairy worms are crawling in your stomach and the backs of your hands prickle with panic. Why won't the damned thing hold still? Your eyes blur and your mouth tastes like copper sulphate and secondhand cigar butts.

As the big tom shears off a slab of flyblown warthog, you take another breath, the urgency of the professional's fingers still impressed on your forearm. Gripping hard, you pull the rifle tighter into your shoulder until you can feel the seam of your bush jacket biting and rasping into meat. That's it. Easy now. Hold it down. Don't jerk. Squeeeeeeeeze off. Right, squee . . . The unexpected blast and thump of the gun recoils the cat out of your field of view but the cross hairs seemed pretty near where they should have been. In the micromoment it takes you to get back on, you see a flash of wrought-iron black and copper slant through the last, starved sunlight angling to your left. You can actually hear him strike the dry, winter earth, a curious cat-soft sound, rather like the sound of a medium plastic sack of cottage cheese curds would make from the same height. That he was dead before he even made the leap seems clear from the great thump on the shoulder you get from the professional, and another from the gunbearer who, in his enthusiasm, is carried away. You don't mind at all.

He lies in the long grass like a Tiffany-set gem, a golden nugget peppered with black rosettes, stretched full in the lean strength of his last leap. He's not even bleeding, although the ridiculously little hole is visible in his armpit. He'll be a head-mounted rug that will bring back the time in the blind whenever you pass him on your way to the living room. He will stimulate indelible memories of the distant smoky waft of burning grass, the twitter of drongos and the dry, snake-cold sound of his own claws on the bark of the *muSassa* tree where a putrid warthog outwitted him. He will also be a very real symbol of your own mortality.

Professional hunters differ in their policies of permitting clients to follow up wounded dangerous game, which frankly astonishes me. Some have no compunction in permitting first-timers to come along to sort out wounded lions, buffalo and sometimes even leopards. I am—you'll pardon the turn of phrase—dead against it. If you want some excellent advice, more than worth the price of this book, swallow your pride. Don't go in even if invited. This is, if you are a nonprofessional, one of the grandest ways of Shakespearean coil-shuffling that you can find, and is highly reliable. If you are an American or European businessman, you simply have no place rooting around thick bush trying to kill something that is far more qualified to kill you. That's the job of the pro. He gets paid—not much—to do just that, but at least he's experienced. Most pick up some very impressive scars learning the process and to place an amateur in the same situation is, to my way of thinking, homicidal.

This doesn't apply to all circumstances, as a wounded buff will often become aggressive without the time lapse involved with a winged cat. Follow-up may not be necessary, as the confrontation will come instantly. Still, and I don't give a damn if you can powder aspirins off-hand at six hundred yards, have the sense to recognize when you are out of your depth. Looking down at a pinkish gray rope of your own guts hanging out of a spontaneous excavation in your belly is not why you came on safari. There's no cowardice implied, *and believe that.* In following up a wounded leopard, the odds are just about even—fifty-fifty—that somebody will get hurt. And, with a leopard, that means badly hurt. Don't let it be you.

This seems a logical place to have a look at the critter himself. A big leopard is about seven feet between the pegs and may weigh anything between one hundred and twenty to one hundred and sixty pounds, although the latter would be mighty hefty. Nine feet seven inches is the number one in *Rowland Ward's* records, an unbelievable specimen that would fit well up in the same record length for lions! He was killed in Ruanda and the date is not recorded. He is or was owned by one J. E. Church, address unknown. That he was a full seven inches longer than the next entry might give some idea of how unbelievable his dimensions were.

After years of association, some of it rather intimate, I

would have to nominate the leopard as the supreme land predator next to man, and certainly the most adaptable of his classification of wild animal. Because of his high prominence as a fur
coat, the idea has long been promoted that he is endangered,
although this has been acknowledged as untrue by those who
originally classified him as such. In fact, the "endangered" status
of the leopard has been downgraded to "threatened" in most
parts of his range, which is about the same niche the professional hunter occupies. For some time, leopard trophies, although obtained on license legally in many locations, were
prohibited from import into the United States. This has largely
been remedied although there are still areas from which the
pelts may not be imported. Since this may well affect your safari, we'll look at some details in a moment.

The leopard, with his large brain capacity, invisible camouflage and absolutely solitary nature, is the master of evasion.
That he lives close to native villages and snacks on items rarely
missed, such as dogs and garbage, makes many think that he's
not even in the area. But he is. He'll eat nearly anything, including fish, antelope, pigs, insects, fresh-water mussels, birds and
also skins, as well as other trophies not carefully protected. In
places where he's under pressure, I have witnessed him jumping
across dirt tracks so as not to leave spoor, and you'll never hear
him call with that itchy, raspy hack of his anywhere near an area
where he has been subjected to traps or dogs.

It's not exactly about hunting, but let me offer a tale of
contemporary interest that occurred quite near where I'm writing this in South Africa. It concerns a newspaper report of the
capture of a leopard in a very populous suburb, and the subsequent information I received on the animal.

On the morning of September 10, 1983, in Benoni, a farming community fairly near the golden city of Johannesburg, one
of the most built-up places in Africa, Elizabeth Boke, a maid,
opened the door of the outhouse on the property of Jessica Bek-
ker, her employer. It seemed jammed. And it was. By a leopard. As Elizabeth realized from the glaring eyes that it was not
the Dalmatian dog she presumed it was, she panicked, dashed
for a nearby car and locked herself in. When nothing happened,
she went next door and enlisted a gardener with an axe to help

her. After one look, he realized the better part of valor and they agreed to call the police.

Two cops arrived at the farm and checked out the situation. While one officer was about to put his head in the window, the leopard gave a chilling roar and leaped through the insect gauze, almost catching the man in the face before running off to hide in another garden. Eventually the cat was darted and shipped off to the Johannesburg Zoo.

Right. Despite what you hear about "endangered" status in the United States, nothing is especially rare about leopards showing up very near or actually in big African cities. I've saved six different clippings of this type just over the past few months in South Africa and Zimbabwe alone. The interesting point is that Dr. Chris Botha, a brother of the South African Minister of Foreign Affairs and Information, came on the scene when he heard of the capture and claimed the leopard was his. Through courtesy of my good pal and international pistol legend, Lt. Col. Mike Malone, I got in touch with Dr. Botha, who told me a very interesting tale of what he believed to be a leopard he knew very well.

It was six years back, according to Dr. Botha, that he was wrenched out of a deep sleep by a terrible row near the pen of his cross-bred Boer bull/ridgeback dog. Grabbing a shotgun, Dr. Botha ran out, not knowing what to expect. He found a leopard cub, about five months old, having a snarling contest through the wire security fence with his dog. As this was only a few miles from Pretoria, in the Magaliesberg Mountains, he was surprised to see the cat, but did not shoot. Remembering that a mature female that had been recently killed nearby had shown signs of lactating, he guessed that this was her cub. Firing into the air, he drove the youngster off and went back to bed.

As weeks went by, more and more fresh spoor of the leopard was noted on the farm. It would frequently come down from the rocky *kloof* or precipice into which the house was wedged to eat the remains of the dog's bones. Time went by and, possibly through association and the barrier of the fence, the cat and the big 130-pound dog got to know each other, to the extent that the dog completely accepted the leopard and vice versa. This is particularly unusual, as leopards seem to love dog flesh. Yet Dr.

Botha clearly witnessed the state of truce late one night, with the dog and the leopard feeding side by side along the fence.

As the cat accepted the big dog, it also came to be on familiar terms with the Botha family. Because the house seemed to block the natural access from the heights of the *kloof* to the expanse below, the leopard actually took to wandering through the house, in through the back door or window and out through the lower end! Often members of the family would pass a full-grown leopard in the passages of the home late at night, but there was never a growl or confrontation, although house guests had to be advised beforehand, which was, I suppose, thoughtful of the hosts.

As the leopard made himself at home, he also wiped out the flock of three hundred guinea fowl on Dr. Botha's property as well as most of his chickens and small buck. The doctor, a reasonable sort, simply reckoned that everybody had to make a living. Many nights, when the Bothas came home late, the cat would be seen in the driveway or often in the garage, where it sometimes slept.

On September 14, 1983, there was a severe grass fire in the drought-stricken region right around the Botha's *kloof*, and five days later the cat was darted in Benoni, sixty kilometers away. Chris Botha had noticed the absence of the leopard but thought nothing of it until he picked up his newspaper and saw the front-page photo of it behind bars. Contacting the authorities, he attempted to have it returned, and thought he could demonstrate to their satisfaction that it knew him. Unfortunately, the gang of press around the cage and the consequent glare of flashbulbs served to sufficiently terrify the cat that he wasn't interested in knowing anybody. Sorry, said the officials, and the cat—now named "Savimbi"—was slated to be released in a remote area with a recently liberated female. This has since been done.

The Botha family took the turn of events philosophically, although the total absence of the leopard in his usual haunts seems pretty weighty circumstantial evidence that "Savimbi" was, in fact, the Bothas' leopard.

It's the essential shyness of the leopard that makes him so difficult to hunt. It shouldn't be forgotten, however, that while the leopard man-eater, like most man-eaters, is fairly unusual, it has historically been the most difficult to kill. Some have taken more than four hundred people, which is several very good-sized cocktail parties.

Leopards are thin-skinned and light-boned, which means that if you put a bullet where it's supposed to go, you won't have any problems. Probably through coincidence, most of my clients have shot their leopards with the .300 Winchester or the .300 Weatherby, and a lovely job they do. I have shot a couple of cattle-killers with the .243 with 100-grain slugs and never had a twitch out of any. Ah, but if you pull that shot and stick a bullet in the guts, get thee to a nunnery.

I wrote somewhere that one of my good pro pals liked his people to use a scoped .375 or even a .458 with solids for their *Ingwe*, which you'll be safe to call the animal most anywhere. He was mauled twice by leopards but none of these proceedings was directly or indirectly attributable to the use of the particular loads. Leopard hunting wants a large objective lens on your scope to gather light; over the years I've found the differences between scopes for this purpose are amazing. If you really want a leopard, bring a high-power objective, light-gathering model and I suspect it will be worth your trouble.

I was hunting up on the Zimbabwe border a couple of months ago with a very fine local rifleman who wanted a leopard. I had offered to give him a hand. I never saw such a place for leopard as this Limpopo River tributary, and it was only four days before we had a big tom feeding. It was an Academy Award tree, locally called "applewood" because of the similarity to the bark of the real one. Only most of the bark had been worn off from the constant passage of the leopard that regularly used it to stash his larder. In all my years, I had never seen one so well worn.

The problem was that the tree was low, in a small, heavily wooded valley with a stream thirty yards away, and if we were to have any shot at all, it would have to be from a hillside above him. This was a major setback, because the light goes first in the valleys and hollows and greatly reduces shooting time. Had we been able to position the blind ideally against a sunset, we would have been able to have a clear silhouetted shot until a quarter past six. But in this circumstance, we were straining at a quarter to six to see anything near the bait.

After the first late afternoon, I brought along my .375 H&H with the big variable screwed up to 9x, and compared what I could see relative to the 4x my friend was using. It gave easily an extra ten minutes of shooting time. That's a lot of time with leopards.

That was the point of this story, but not to leave you hanging, we did not get the leopard. He was feeding very well and regularly but we ran out of minivacation and had to return because of business commitments.

Interestingly, a genet cat came early every evening for a snack, and we could have taken him easily but for fear of frightening the leopard. The last two evenings, he would eat a bit, glance around over his shoulder with his infra-red vision, and completely panic. There is no doubt, at least not in my mind, that he saw the leopard coming just as we lost the last shooting light. Another night or two and the leopard would have been permanently resident before my pal's hearth, but it was not to be.

Having written in great detail on the subject of leopard blinds and baiting in *Death in the Long Grass*, I don't think another complete inspection of the principles involved is necessary here. The essential elements are to hang a natural bait in a proper tree that has enough cover around it for the animal to approach unseen and, when the leopard has established a feeding schedule or routine, to intercept him from a blind.

Artificial baiting isn't always necessary, as the best possible chance of getting your leopard is to find a fresh kill he himself has made and placed in a tree to keep it out of reach of scavengers and other large predators. This doesn't happen very often, but when it does, you're really in business! A very casual blind can be erected, or cover taken in natural surroundings. I once had my men move quite a good-sized tree ten feet from where it was growing to open a field of fire, this done at midday when the cat was somewhere away from his feeding area. We got him too, a record-book tom.

Knowing of the leopard's love for baboon meat, many hunters hang dead baboons as baits. This is a mistake and generally a waste of time. A baboon, even a big one, is just too small to "hold" a leopard and leave enough to eat that the cat will return the next evening or morning. The best bet is either warthog, impala or any other small antelope. I only tried zebra once and was successful with it. Leopards will really eat anything, although I think they prefer fresh meat to rotting carcasses. The impression that leopards like really maggoty meat is probably attributable to the fact that they, with their very moderate sense of smell, can't find a fresh bait very easily and only locate it when it gets "high." From then on, though, they will invariably eat the fresh meat that is used to "top up" the bait first.

Naturally, it's important to secure the bait properly so the leopard can't tear it free and carry it off. When this happens, it means a three- or four-day delay until you can get him back again with another offering. He should also not be able to eat his fill, the bait being wired in such a position that it's awkward for the cat to feed comfortably. If he can only manage a light snack, he'll be hungry enough to show himself in daylight when you will be able to get a shot. For this reason, I usually tightly wire the bait to the underside of the branch, making it difficult but not impossible to reach.

When that magic moment does arrive and you're looking through the cross hairs at the dappled grandeur of a big male leopard, don't try to be cute because the shot seems easy. Take the center of the chest and make sure your bullet goes where you want it to go. There are no second chances with leopard. The best thing is to pick out a particular rosette over a vital area and to try and place your bullet smack through it. Considering the distance and the quality of your sights, this should be no problem. Of course, leopard fever doesn't always bring these things to mind at that moment.

I recall a very old episode of "The American Sportsman," ABC Television's sporting adventure program before it was castrated, and the viewing matter shifted from elephant hunting to stunt flying and game viewing with actresses. The segment that sticks in my mind featured a well-known movie star hunting leopard in Kenya, and had some excellent footage of the details. Of course, the leopard did show up and the star fired. By what in retrospect seemed a miracle, the cat fell out of the tree stone dead. There was a rash of mutual back-thumping and congratulations, at which point the star walked over to the tree and made the comment, "I wonder where I hit it?" A chill went up my spine and undoubtedly that of most pros I know who might have been watching. He should have been able to decide accurately which ventricle of the heart his slug would penetrate, hardly leaving a question of "where I hit it." Brrrrr!

Before we shuffle off from the leopard, there are a couple of important matters you should be aware of if you are hoping to include a *Chui, Nyalubwe* or *Ingwe* in your collection.

Not too long ago, the leopard, mostly through antihunting pressure, was classified as endangered despite the findings of the preservation organizations' own research. Ranked as endangered, there were several seasons when an African leopard could not be imported into the United States, no matter how legally he had been hunted in Africa. So the majority of African leopards living near cattle, sheep, goats or the like were cheerfully poisoned or hunted down with dogs, as they no longer had a commercial value but were a financial detriment to the stock farmer. In fact, with their international "protected" status, they were taking a great deal more pressure than they ever had under sport hunting, which is interesting if you give it a minute of thought.

Happily, the realists triumphed over the emotionalists and the leopard has been reduced to the status of "threatened" (and who ain't?), which means he can be exported from much of his African range, provided that proper documentation stating he was not poached is included in the importation documents to the United States. *However*, it's up to you to make certain that he may be imported from the area *you* are hunting, which could be a prohibited zone.

You might also bear in mind that the cost of a leopard license in Sudan, for some unknown reason, is the cool equivalent of U.S. $3,000 —as it also is for oryx at the time writing. Perhaps a Sudanese leopard would be worth that kind of money to you but it wouldn't be to me.

From time to time, weird local laws are spawned in various countries that influence leopard hunting. The first I was aware of was in East Africa in the 1960s, which forbade the building of a blind near a bait. I can't remember exactly, but I actually think the rule was against baiting in any manner. Naturally, most of my professional pals got around to abandoning some antelope or pig carcasses in convenient spots and found equally convenient bushes to sit beneath. What the logic was in a country where 90-plus percent of the total number of leopards taken were poached, I don't know. Only those killed from blinds over bait by legitimate sportsmen provided income to the state, yet these were prohibited from fulfilling their financial role.

A similarly odd thing is currently in effect in Botswana, where the government hosted the 1983 CITES meeting for the year. In deference (presumably) to the international conservation group, Botswana also prohibited baiting, despite a considerable upsurge in the leopard population and increased complaints from cattle farmers because of damage to their herds. According to a well-known safari firm, their professional hunters are now "tracking" leopards. They claim good results. Pardon my scepticism.

SIXTEEN

Rhino

I wish I had something clever and encouraging to tell you about rhinos in general and African rhinos in particular, but the fact of the matter is that they've been heading downhill for the last ten thousand years, since they became extinct in North America and Europe. Man, especially early firearms hunters, has had an effect, one of the rare examples where simple greed in fact hurt two major species. In this case, it's the so-called black rhino, *Diceros bicornis*, a prehensile-lipped browser, and the white or wide-lipped rhino, *Ceratotherium simum*, which is primarily a grazer. The white rhino is the only species on license today, the black being protected entirely, which is ecologically interesting as, for many years, it was the other way round.

Since the middle of the last century, a proper patchwork of problems has descended on the rhinos of Africa, neither species having been able to deal successfully with any of them. Some might take exception, but it seems to me that the inability of the rhino to adjust to other than Pleistocene times and conditions is a pretty obvious indication that it would have been on the way out with or without the pressure of man, although there's no doubt that poaching hasn't been very beneficial. Like the elephant, the rhino is cursed with a high commercial value, in this case the horn, which is prized as a supposed aphrodisiac in the

Far East, and also as dagger handles in certain Arabic states, especially North Yemen.

Although both species of rhino are closely protected, many tribesmen are glad to take the slight chance of getting caught for the possibility of picking up an easy four or five years' pay with a well-directed spear, poisoned arrow or musket ball. Rhino horn is relatively low-bulk, easy to hide and ship and is worth many times the same weight of ivory.

Such a small proportion of the readers of this book will collect rhinos that it's not worth an in-depth discussion of the animal. White rhinos are still on license in parts of Africa, though, especially in the Republic of South Africa, where they have been carefully nurtured for decades until their numbers are now threatening to become a nuisance. Many of these animals, both black and white, are being exported to areas where they previously ranged years ago, and there are plans through Game Conservation International to import some to Texas. As usual, income generated by the very few that are hunted by sportsmen at very high fees justifies the expenses of the rest of the population. At the moment, if a rhino permit is available, it will cost between $5,000 to $8,000 (U.S.).

I have never been in on the shooting of a white rhino, but considering that the black has a much worse reputation, I think it would be safe to say that neither takes a great deal of killing. In my experience, the buffalo, smaller by far, is easily twice as tough. I suppose bulletproof rhinos do come along from time to time. The shoulder shot is, again, the best bet, although some hunters like the neck shot because of the large size. The straight-on charging angle is one of the more difficult as the horn protects the brain very well, and although a slug in the horn will most always turn the rhino, it doesn't do much for the condition of the horn as a trophy. A good choice is just to the side of the horn and into the chest or shoulder. A rhino turns easily, although he also charges more often than any other animal I know. Give him a thump and he'll normally sheer away and offer a better angle for a killing shot.

Don't forget to carefully check the status of the rhino for purposes of importing your trophy into your home country. The fact that you may be able to take one quite legally in Africa does not necessarily mean that you can import him!

By the bye, I always thought black rhino filet among the best cuts of meat I have ever had, back when they were on license in Zambia. Quite the equal of filet mignon, especially sliced and served cold on slabs of fresh bread for lunch with a hint of garlic butter. Ah well, it was always fun to open the *skafu* box and thunder, "Oh no! Not rhino on rye again!"

SEVENTEEN

Common Game

Although it is neither the intention nor implication of the author that this be a guidebook to the game animals of Africa, it seems, on the other hand, not unreasonable to have a quick scan over the more common species as well as a few of the exotics. Since you'll probably want to get into the subject in far greater depth, I would suggest that you pick up a copy of the latest *Rowland Ward's Records of Big Game*, now produced by my good pal Bill Askins of Game Conservation International (The Petroleum Center, Suite D-211, San Antonio, Texas, 78209, U.S.A.) and the latest records of Safari Club International, which has its own system. I would like to explain that I extoll the virtues of neither measurement system, nor do I criticize either. Both have strengths and faults. After my years as a professional, though, before there was any recognized method other than *Rowland Ward's*, I tend to think in terms of the more senior and widely known system rather than the new one, through familiarity. You, however, may take your choice.

The reason I am so anxious not to get sucked into explaining the detail involved in trophy classification is that, for both scientific and sporting reasons, the determination of what race or family of game an individual of the same general species represents depends on so many factors and geographical break-off points. Politics and nationalities of humans may be handled neatly by the concept of borders but borders, at best, rarely exist in nature. Just by way of quick example, there are eight brands of hartebeests, three classifications of impalas, twenty-two closely related races of duikers, nine dik-diks of two generic groups, et cetera, ad nauseam. Your purchase of a good game guidebook will greatly expand your knowledge of African game and its particular racial and familial locations. That is not really my purpose. I see my job at this point as that of giving you some idea of what's involved in hunting the more obvious species, not how to look like a zoologist.

Speaking of zoologists, there will likely be many gaps in the field taken for shock therapy leave when and if they have a look at the peculiar order in which I choose to offer highly diverse species for your inspection. Since it is among the most populous and well distributed, we might just as well kick off with the impala.

A comment of a client many years ago has always stuck in my mind as undoubtedly true. A rather sage gentleman who took most of my money during the trip under the guise of teaching me gin rummy, he observed that, were it even reasonably scarce, the impala would be more prized than the practically supernatural bongo. I suspect he's quite right. Considering the length and the unquestioned lyrate, swirling beauty of the horns of a good male, particularly in terms of the body size of the whole beastie of between 120 and 180 pounds, he is purely spectacular. The grace of the impala is legendary, even confirmed by Chevrolet, but then I don't think they would have done all that well marketing a model called the lesser Yak or the Aardvark.

Considering the constant need for camp meat and the generosity of most countries' licenses with this species because of his large numbers, you will probably collect more than one impala, but this will depend on where you are.

The shot best taken is any through the shoulders or central chest, and since this is a continuation of our previous observation, unless otherwise noted, this is the standard formula for any species from here on. Impala are fairly easy to take with a chest shot but, as in the case of most other animals, it must be well placed. Break a leg and you may well be looking at the beginning of twenty or more miles' spooring. Even smacked with a

.375 H&H in the right spot, some impala will often go more than seventy-five yards before giving up the ghost, which, if it doesn't impress you, sure does me!

Impala are excellent eating, especially the hams and the filets, but the real prize is the liver. I don't believe the veal has yet been born that can match the delicacy of impala liver.

If you're up in East Africa, you'll find similar-sized animals that are hunted much like the impala. Chief among these in Tanzania and parts of Ethiopia would be the Grant's gazelle and his cousin, the Peter's gazelle, as well as the Robert's with flared horntips and the smaller Thompson's gazelle, which, to me, has always resembled the southern African springbuck. These, coupled with the puku of Zambia, the bontebuck and blesbuck of the far south and the other medium-sized plains and open bush dwellers, are all herd animals and are not really tracked but stalked after a binocular inspection to determine that there is a shootable male. Most places, the males are called "rams," although you will sometimes hear the term "bucks." They are all very tough and fine bullet placement is vital.

It'll take you a while to learn from a glance which is a shootable specimen and which is not, but that's one of the prime duties of your professional hunter anyway.

The next classification from a hunting standpoint would be the heavier plains game, typified by the zebras, wildebeests, hartebeests and similar animals, weighing anywhere from a few hundred pounds to as much as five hundred pounds. Next to the Cape buffalo, at least in my experience, the toughest customers you will run across will be the zebra and the larger species of wildebeest, both of which will soak up lead like a sandpile. Any of the heavier .30-calibers are fine for this league, but remember to use weighty bullets, as these antelopes and zebras require good penetration and reliable performance.

The African pigs are really in five clans, but we might as well exclude the European wild boar, which is found in Morocco and North Africa but not really farther south, unless introduced. This leaves the warthog, the bushpig, the giant forest hog and the red river hog. Your most likely experience will be with the warthog, considered by many to be the ugliest animal on earth but somehow always rather charming to me despite his cosmetic shortcomings.

Don't get casual around any of the pigs. Without exception, they are capable of sorting you out so a computer would have trouble figuring out which end your legs should be sewn back on. With modern firearms, it doesn't happen all that often, but not for lack of their trying. In the sweltering, tropical beauty of the South African Lowveld, nestled below the escarpment of the snaggled Drakensberg Range, kids are taught not to worry so much about the lions and buffalo but that the two animals they must respect are the bushpig and the bushbuck.

Once, in Zambia, I saw an impressive example of the courage of a warthog, a female that had one of her piglets pounced upon by a lioness. The cat killed the baby but the smallish sow charged and slammed into the lioness' flank, giving a nasty slice that knocked the *Simba* completely off her feet. Of course it was all for nothing as the lioness broke the pig's spine with a lightning return blow and then, in what rather seemed like spite, hunted down and slaughtered the remaining two of the gallant porker's litter. Well, you can't always expect justice.

As I've mentioned earlier, until recently I haven't had much experience of the bushpig, which is nocturnal while the warthog is diurnal. However, my ofttimes host in the Lowveld, Ron Selley, raised a young female bushpig to maturity and it was as tame as a dog and just as smart. Although it had had its fighting tusks removed by a vet, it was certainly a match for the biggest dog. This is not conjecture, either, as it would routinely kill any strange dog on Ron's property but would put up with his two big combat pooches from Rhodesian war days, Brutus and Tuffie.

That bushpig was truly one of the most handsome and exotic hunks of wildlife I have ever seen, if you wish to consider about one hundred and eighty pounds of almost literal pig iron attractive. It was covered in the most delicate shading of stiff auburn body hair with a long, rich, rufous mane that somehow gave it a prehistoric look. But after even a few minutes with the bloody thing, although it clearly would have taken up a life of sin to have had its stomach rubbed with any frequency, there was never any question as to who was in charge, and it wasn't me! Had you seen the unbelievable speed that animal could churn up in a bluff charge, you would appreciate the respect that bush dwellers give it. It was fearless, as tough as seasoned oak, and would eat anything, warming up with an hors d'oeuvre of

empty beer cans before finally making a main course of my top
leather imported gun case: all that without proper tusks, too. I
might have fed that case to a famine-stricken passel of Bengal
tigers with less impressive results!

The prospects of having bumped into that brute in the wild
state, on a nice dark night in somebody's cabbage patch while
she was still in possession of her choppers would have made for
a highly interesting though rather short evening, I do believe.
Alas, poor Miss Piggie may have either gotten a better offer
from a lovelorn Mr. Piggie or, if certain dark rumors are true—
of some local gentlemen being seen with large quantities of red
meat—she may have wandered into a snare or caught a musket
ball when Ron wasn't looking. Personally, I think it's just as
well, despite a fine attachment between us, developed through
several long, hot and beery afternoons under Ron's big syc-
amore fig. Sooner or later, I suspect she might have eaten him,
if not me, and I'm not entirely joking. . . .

I don't think anybody would object to the observation that
the warthog has the longest and thickest ivory of all the world's
pigs, and mighty impressive it is too. It seems to have been
largely forgotten that from South Africa to Somalia, during
colonial times, "warthogging" from horseback with classic
"jobbing" spears was quite a pastime and cost many a rash man
a broken neck, a disemboweled charger or some wonderful
cocktail conversation scars. Personally, I'm far more afraid of
"tame" horses than of wild pigs, which at least don't kick, so
I've never given it a try, although it must have been grand.

Warthogs, given proper emotional justification, will "come
for you" with great enthusiasm, although there is a greenhorn
trick you might keep your eye open for if you're not fond of
being on the receiving end of practical jokes. Warthogs, where
the soil type is sufficiently stiff to permit aardvarks or ant bears
to burrow, will live in their borrowed or usurped holes. As evening comes on, the pigs will back down with their tusks facing
toward the opening, stacked one above the other in some sort of
predetermined order best known to them, usually the young
deepest down and the old boy, with a face full of ivory carving
knives, on the top, although sometimes a female will cap the
hole. Apparently claustrophobia is not a common trait of warthogs. When I started off my career in Zambia and Botswana,

both sandy regions where proper holes were impossible to dig, I was unaware of this night-stacking. When, however, I first went to Rhodesia, a pal of mine stepped up to one of these dens at sundown and fetched it a mighty thump from above with his booted foot. Thank God I wasn't on the "live" side of the hole as, with a tremendous explosion of dirt and squeals, five warthogs erupted like dusty Minutemen missiles, about two and a half feet from my toes.

Fortunately, they must have been half as surprised as I was because nothing doubled back to bite me as an afterthought. So if you see anybody thumping the top of a warthog hole with a sly grin, make damned sure you're not downrange. Not if you're fond of your shins, that is.

So far as my experience is concerned, both the giant forest hog, which is generally from tropical central Africa, and the red river hog, from the western areas, are fairly remote. I have never hunted either, although I would dearly love to collect a giant as they are wonderful-looking animals at around five hundred pounds, rather like bushpigs after two years on Wheaties and chicken fat.

So that you won't be surprised on eating your first warthog, they do not have the subcutaneous fat that domestic swine accumulate, being really quite lean, although certainly delicious. As a rule, the meat does not cure as well for biltong as does the red meat of the antelopes and buffalo, or at least I would surmise this is why I have never seen warthog biltong. The tendency to decompose, while horned-game meat dries, is one of the reasons I so greatly prefer warthog for leopard bait, although as a fresh roast or filet with garlic butter, you won't find much better.

One thing to look out for in certain regions in all game, particularly warthog, is parasites in the meat. Some have them obviously and others are completely free. I'm not sure which parasites they in fact are, possibly trichinosis, but they are usually visible in cysts. I have never heard of anybody becoming ill from ingesting them when well cooked, great care being taken to clear the flesh of their presence before preparation. Don't, however, count on it. It may not be a very appetizing prospect, but with a little care, you will be satisfied that your meat is clean. Every safari company with which I have been associated was always very careful and fussy about this.

*   *   *

The smaller antelopes, particularly the duikers (Afrikaans for "diver," for the way it disappears in alarm into the dense bush), dik-diks, klipspringers (literally "rock jumper"), oribi, steenbuck and similar-sized antelopes are about the bottom of the range of horned game. All are generally shy and live in small groups of usually two animals, as opposed to the herds of most of their larger cousins. Ranging in size from scrawny fox terriers to boxer dogs, nearly all are attractive and interesting. Although they are normally challenging shooting, I doubt you will have all that much interest in collecting more than one representative head for your collection over a lifetime, even though a man could spend a fortune and another lifetime just taking all the duikers, some of which weren't known to science until the 1920s.

Since there are so many of these small buck throughout Africa, and as one may be "royal game" protected in one area and very common in another, there's little point in going into their hunting in detail. Most are taken by chance as encountered while hunting something else. So, in a word, the small antelopes are really the icing on the cake, whereas the cake itself is mostly the medium and big game on a general safari.

While we're on the "lesser" game, this might be a good time to bring up varmints, which many clients don't think of when considering an African safari.

Baboons of several varieties are largely considered vermin for the great damage they do to crops. What is not appreciated is that, for animals considered to be essentially vegetarians, they are also great predators and as I write this, there have been press reports of severe outbreaks of stock-eating by baboons in both Zimbabwe and Kenya. Goats, sheep and the occasional calf are all killed by baboons whenever they have a chance. Baboon hunting, unless a troop is come upon by chance, is rather like the military art of sniping, and should you have a bit of spare time, you might enjoy taking on one of the cleverest targets in the world.

Hyenas, long considered useless, tend now in many areas to be protected. They're hardly any sport to hunt under most conditions, and the bush would be ever so much poorer without their wild chorus and sanitary duties, although they are also effective killers of even the largest antelopes.

I've never had any experience with using the "dying rabbit" calls so effective on coyotes, bobcats, badgers and such in the States, while hunting in Africa. A couple of friends of mine have, though, and report that the ruse is very effective on jackals, smaller cats such as servals, genets, civets (the latter of which are not really cats) and other minor predators looking for a free lunch. The problem seems to be that, considering the fauna of Africa, you never know what kind of puddy-tat may be creeping up on you to attack the "dying rabbit." I know it will attract leopards, and see no reason why a lion or two wouldn't saunter over for a canapé of hare, which could lead to serious consequences for the unsuspecting hunter. One man who tried it still occasionally goes varmint-calling. The other told me that after the scare he had with a leopard practically in his lap, he'd never try it again. Can't say I blame him!

Aquatic game would certainly include the crocs and the hippo. I advise you to check carefully on the problems or lack of them in importing a croc trophy, as the species has been lurking around the endangered category for some time. As with the elephant, this would be accurate in some watersheds but ridiculous in others. Another thought you should have in mind is that even if you manage to import your croc skin where you live, you're going to have hell's own time getting it tanned. I don't know the technicalities but apparently croc belly skins, normally the only part taken, require a different tanning process that most taxidermists don't offer. Possibly you might find somebody who handles legal alligator hides in Florida or Louisiana to do the work for you.

Hippo tusks make very pretty trophies, especially when nicely mounted. Due to the incredible thickness of the hide, this is also the best source of the classic African *sjambok* whip, which is trimmed from a length of the hide after it has been dried hanging and weighted from a tree. You will normally have to arrange for these to be made for you in camp and probably sent to you later but they are worth the trouble. As resilient as spring steel, yet with the appearance in the raw state of freshly barked saplings, they are quite a conversation piece. They are also available commercially in many African cities, decorated with local beadwork and stained dark. I think they're more interesting in the rough state, but take your choice.

Under normal circumstances, shooting a hippo is not quite up to chasing lions in thick cover. If you can catch one early in the morning or at dusk as he comes out into the heavy bush to feed, though, it's quite a different proposition. Just remember, if you're inclined to be casual with such a funny-looking critter, that he kills more humans every year in Africa than the buff and the elephant put together. Whatever you do, don't get between him and the water or you'll almost certainly be charged. The speed of a hippo on land is unbelievable, so you'd better hit him hard in the forehead and keep doing so until he's down.

Before proceeding to some of the more classic glamour game, let me reiterate that I haven't forgotten the grysboks, reedbucks, tiangs, royal antelopes, lechwes or any of many more species that you might encounter on safari. It's simply that there's not that much space in *any* book to have a detailed discussion of every minor African game species, and I don't want to create an encyclopedic atmosphere here when we might be having a cold beer instead.

EIGHTEEN

Glamour Game

As long as there are crying jackals, dying campfires and tired hunters reviving themselves with a bit of Scottish holy water, there will always be a discussion as to which of the grander African antelopes is the most magnificent trophy. Some, especially those who have hunted him, will nominate the bongo of the deep rain forests and strangled, nettled slopes of the central and East African mountains. Few others would deny he's about the toughest to take in fair chase, unless it were the mountain nyala or the Abyssinian ibex of Ethiopia's Simien massif. But not many hunters have had a crack at these rare jewels. I believe it really comes down to just two antelopes as the most impressive trophies, at least from sheer appearance. I therefore nominate the sable antelope and the greater kudu.

The greater kudu, with his massive yet delicate spirals of deep nutmeg brown, tipped with almost translucent ivory, seems to me the handsomest. And he's not the only one of his dynasty that is beautiful, coveted and hard to take. He's part of the large family of spiral-horned antelopes in whose ranks are many of the greatest prizes of the chase.

Among his clan are such cousins as the largest antelope, the eland, counting four recognized varieties, the closely related bushbucks and the larger nyalas, the aquatic and rare sitatunga and the two main races of bongo. That's pretty fancy company to keep!

The smaller lesser kudu is especially beautiful, although not so impressive in his headgear as is his big relative. He is found from Tanzania to southern Ethiopia, where I took a real honey some years ago. Most places you will hunt today offer greater kudu, or to keep it simple, kudu. The largest specimens are the southern race, particularly as found in South Africa, Zambia, Botswana, Zimbabwe and South-West Africa/Namibia. The East African race is a bit smaller, somewhat rarer and the least impressive, although the western subspecies, living from Chad to near Somalia, is still breathtaking.

Kudu hunting appeals especially to Americans used to the wiles of their white-tailed deer. An animal of rocky, hilly, heavily bushed country, but capable of existing in a variety of non-jungle terrain, a good kudu bull of better than, say, fifty or fifty-two inches is a tough proposition, as you will find if you thumb through Hemingway's *Green Hills of Africa*. For an animal pushing seven hundred pounds for a very big bull, the kudu has a surprisingly small track and an astonishing way of laying back his long horns and ghosting through cover that would confuse a pygmy. He's got ears bigger than your shoes and eyesight like your mother-in-law's. How he can maneuver horns up to the record length of half an inch short of six feet through dry thorn without a sound is a question I have never been able to answer.

Speaking of kudu horns, the miracles of nature never cease to fascinate me when I look down the central axis of a kudu horn. Unless the horn is somehow malformed or damaged, you will see a perfect, empty circle, as if a mandril that the horn grew around had been removed. The precision of the spiral is really incredible.

As my late friend Warren Page used to point out, nobody ever shoots less than a fifty-five-inch kudu because there are so many ways to measure the beast's horns. Considering that fifty-two makes the bottom of the record book with *Ward's*, you'll get the drift. Even when *Rowland Ward's* was pretty much the only authority, so many people insisted on *mis*measuring kudu horns that there used to be at least four pushing fifty-eight inches pretty hard at most cocktail parties I used to go to. The only official method of determining the length of a kudu horn until recently, when the Safari Club International system was devised, was to measure along the *outside* edge of the surface of the horn and *never* to wrap the tape around the spiral, following it up the length of the horn. Of course, if you do the latter, the measurement will be considerably greater and you will only be half fibbing if you say that was what your kudu measured. The measurement of the circumference of the base of the horn and the distance between the tips was also taken. This wrap-around method was so freely abused that *Rowland Ward's* used to go to the extra expense of printing this common error in red ink in their minimum measurement schedules, but there are some people who never used any method other than that which gave the longest tape measurement.

Despite his bulk, the kudu is legendary for his evasiveness. He is usually found with a harem of cows and calves, which are extra eyes for the old boy. Some are found in bachelor groups, and a few of these little congregations are composed of absolute monsters. I photographed one such gaggle across the Letaba River in the Kruger Park a couple of seasons back and even with the telephoto you could see there was some real talent present.

Like most professional hunters, I've had clients place a number of greater kudu in the book, but in my own case nothing absolutely outstanding. The two best I ever saw were one at Matetsi in Zimbabwe with Geoff Broom when we didn't have a client, the other being on the last day of a Botswana Okavango safari with Bob and Vi Welch. It was early in the morning and Bob was already dressed in his business suit for the drive back to the airport when, not a mile from camp, we spotted, if I recall, six very good bulls, one being outstanding. Bob and his family had done very well on everything else, but we had been snake-bit with kudu. At the eleventh hour, there stood this brute in the early dawn with his horns swirling like giant sticks of wet licorice two hundred yards away. Considering that we actually had to unpack to get at one of his rifles, it was remarkable that we even got a shot after a stalk. We did, though, and the bull turned just a fraction of a second before Bob shot. It was a fair miss, but that's the way it goes with kudu.

Sometimes, though, despite their reputation for slinking stealth, kudu can be idiots. Charlie Askins and I once got close enough to a pretty good one in Rhodesia to kill it with a thrown boot, although he did use his rifle. Two days later, another one acted the same way and Charlie thumped it with his outlandish 8 mm Magnum Wildcat at about thirty yards.

Kudu are reasonably territorial and if you can find big spoor, you can normally be fairly sure that the old chap will be hanging around not too far away. Then begins one of the finest parts of African hunting, as kudu tracking in the dawn or late afternoon is to ordinary hunting what fresh truffles are to dried mushroom soup.

Since kudu cows don't have horns—well, at least *one* did, which was picked up and recorded by Selous after she had been pulled down by a pack of wild dogs in 1888—there should be no confusion with the sexes. However, it's still very quick business, as often your only chance for a shot will be over that heartbeat of time when a big bull pauses to look at you before bolting. This really doesn't give time to inspect the horns carefully unless you have had a chance to glass the animal earlier. Since there may well be several bulls that, at a glance, will all appear good, you are really taking a chance at collecting what merely seems the biggest. There's not much you can do about this, though, except to make as certain as time allows that you haven't pulled down on a poor rack in mistaken haste. That's a decision your pro will even have difficulty in making for you, because it works both ways. A perfect shot may prove to have been at the wrong animal and a purposeful pause may see a real whopper hunker over the lip of a hill before you can be sure. Well, that's hunting. . . .

The finest single trophy I ever had a client collect was the 35½-inch Livingstone's eland, taken by George Lenher with me in the Luangwa in 1969. At the time I think it was number five or six in the book, and even after all these years it ranks eighth, which ain't too shabby. Still, it was a classic case of the luck involved with coming across a really exceptional specimen of any game animal. Can you imagine the odds, given the extent of your visibility in bush country and how many millions of miles you'd have to walk with perfect intercept timing to come across a number one record animal of any species? What, for that matter, are the chances of you and the animal even being alive in the same time period, let alone your crossing paths when you were armed, ready and shooting properly? Obviously, trophy hunting is largely luck, coupled with top field skills and plenty of time on safari.

George and I, in company with pro Ian Manning and George's father, Samuel, were actually poking around for a lion that morning when we looked up and saw, walking toward us, what looked like one helluva big eland. Turned out it was, and George cooled him with his .404 Mauser. Oh, there was a little chasing around but it was really that simple.

Or, on the subject of record eland, consider the story that a good friend and professional hunter in Zimbabwe, Brian Marsh, also the author of a hunting novel, *The Last Trophy* (St. Martin's Press, New York, 1982), tells on himself. The number three entry in *Rowland Ward's* is a 37¾-incher taken in Matetsi, then Rhodesia, in the late sixties. It bears Brian's name, although he clearly states that he did not kill it. The best ever taken in that country, the entry was submitted by a friend without Brian's knowledge after the skull and horns were found wedged in a tree at a cropping camp Brian ran. The giant had, in fact, been killed quite unceremoniously by a black cropper named Zachariah. Before leaving this, let me make it most clear that Brian never claimed to have killed the animal, in fact he emphatically denied it in a magazine article, but of such are records made. Of course, it must be remembered that there is a great geographical value to game records, as they provide information on where the best heads have historically been found, as well as credit to *either* the hunter *or* the owner, who are not necessarily the same person, nor are they implied to be so.

Eland, for their size, are not especially difficult, but because they are so big and strong, I would recommend nothing less than a .338-class Magnum or a .375 H&H on them. When wounded or frightened, they will swing into a peculiar trot that takes them for tens of miles and are one of the hardest animals to follow up if for no other reason than the distances involved. They are in my opinion the best eating of all the African antelopes, finely textured and with a delicate, distinctive flavor some hunters compare to the choicest beef. I would say that there is a difference, eland being far better, but then how would you explain the taste of lamb, for example, or pork, to someone who has never tried it?

You probably won't have to rush as much with eland as you will with your shot at kudu bull, which is just as well because both sexes have horns. What's worse is that to the inexperienced eye the cow's horns are often longer than those of the bull and may appear more shootable. The bulls are distinct through their heavy forelocks and dewlaps and their horns which, if you have a chance to compare, are much more massive than those of the cows. Older bulls take on a peculiar dun-blue color, while the females are generally browner. All have striping much like a kudu but this may become considerably muted with age. It's interesting that the eland, despite his near ton of bulk, is one of the greatest jumpers of all the antelope, easily clearing fences that confine most other game species on reserves. The horns are twisted rather than corkscrewed like the kudus, and are very thick, although they tend to wear down heavily with age. Usually found in herds of what may be well over one hundred, lone bulls also occur.

There is also the giant or Lord Derby eland, found from northern Cameroon, through southern Chad (now off limits) and on into part of the Central African Republic and Sudan. He is highly specialized safari fare, particularly for the first-timer, so we won't elaborate.

The bushbucks are unquestionably my favorite of the smaller antelopes of the *Tragelaphinae* or spiral-horned group, and are found in many races over most of safari-active Africa south of the Sahara. The bushbucks, normally between 80 and 175 pounds, are among the most attractive and the handsomest of the smaller bucks, usually vividly marked with a variety of patterns or stripes, depending on their particular species. To call the bongos super-bushbucks would be no real error, and to similarly designate the sitatunga of the deep, wild swamps from the Okavango to Lake Victoria's islands, the Sesses, would be equally reasonable. The bongo is by far the largest of the bushbuck clan, a big bull averaging about five hundred pounds. The nyala of southern and South Africa is another especially attractive larger member of the bushbuck clan.

The specialized mystique of bongo hunting is not really appropriate for this book, save to say that it's not a sport for the casual safari-goer. It's some of the toughest, most uncomfortable rain-forest, high-altitude hunting a man can do. That you *probably* would not take the time and trouble to try for a bongo on your first safari or two is as axiomatic as suggesting that you *probably* would not buy your eighteen-year-old daughter a Maserati or a Rolls-Royce in which to learn to drive. Sure, it's done, but it's unusual.

All the bushbucks, as we've mentioned, are potentially lethal. Wounded, they're almost without exception fearless and aggressive, and many hunters have been killed or badly gored by them over the years. I recall once, with the late Jack Block at his home at Lake Naivasha in Kenya, seeing a captive bongo from the Aberdares Mountains repeatedly charge the heavy fencing to get at us. It was a very impressive performance, take my sworn word!

Not being herd animals, the bushbucks are largely taken by quiet loafing through thick cover or even by still hunting. The sitatunga, being aquatic, is hunted mostly by boat, raft or canoe, which, as for the bongo, is pretty specialized sport hunting.

An important consideration concerning which rifle to use for bushbuck would be not to forget that they are a dense-cover animal and there will be plenty of bush to disrupt or even vaporize a very fast bullet. Stick with heavier, medium-velocity loads like the .30-06 with 200- to 220-grain bullets or even the .375 H&H. All do a fine job in thick bush. Even the .458 is popular with bongo hunters who have learned to handle it.

We discussed the sable antelope at the beginning of this book, but that's no reason not to reintroduce him here as we leave the spiral-horned game for the straight and scimitar-horned species. If the greater kudu is sly, tricky and smart, as well as handsome, then the sable is bold, savage and noble in his turn. As gleaming, glossy, grackle-purple as waxed anthracite, with a harlequin, two-toned face coloring more like war paint than markings, and great, black, knurled, sickle-gaffs that will disembowel a lion in one sweep, he is my vote for the most impressive of all Africa's horned game.

The best shootable sable are found in Zambia, Botswana and Zimbabwe, the East African race being a bit less well horned. The unpopulous giant race of Angola, found only between a pair of remote rivers, has long been strictly protected, but considering the disruption of the country over recent years by war, they may well be extinct through poaching and habitat deprivation.

Based on my own observations, the old bull sable who has broken away from the herd to live out his days in exile is about the most territorial of all the large oryx clan, including the roan, sable, oryx, gemsbuck and the addax of northern Africa. The South African *blaaubok*, extinct for generations, along with the quagga, was also a member of the oryx or *Oryginae* tribe. It is for this reason that I believe that the sable is not so difficult to hunt as the greater kudu, which covers a larger territory.

Very often, a single sable bull will be seen at a certain time of day practically in his same tracks near some landmark, an old tree or a peculiar rock that he seems to recognize. Of course, this is not to say that big sable are pushovers for the hunter. Hardly. Some are shyer than bushbabies and fully as difficult to spoor down, should they take a whiff of the hunter's scent or catch sight of you.

I have written a lot about sable in earlier books and have related how they have killed lions in game-lodge swimming pools, wiped out whole packs of dogs in seconds and ripped the stuffing out of many men foolish enough to come within their wounded or irritated reach. Like all the bigger antelopes, except kudu and eland, they are extremely tenacious of life, as Selous once noticed when he put a .93-caliber, 4-gauge, quarter-pound bullet through the chest of one lengthwise. It went a full one hundred yards before dropping!

A close cousin of the sable is the roan, also with curved horns and a temper to match their sharpness. The roan is more widely distributed throughout Africa generally than is the sable, and although the horns of a good male are quite a bit shorter than those of the sable, the roan is chunkier and, if anything, even more deadly in confrontation than his black cousin. They look similar in shape but are completely differently colored, the roan being named for his tone of hide as the sable is for his.

Next to the elands, it is said that the roan is the biggest African antelope, at an average of a bit over 600 pounds for a bull, against about 500 for a sable male, this according to *Rowland Ward's Records*. I've always argued that this isn't necessarily so. The greater kudu is without question taller at the shoulder, *Ward's* even making a comparison of sixty-six inches against fifty-seven inches for both roan and sable bulls. *Ward's* also gives a weight of between 650 to 750 pounds in its description of the greater kudu before the chapter with measurements, which I suspect must be divined from exceptionally large males and not average specimens. Yet this is from 25 to 125 pounds more, by their own findings, than the roan for which they claim number two size among the biggest antelope. Essentially, this pronouncement goes against their own information and opinions and was probably a matter of one editor being not exactly in step with the next for their seventeenth edition (1977). If I were to make a choice, it would be the kudu after the eland, the latter even considerably outweighing a bull buffalo under normal circumstances. Ah well, considering how marvelous all the species are, rankings as to size really don't carry much swat with experienced sportsmen.

I have personally had less experience with roan than with sable, even though I have had, according to my diaries, about thirty-five roan killed on safaris I was in charge of. To me they seem wilder than sable, although not as strikingly marked. Certainly, although the roan was in shorter supply in most of my areas than was the sable, he was also harder to collect. I don't think he's a comparable animal to the sable in looks, but there are no two ways around it that, between the sable and the roan, you don't want any eyeball-to-eyeball experience with either.

A good thing to look for in hunting either sable or roan is "height" in the horns as an indication of length. It's the best give-away as to what will tape out as record-book length. If the horns "tower," rising a proportionate degree before tilting back, he's probably worth taking, everything else being in order. There is a great deal of individuality, especially in sable horns, which makes most individual bulls recognizable one from the next.

The first member of the oryx family I ever saw was in Ethiopia, at that time still under Haille Selassie, in the late sixties. I was hunting with the late Chris Pollet and the Swiss hunter Karl Luthy, in Sidamo Province for the first time. This particular species, or better said, race, was the Beisa oryx, one of the three submembers of the clan, which actually encompasses five different animals. These are the Beisa, the fringe-eared, and the southern African gemsbuck, which is the largest in the horn department. The other two oryxes are not worth mentioning here in detail as they are not common fare, given Africa's political situation. The scimitar-horned oryx is a north African desert animal with curved horns rather than straight, and the Arabian oryx is quite rare and pretty well out of reach for hunters.

Another oryx, technically speaking, is the addax of Libya and the Sahara regions. He unfortunately falls into the same category of not being worth the printer's ink or your time to discuss at this point.

Like the allied sable and roan, the lance-horned oryxes are among the most dangerous of antelope, so savage when pressed or wounded that most lions won't fool around with them unless the oryx is *in extremis*. They are clearly herd animals, not tending so much to the late-life bachelorhood that the more liberated sable and roan adopt, although the occasional old boy kicked out of the group's status of extended connubial bliss isn't especially rare.

Zoologically speaking, the fringe-eared and the Beisa are today considered to be variants of the same family, but the record-book minimums are different. In *Rowland Ward's*, a minimum of thirty-four inches for Beisa and thirty-two inches for the fringe-eared is stipulated. Sometimes one wonders why the biologists and the trophy recordkeepers don't get together. To enshrine a gemsbuck, you'll have to take one of at least forty-two inches, unless it's the Angolan subfamily, which requires only thirty-five inches. Unless you have a Russian or Cuban passport, the latter is unlikely at this particular time.

There is an overlap between the Beisa and the fringe-eared, with the Tana River of Kenya being a rough delineator. The Beisa reigns to the north and the fringe-eared to the south. The gemsbuck is typical of the dryer regions of South-West Africa/Namibia, Botswana's Kalahari and South Africa, and can live its whole life—so the biologists tell us—without actually drinking water. They subsist very well on the *tsama* melon, a staple of the Bushmen, as well as on wild cucumbers and other water-bearing tubers, much as kudu are reputed to do in very dry regions. As long as we're speaking of water in so-called deserts, bear in mind, should you decide to hunt there, that the Kalahari (or any of its variant new African spellings) isn't a Hollywood-style desert but merely a huge area without surface water. There are plenty of trees, grasses and shrubs, so don't expect something out of Lawrence of Arabia with Omar Sharif behind the next dune.

The best gemsbuck I ever saw was in, of all places, the then-Rhodesia. I had a good look at him—thoroughly protected, of course, as well as rare in the Matetsi area—and I still would bet that he went at least forty-three inches. He just wandered through the concession we were hunting at the time, many hundreds of miles away from where he should have been in Botswana, South-West Africa/Namibia or South Africa, but I saw him several times. When you make a living judging trophy horn length, after a while you get to be pretty fair at it. When I tell you he was forty-three inches, I'm knocking at least an inch off my true estimate. The all-time record gemsbuck is, incidentally, forty-eight inches, a cool four feet.

The oryxes are essentially open country animals, even though they're sometimes found in pretty stiff bush, especially long grass. As such, their eyesight is first class and they are shy to boot. Most of your shots will be on the long side for any of the members of this 450-pound-class animal. Whereas any of the hotter .30 magnums are enough gun with correct placement, especially considering that deep bush is not too much of a factor, you still wouldn't go wrong with a .375 H&H with a good telescopic sight. They're all magnificent trophies and among the most exotic-looking game animals on earth. Happily, they have few problems with being endangered, except in war-swept areas where "meat's meat."

Although it is not a member of the oryx group, it would be unreasonable to conclude this chapter without reference to the waterbuck. This is the grand, shaggy, parenthesis-horned antelope of the bush, normally found close to water. I suspect that the name waterbuck comes not just from their constant proximity to streams or rivers, but also from their habit of taking refuge there from attack. I have twice seen them in small pans or ponds fending off the ferocity of wild dogs (*Lycaon pictus*) and guarantee that they lack for nothing in ferocity when compared with the entire oryx group.

I remember with spine-shivering clarity one day in Zambia when I came up to a "dead" waterbuck, chest-shot by my client. Happily, I was obeying my own survival rules. It looked as dead as Russian capitalism but swished a pair of pig-stickers past my shins close enough to jog my memory and brow with sweat today. If I had been wearing long pants, those smooth pointed, bayonet-tipped sickles would almost certainly have gone through them. A reasonable waterbuck being something above twenty-eight inches over the forward-tilting horns, I suspect that would have smarted. Since I had recently had a very nasty thing with a "dead" buffalo, I happened to have my rifle's muzzle against the base of the skull of the waterbuck and gave him 300 grains in about one six-thousandth of a second. He didn't like it but I sure did. This incidentally, is not the waterbuck incident mentioned earlier. They just don't seem to like me.

With all deference to those who have taken really good waterbuck, I wouldn't count the species as especially difficult to hunt. They are usually found in the same area of a couple of acres but can be as elusive as leprechauns if they have a hint of a hunter.

Actually, the waterbucks are part of the kob or *Kobus* group, including reedbuck, puku and similar horned fare. There are essentially two types of waterbuck. One of these is the "common," often seen referred to as the "ellipsiprymnus" in older hunting books written by people who obviously had more time for etymology than we do. Where I spent most of my time in the hunting profession, the main species was the common one, with the bull's eye circular tail ring around the rump. The more northern version is the Defassa waterbuck, lacking a ring around the rump but having a white tail patch. Most clients, upon seeing the common waterbuck, would usually classify him as the "bull's-eye" antelope.

The waterbucks of most any group are rather heavily built, in my opinion heavier than the 350 pounds often suggested by animal encyclopedias, although I've never weighed one. They seem to my eye like fine Scottish stags, shaggy and gray rather than reddish, but with a similar demeanor. The horns tilt forward and are deeply knurled or ridged, making especially handsome mounts.

You'll notice that, like most of the large classifications of antelope, there are many different races based upon relatively minor physical divergences. The same is true of the waterbucks, but if taxonomy isn't your bag, just go by the guide book.

I have an almost unnatural passion for venison, which is just as well as I used to live on it ninety-five percent of the time, year on end. But one animal that was normally not eaten at the safari table was waterbuck. Probably because they live in such insect-infested areas, the long, greasy coat of the waterbuck is thick with a natural bug repellent. Undoubtedly because this comes into contact with the meat while the animal is being skinned, the reputation has gone out that waterbuck is unpalatable. Well, I'm not going to take a stand on the isssue, but after years of refusing the meat, I had some a couple of months ago that was carefully skinned to be sure that the hair grease did not come into contact with the meat. I won't say it was eland or kudu interior filet, but it really was excellent. Yet, having refreshed my memory with a few antique books, I note that the fat was supposed to "congeal between your teeth." I now don't think it's so, but merely a matter of the meat becoming gastronomically fouled by skinners whose hands are covered with the hair grease while skinning out the animal.

These, then, are at least my preference of the best of the safari feast of beasts, the real glamour game, the horned super stars. Sure, many have been left out, but you can flesh out a six-month trip on the skeleton listed here. I suppose they're really the backbone of safari, after the Big Five, for there's no doubt that you'll spend as much time after the spiral-horned will-o'-the-wisps and the sword-skulled oryxes as you will after lion, leopard and the rest. Hell, I wish I were going with you.

NINETEEN

Bird Shooting and Fishing

The last of the day is dying a bloody death beyond the strange snaggle of central African trees, its gore tainting the surface of the water hole with a glow like that of a distant bush fire. A pinch-bellied jackal *yap-yap-yowrrrls* somewhere in the balding winter hills, impatient for the killing time of night, and the hollow clatter of roosting hornbills floats metallically on the soft evening breeze. You check the chambers of the double for the third time, thumb on the safety slide. Hunched behind the flimsy blind, you yearn for a smoke while thoughts of the little collection of neatly lined amber bottles on the starched white tablecloth back at camp are a vision of Paradise. A little longer. Not quite yet.

You glance sideways at the camouflaged form of your professional hunter who is scanning the dimming front with bloodshot eyes, his big double also ready, squat shells close at hand. Will they come? What if there's a mass charge? After all, this *is* the dark heart of Africa. Behind you, a gunbearer with an unpronounceable name full of clicks and pops watches the tree line with an occasional glance to the rear. And then they're almost on you, ghosting in from nowhere straight at you.

"Now! Take 'em!" whispers the hunter, and the blob of barrels swings up.

A visible lash of flame blends with the unfelt kick and the echoing boom of the gun. The male falters, then falls. In your excitement, you don't even fire the second barrel. By God! One shot!

"*Tola na buisa lo nyoni,*" instructs the white man, slapping your back. "Bloody good shot, old boy. Most chaps don't do well in this light. But you'd best stoke up that blunderbuss because there are bound to be more of the blighters along directly."

You drop a fresh round into the cavernous chamber, the empty ejecting in a delicious waft of powder smoke. The gunbearer is back, proudly presenting your trophy. Oh man! He's more elegant than your big kudu, more sharply marked than the lunker sable bull. The feel of his exotic, streamlined shape is as wondrous as if he came from Venus.

"Fine, big male," admires the pro. "An easy seven ounces. Maybe not *Rowland Ward* material but a nice start. You really—Watch it! Here they come again!"

The sanguine horizon is freckled with dashing, wheeling blots of motion, the muted swish of their coming eerie in the weird afterglow of light. You pick up a crossing shot and swing ahead. As the gun fires, in the same instant the target zips downward toward the shore of the water hole, untouched. Holding under, the second barrel bangs, just as the *nyoni* flutters and stops in midair. Another miss. Reload. Swing and fire. Again. Again. Nothing falls. You stop to shake a shell, wondering if this is not a monstrous practical joke. Nope. The pellets rattle ready in their plastic shell casings. 'Tain't the shells, me boy. The problem lies with the nut behind the stock.

Your hunter is also firing now. Dark shapes fall in neat slants to bounce on the hard ground. One, you see, drops into the water and disappears in a savage swirl. A Labrador wouldn't last very long in these parts, you mentally note.

The first box of No. 7½s is as empty as your bank account. ("Safaris aren't all *that* expensive, darling.") But why are there only four shells left in the second carton? Must have spilled some. Holding carefully on a suicide-bound speedster, you touch off just as he flares. A second barrel improves the lead content of some topsoil a few hundred yards away. A miss at an easy passer—too easy?—and then the final round at the leader of a whispering squadron. The fifth bird behind him explodes in a flak-burst of feathers, spinning slowly down on death-frozen wings to plop softly in front of the blind. You see little point in mentioning that the ill-fated recipient of your last shot was six feet behind the one you were firing at. Nice going, Champion of the East Chilblain Trap and Skeet Club. Well and truly done, Mr. High-Over-All. Oh well, that's what conservation's all about. Limit your kill, don't kill your limit. Small danger of that!

That awful evening was many and many a martini ago in a small, central African country that's changed its name with sufficient frequency that I doubt the head of research of Rand McNally could tell you the correct spelling. I was the gunner. The creature that led me to a New York psychoanalyst is the African sand grouse. I *hate* sand grouse. I *love* sand grouse. You will observe that I am still confused.

"Sandies," or as my bwana that trip called them, "tricky little brutes," are normally perceived by shotgunners who read about Africa as great game birds. Not so. Ask anybody who has hunted them. People like Bob Ruark and Russ Aitken who wrote so charmingly of them can only be ranked among the hopelessly naïve. Or perhaps their Africa hadn't gotten more politically involved at that time than the parboiling of a few plump Congo missionaries or the development of Mau Mau as the Kenyan national sport. Some ornithologists don't believe me when I reveal the findings of a recent, personally conducted survey of the political affiliations and ambitions of the sand grouse. There being no point in beating about the bush, I must state positive evidence that vast numbers of this supposedly non-dangerous species have been recruited into the Communist adventure in Africa. I have personally captured several that sneeringly admitted being trained in Cuba, Albania and, in one case, Moscow itself. After indoctrination, they had been sent back to their homelands to rattle the confidence of the visiting Wall Street capitalist warmonger American bird hunters. They are succeeding too. I had much of this on tape but it was inadvertently erased by my secretary while being transcribed. However, I do remember enough details to give a couple of examples of what's *really* going on.

One well-known competition pigeon shooter returned from a sand grouse hunt in Botswana not more than a year ago in very bad shape. The first thing he did was have his wonderful collection of Purdeys and Hollands recycled into IMPEACH AUDUBON buttons. Clearly unwell, he gave his wife her own checking account and, at last reports, was spending the rest of his life in meditation somewhere in the Carpathian Mountains. The rumors that trickle out with remote villagers is that he spends all waking hours in the lotus position, endlessly muttering, "Why? Why?" He also drools a lot.

Or take the case of Mr. X, an accomplished ruffed grouse, duck and dove gunner in America. He went through four boxes of shells one afternoon on Zimbabwe, killing exactly one sandy; the wrong one. He was last reported living in a large, hollow baobab tree, having thrown his shotgun into the water, bitten his professional hunter twice and fled, naked and screaming, into the bush. He was still up that tree, crowing at sunrises, in late 1982, three years after the terrible incident. Parliament is reputedly debating whether he should be granted citizenship based upon extended residency, or whether he should be declared a protected species. It seems he's becoming something of a tourist attraction, rivaling the Victoria Falls itself as a source of foreign exchange. I find it particularly significant that leaks from the Department of National Parks and Wildlife indicate that he also drools a lot. Now, I ask you, isn't that clearly a pattern?

Since all misconceptions have been subtly dispelled concerning the sand grouse, let's get down to hard facts. For starters, he's neither a grouse nor sandy (although he *can* be mighty gritty when dropped on the ground on the way from the kitchen, then carefully replaced on his platter by the camp waiter). He comes in a fairly wide variety of species—all absolutely unprincipled—ranging from the Sahara south to the Cape. If you had to categorize him, he's rather a cross between a wild pigeon and a Scottish red grouse, invariably with handsome markings that include a bold bar across the chest and a mottled back that blends with the ground when he's dusting or feeding. In central Africa, where I have done most of my hunting, the banded species is the most common, although there are other varieties such as the Namaqua, found farther west. Around the rest of the continent, there is also the fairly rare imperial sand grouse, the black-faced and the pintail. None gives nor asks any quarter.

Rather than play "What bird is that?" with you about watering habits and such, let's just say that sand grouse are unlikely to share any intimate air space with your shot charge because they're so shifty in their flight patterns. One moment they're howling through the air like teal in a tornado, afterburners smoking; the next—one-thousandth of a second before you fire—full flaps are applied, and the grouse flutter like anemic butterflies to the bank to drink. The trick, if there is one, is to kill—excuse me, I meant *shoot at*—your birds as far away as possible, while they're still going at a relatively constant rate of speed.

Of course, there are many more ways in Africa to end up talking to yourself than hunting sand grouse on purpose. If that great land is a smorgasbord for the horn hunter, then it's an absolute groaning board feast for the scattergunner suffering from masochistic tendencies. Duck and goose shooting is often excellent, ranging from the streaking gargany teal, which fly so fast that their passing can sound like a sail tearing in half, to the spur-wing goose, which can weigh as much as a shot put and packs a pair of switchblades in each wing joint that could subdivide a Cape buffalo. Having once in my ignorant youth tried to pick up a crippled spur-wing, I am, now that the stitches have healed, firmly resolved to finish any others with my .470 Nitro Express, with a 500-grain solid bullet, probably delivering a frontal brain shot in full charge. I'd as soon handcrate honey badgers as fool around with a gut-shot spur-wing.

Waterfowl are plenty of fun but are casual shooting, unless you are lucky enough to get a crack at the Nile Delta or Lake Ngami. No decoys are used and there's rarely a boat at hand. Pass-shooting at dawn and dusk along rivers and near waterholes can provide some hot action, but many birds are lost to crocs.

Which brings to mind the fact that bird dogs, either pointers or retrievers, are practically unknown in central Africa and for a lot of very good reasons. The main consideration is that they tend to survive only a short time before a leopard takes them as a late snack, a croc pulls them down, they become indiscrete with a cobra or puff adder or die of nagana, the tsetse disease fatal to all domestic animals.

Of the ground-dwelling game birds, the primary groups are the spur-fowl or francolin, the tiny "button" quail (which aren't much either for size or sport, some grasshoppers being larger and better fliers) and the Spotted Terror, the guinea fowl. By far the sport most resembling American upland shooting is with the francolin, which are found in two main species, the yellow-necked of the Kenya/Ethiopia area and the red-necked, which ranges south from there. About the size of a chukar or Hungarian partridge, they act more like ruffed grouse and, if such a thing is possible, taste even better. In my areas, hunting them is done in two ways—walk-up, and driving the *vleis* or dried-up marshes in the winter season.

In early morning and late afternoon, like their cousins all over the world, francolin come out of heavy cover to feed in the edges of clearings and dust in the game trails. It's a shame pointers can't be used for them in most areas, as I believe they would hold well for a dog. But a bang-up hour or two can still be had walking up the birds. A reasonable bag, there being no limits in most places as there's almost no gunning pressure, for two men would be ten to twenty birds in an hour or so. As good, fast fliers, twisting and darting around the bush, they can be as tough to hit in cover as winged ectoplasm.

Oh, I forgot something. The local chap walking behind you with your shell bag had best be packing your heavy rifle too. One fine morning, combing some grass with a skeet-bored 20-gauge (even though I advise you to bring *only* a 12-gauge shotgun), I damn near stepped on a lioness that had a badly cut and infected foot from which a broken length of poacher snare was still dangling. Turned out she held me responsible by proxy and, after dashing off a few yards, turned and charged without benefit of preliminaries. I had no choice but to hold on the bridge of her nose and give her both barrels of—if I recall—No. 8s. Considering that I had to wait until she was no more than about a yard away, you will appreciate that she might as well have been hit by Skylab with all the damage those two practically solid clumps of shot did to her profile. I don't know if anybody else has ever killed a full-grown lioness with 20-gauge target loads before or since but I do not recommend it. Very bad on the nerves.

Driving francolin is also interesting shooting. Lacking a bit of the formality of Scottish grouse drives or Spanish *perdiz* beats, the principle is still the same. Safari personnel take up at one side of a *vlei* and as many guns as possible cover the other side. Whooping and clanging cans, the beaters drive the birds ahead, hopefully into the guns. The action is fast and tough when francolin build up some speed—very challenging shooting. I don't do it anymore, however, since I have had one beater mauled by a leopard and another flattened by a boar warthog that hadn't read the script.

And then there are the guinea fowl. Any similarity between the domestic barnyard variety and the wild African *hanga* or *mpangele*, living or dead, is purely coincidental. If you have problems with sage old ringneck cocks playing a running game, you had as well take up roadrunner hunting as tackle guinea fowl.

The most familiar of the guineas is the helmeted brand, which has a thick, boney crest on its head that would bend a .375 Magnum solid. There are other types, less common, such as the vulturine from the deserts of northern Kenya and Ethiopia as well as a South African variety that looks like a black Harpo Marx toupee with legs. All are dirty, lowdown, conniving life members of the Frustrate American Hunters Club, an international organization secretly funded by a large group of heart specialists and orthopedic surgeons to promote business. If the guinea fowl and the sand grouse ever form a coalition, brother we're *really* in trouble!

The lilting call of the bull guinea fowl sounds like an unlubricated coffee grinder digesting a load of glass marbles. But it stirs the quivering heart of the congenitally optimistic hunter into grabbing his shotgun, track shoes and nitroglycerine tablets, and sallying forth bravely in hope of a shot or two before cardiac arrest or cerebral hemorrhage occurs. As a personal observation, guinea fowl hunting on foot is too cruel to be incorporated into the Olympic decathlon but would probably have been just right for the early Roman games or the Spanish Inquisition. The problem lies in the fact that guinea fowl have some sort of terrible aversion to flying until they are at least a quarter of a mile from the hunter. Sometimes in flocks of a hundred or more, they can sucker you along at a tantalizing, just-out-of-range pace until you've covered enough ground to make the marathon look like a stroll to the men's room. Just as you're about to drop, they'll finally flush, about eighty yards out. If there is a hill handy, especially a steep, rocky one bound to contain enough cobras, mambas and other sweethearts to start a private serpentarium, they'll without exception fly straight up it, waiting for you to reach the top before . . . Well, I just can't bear to go on.

About the only way to effectively shoot guinea fowl, excluding the use of claymore mines, is either to stalk them up close or happen on them in heavy cover. Stalking is roughly as effective as trying to catch Canada geese with your bare hands and a burlap bag, blindfolded. Another method that I have developed to place some guinea breast on the table and which *does* work is to hide in the stubble of a native farm field where a flock is known to feed, and then pass-shoot birds as they trickle out of heavy bush on cupped wings to feed in the early morning or late afternoon. That, neighbor, is some good fun.

Guineas are tougher than tax men, and to catch a winged one is quite an accomplishment without a Kawasaki and a big net. Thus, in the interest of trying never to be guilty of wasting game, a wounded guinea is best fed another barrel to anchor him or as with a crippled duck, it'll be bye-bye.

Because of space limitations and my tight shock therapy schedule, it's impossible to get into the terrific dove and pigeon shooting in much of Africa. It is largely overlooked because of the cost of shells and their preferred use by most sportsmen on safari for more exotic or meatier table birds. For sure, it's a lot easier to sit popping swarms of doves than it is hoofing after guinea fowl or bush-busting for francolin. But, for me, I would rather spend that magic half-hour beside the evening water hole, mourning the passing of another African day. I'll be watching, waiting for that first blot on the riot of color that is the horizon to grow from an indistinct blur of motion to a darting, twisting target that will almost surely grant me lasting humility.

We've discussed to a minor degree your choice of a shotgun for general African bird shooting, but the most important aspect that I can think of is to choose one that offers an option of choke such as the Winchoke system or any of the others now on the market. You'll be trying to knock down wide, fast ducks and geese but you'll also be taking sand grouse that may want to light on your hat in the dusk. I remember at one particular spot on a Zimbabwe river, a smooth, clean sheet of rock that flared down to the water's edge, sitting still, and actually catching with my hands double-banded sandies that would light next to me. I am also in recollection of having tried the same thing with a yellow-billed hornbill that had settled down for the Botswana night on a branch under which I had driven my hunting car. Like a damned fool, I reached up and grabbed it. Well, I'd as soon have tried to give a wounded leopard an enema. It bit my hands nine ways from last Sunday and surely cured me of any future impulse gestures with live African birds. Squalling with indignation—and victory—it fluttered away, possibly to savage the next lion it ran across.

I know I said that a discussion of pigeons and doves wasn't worth the trouble as they are so populous, but since moving to South Africa, I have run across a game bird that I consider one of the most sporting I have encountered anywhere. Considering that I have shot mourning doves in the United States and Mexico, the white-wings, scaled pigeons and red-billed pigeons of Yucatan, white-crowned pigeons of Cuba back when, wood pigeons in Ireland and England, a variety of doves in Argentina, Columbia, Nicaragua and British Honduras, forest pigeons in Brazil, as well as band-tails in the American Northwest, not forgetting at least six varieties of doves and pigeons in various parts of Africa, my nomination for the best is the South African rock pigeon.

They're big, handsome birds that look as exotic as most African game, boldly speckled and with an eye patch redder than a parson after a week on Sterno. The really interesting thing about these devastators of so many crops—especially the local sunflower fields—is that they are actually city dwellers! Some of the oldest cave deposits in southern Africa, the same that have yielded the remains of *Australopithecus*, clearly show through cave taphonomy that the rock pigeon (*Columba guinea phaeonota*) was contemporary with and often a prey of the baboon-murdering little brutes who eventuated into one or another species of thee and me.

Rock pigeons, originally living in the *krantzes* and caves of the mountains, have apparently considered the erection of Johannesburg and Pretoria as private roosts and, by looking out of the window right now, I can confirm at least four nests on ledges and crannies less than twenty-five yards away from our apartment.

Each morning, "rockies," as they are locally dubbed, fly for up to thirty miles one-way to feeding grounds, usually in groups of five or six and up to as many as the eighty or so I have witnessed. When they happen to be coming straight over the shooter, they display that characteristic which I think ranks them as the most difficult of the pigeons to "double" on. If a flock is heading right down your throat, and you fire at about forty yards, you will find the opposite reaction of most other game birds, especially ducks. The flock will flare like a gaggle of F-15s on detecting a bevy of SAM missiles, dropping straight toward the ground and roaring at phenomenal speeds past you while you try to catch up with your swing. I don't know why this is, unless it's a reaction to hawks or eagles that other doves and pigeons haven't mastered. To describe it is impossible as you wouldn't believe me unless you saw it. But if you really want some humbling wing shooting, get hold of somebody in South Africa, especially in the Transvaal, who can fix up a bit of "rocky" shooting. The season normally starts in January and goes for several months.

Many people sing the praises of the rock pigeon as a culinary delight. I am not one of them, but to be reasonable, I don't like squab as dished up in most New York restaurants either.

Shot sizes for your safari will vary. If you will be in an area of considerable waterfowl, then you'll want to arrange for or actually bring a good supply of No. 6s. Many gunners like much coarser shot, but I believe that the smaller stuff, provided that it is capable of doing damage at reasonable wing shooting ranges, is a distinct advantage. For doves, No. 9s are just the ticket, and as big and tough as rock pigeons and the like are, I don't believe you would curse me overly were you to select No. 8s. I have a lot of pals who shoot loads as heavy as No. 4s on "rockies," but when the day finishes, I don't see that they have any more birds than I do, although it's noticeable that they seem to have quite a few more body-hit cripples that are lost. Density of pattern with an *adequate* pellet is the answer to me after many, many thousands of game birds on four continents. Oh, just for the record, should you be a fan of the American No. 7½ shot size, it's called the No. 7 in Britain and also in previous colonies such as South Africa. It's not a bad compromise either.

It's certainly not my job to advertise shell brands but I would suggest, if you're an American or a European, that there are really first-rate shells being produced in Cape Town under the trade name SP, and I promise you that they're as reliable with their plastic shot collars as any American shell I have traditionally used. At the moment, they are paper-cased—so what?—rather than plastic-hulled, but I'm not sure in my real heart of hearts, as the pastor used to say, that I wouldn't use them if they were available in the States. Just as we mentioned earlier, be sure to have an appropriate supply laid in by your safari company before your arrival if you plan on some serious bird busting.

Probably the biggest flying game bird in the world, at least on a size basis, would be the kori or royal bustard. Once common, it is historically considered to have been the grandest eating bird on earth, although I have never tasted one. In fact, I saw the first in my life only a couple of months ago when hunting a cattle-killing leopard in the northern Transvaal in South Africa. I had always been rather suspect of the reports of a male kori bustard weighing between thirty-five and fifty pounds, as reported by many naturalists, even of the caliber of Russell Barnett Aitken and, much earlier, Major Boyd Horsbrugh in his classic *Gamebirds and Waterfowl of South Africa* (London, Witherby, 1912). However, the one I saw made me a believer! I promise you that if they were parakeets, they'd be man-eaters. This magnificent heavyweight has been completely protected for many years everywhere in his range, but if they were in good supply in the States, a million quail hunters would take up smelt fishing in sheer self-defense.

Well, why not? If the kori bustard is supposedly a major contender, it just wouldn't be fair to omit the ostrich, which is frequently available on license and is a source of some of the world's finest leather. Like the bustard, he's a rifleman's bird, usually offering—if any—a very long shot while pacing along like Secretariat feeling the spurs. Actually, I have had very few clients take ostriches, although they are thoroughly sporting. Like everything else in Africa, they bite too, and will kick your gonads through the top of your hat any time, given the chance, provided they don't peck you to death before getting around to it. Today, they are largely raised commercially but there is no dearth of the original item in most big game areas.

I've never eaten any ostrich meat in Africa, although the stuff is often seen offered commercially, dried into biltong, so I guess it must be okay. I did, however, once do something fatally rude to a Patagonian ostrich, a *nyandu*, better known as the *rhea*, and must say that it was pretty good fare. Naturally, the practical joker possibilities of an ostrich drumstick are obvious, as I can tell you, having been on the receiving end of such a ploy.

One nice item to pick up at curio shops in Africa is an ostrich shell that has been "blown" dry and emptied. To non-Africans, they make grand conversation pieces and are often made into all sorts of items, including sterling silver tea sets in the manner of the art of early sailors when they visited South Africa. The plain shells are usually quite reasonable and make very nice gifts.

There are really quite a few categories of African fishing. To more than generally cover them would require a lot more space than I can afford in what is essentially a hunting book. I am personally a light tackle man, and when living in the States, specialized in giant tarpon on the fly in the Florida Keys, mostly with the Grand Master, Cal Cochran of Marathon. There *are* tarpon of reportedly prodigious dimensions in some areas of Africa's west coast but there is not really a practical way to fish them as the sporting industry isn't organized. I know that a few of the best American tarpon anglers went over for a look-see but were disappointed in the primitive quality of the facilities. If you want to heap local politics on top of this, you're better off to forget the project, at least as far as *Tarpon atlanticus* is concerned.

Tropical fishing in Africa is damned interesting, however,

and this is the brand you'll be most likely to encounter on safari. The head of the list, and I don't think many would argue, is capped by the tigerfish, a prehistoric nightmare of teeth that would unnerve an orthodontist, propelled by a gold and black red-finned lump of muscle that would make the great white shark look like a sissy if the tiger were half the shark's size. They have always reminded me of the *dorado* of northern Argentina in their ferocity with a lure or cut bait, great jumpers and game to the last. My personal opinion is that the tiger is the most exotic mounted fish one can treasure. They're usually taken by trolling with a spoon and are found in shoals only in rivers flowing east, which is kind of interesting. Certainly, you can cast for them, but trolling seems to be the most successful method.

If you rent or borrow tackle on safari, you'll mostly find that it will be heavier than that which you would have brought with you. Considering that fishing tackle is relatively light in weight, you might consider putting together a well-backboned spinning rig suitable for American bass, about a seven-foot rod and a medium reel with extra spools in six-, ten- and twelve-pound breaking strength monofilament. Most of the lures that work well in the States will also serve here, particularly "Finnish" minnows of the Rapala and Rebel brands. A good selection of spoons from medium to fairly large would also be in order, as well as some light wire leaders and swivels, as you must remember that they're not called tigerfish just for their stripes.

My opinion of the best-eating freshwater fish in the world is the African *Tilapia* bream, which will also take small spoons and spinners as well as streamer flies. It is widely distributed in southern Africa and a fine fighter to boot. Your outfitter will be able to advise you as to the fishing available, depending on where you are.

Africa sounds like a very odd place to encounter trout but in fact there are high-altitude areas that offer some very decent trout fishing. The Drakensberg Range of South Africa is especially notable as is the highland region of Kenya, particularly the Aberdares, and the eastern highlands of Zimbabwe, bordering on Mozambique. A rough rule of thumb: where tea grows, trout grow, too, as altitude is the factor. Like most anywhere else, much of the better water is held by clubs or hotels but arrangements can be made for a couple of days' fly fishing. In South Africa, I would suggest you contact a fine tackle store called:

The Fly Fisherman
6 Harwin's Arcade
Pietermaritzburg, Natal
Republic of South Africa 3201
Tel: (0331) 21855

The gentlemen running this store carry much American tackle and are in a position to give you reliable hints as to where to find some action in the South African mountain streams as well as advice on local flies. A visit to the Drakensberg itself is worth the trip, never mind the browns and rainbows of their beautiful streams. In Zimbabwe and Kenya, most larger hotels or tour operators will be able to steer you properly, troutwise.

There is quite a good amount of deep-sea fishing off East Africa in locations such as Pemba and the other islands off Kenya and Tanzania in the Indian Ocean. Of course, most hunters realize that this aspect of a safari extension is almost a trip in itself. Frankly, farther south in Africa, most Americans who have fished Baja, California, Montauk, Chubb Cay and the Bahamas will find that, except for billfish, the fishing isn't as good, or at least that's my experience. To pay the charter prices for the chance of a local South African "tunny" or even a few isn't really the cream that Africa offers in other areas.

For the hunter/fisherman who would like to try a touch of each, there are packages run by well-known outfitters especially geared for this form of sport. Not to make an endorsement, but by way of an example I would suggest a trip run in cooperation between Botswana's SafariSouth and Sporting International of Houston, Texas, which gives approximately three days each of excellent wing shooting and fishing for tiger and bream in northern Botswana waterways as well as abundant game viewing. Obviously, my description should not be construed as a valid representation of the trip, but the details are available from the joint outfitters in the appendix. The price, as I write this, and based on the exchange rate of the Botswana pula and the U.S. dollar, is $5,290 per person for a group of eight people, either fishing, bird shooting, game viewing or all three. With the exception of international air fares to Johannesburg in South Africa, pre- and post-safari food and accommodation, personal items and deviations from the normal itinerary, the whole shootin' match is thrown in. This includes shotshells, fishing tackle, all staff, accommodation, incidental park fees, boats, air charters both ways between Johannesburg and Victoria Falls, Zimbabwe, wine, liquor and nearly anything else you can think of that you would normally require. At this price, considering the inclusions, it ain't a bad deal at all.

Although there are packages available from several of the larger safari firms, don't forget that nearly all will be happy to quote on shorter or longer trips just for fishing or birds or both, and also for much smaller groups, down to one or two participants.

Really, if you have an interest in wing shooting or light tackle fishing, don't forget this aspect when booking your trip. It's some of the very best in the world.

TWENTY

Photography and Game Viewing

After your first few days on safari, you will have learned the one Great Truth Hemingway left out: You can't hunt and work a camera with wildlife at the same time. Yet your camera is one of the most important accoutrements of your trip and is certainly worth this chapter.

What most foreigners don't seem to realize is that there are, speaking just in terms of wildlife, two *completely different* Africas; that of the major group tour and the real MMBA (Miles and Miles of Bloody Africa) that you'll find in your hunting concession. Let me try to set up the boundaries.

The national parks and reserves probably spawn more antihunters than any other single factor among the loads of TV-oriented tourists, because they don't somehow seem to notice that the animals they are looking at are as tame as in most zoos. They really believe that these semicaptive, multigeneration-bred animals, constantly inured to the presence of humans under the practically artificial circumstances of parks and reserves, are representative of the actually *wild* game of the rest of the continent. They envision hunters slaughtering the same animals that eat sticky buns from their adoring hands, and come to the obvious conclusion that hunters must be interested in little but Bambi's blood. Well, enough of them have broken the rules, gotten out of their cars and gone over to pet "Elsa" or whatever other lion may be in vogue to have been well and truly educated. Of course, you don't hear much about this except from rogues like me. Bad for business and foreign exchange, you know.

Still, and make no mistake, there is a huge value to anyone concerning both aspects of African wildlife habitat. The fact that they are not identical takes away nothing from either, given that they are appreciated, each in its own right, for what they are. If you are going on safari and don't avail yourself of a visit to some of the really magnificent parks, you will have wasted a facet of the trip that will unquestionably yield the best photographs and perhaps the clearest view of wildlife that you'll experience.

We've commented earlier on the value of a good light-weight tape recorder, but it's quite secondary to the photos you will bring back. And, with a little common sense, you needn't be a Phil Kahl or other world-known shutterbug to get results that may become heirlooms. To have the opportunity to visit a good game park or reserve and pass it up either on your way to or from your safari would be a shame, considering how far you have come.

Although I have had hundreds of photographs published to accompany articles, I don't really consider myself a professional photographer. Maybe that especially qualifies me to share the following series of thoughts, as I doubt that many safari clients are particularly adept with a camera either.

Since this is a book on hunting safaris and will involve the photography of slain trophy animals, maybe a word of my own philosophy is in order. I believe that if an animal is worth shooting, it is worth respecting. You'll find this in the wildest societies, from the praise ceremony of the Old Nandis over the speared carcass of a lion to the German custom of honoring a game animal and its conqueror by wearing a sprig of foliage dipped in the trophy's blood in the hatband. Some of these ancient rites are far more involved and undoubtedly come down to us from the concepts of sympathetic magic, meant to produce success in the hunt. To my way of thinking, these mini-ceremonies are meant as respect and praise from the hunter to a worthy adversary. The "hero" photograph is not. Bad taste is bad taste in any sport.

Most people who take a fine trophy animal will want to commemorate the event on the spot with a picture. This seems simple enough but if you will take a second to consider who may be seeing that photograph in years to come, it's worth a bit of preparation. The first thing, in my opinion, is to clean things up. Look, bullets do cause blood, and those who are not hunters will react much more negatively to the sight of the stuff than most hunters, who realize that you still have to break eggs to make the proverbial omelette and that lamb chops are not manufactured from plastic. A gory color photo of a recently taken specimen certainly isn't attractive for its own sake, no matter who is viewing it, so have your field staff tidy up. You'll never convince an antihunter that killing isn't the real object of hunting rather than the secondary result of the chase anyway, but there's no need to unnecessarily fuel the flames of emotion on the issue.

The concept of respect for your prey will come clearly through the pictures you take by the implied relationship between you and the animal in your pictures. Don't sit astride a fallen trophy as if it were a side of beef. After all, it's a special animal that you have come a long way to hunt and kill under a strict code of ethics. You have taken its life to treasure it and the memory of conquering it on its own ground by ultimately mounting it as a trophy in your home. To have yourself photographed with your foot on the animal's body in the classic 1910 Teddy Roosevelt position isn't done in polite—or responsible— hunting circles today.

Because their business is so involved with it, most professional hunters are pretty fair photographers. They'll normally take your trophy pictures of fallen game, although experienced gunbearers are no mean hands with cameras either. First, they'll clear away any intervening grass or bush that would otherwise obstruct the shot and then do whatever is necessary to get the light from the correct quadrant. Since most game is killed when the sun is low, either morning or evening, this can take a bit of doing with an animal as heavy as a buffalo. I don't know of any elephants that have been shifted to accommodate the proper angle for a snapshot, though.

The rules for this type of picture are fairly simple: just fill the lens. I've seen so many trophy pictures taken from such ridiculous distances that they are hardly discernable. Most all of my work has been done with 35mm single lens reflex (SLR) cameras, but I see more and more motion picture cameras on safari, whether 16mm or 8mm or the more popular Super-8. The only advice I would give here after seeing some of the results is that the shots taken by amateurs are normally far too short, giving a jerky appearance to the final product. I would suggest that at least ten or twelve seconds be the minimum take; much longer on an action or scanning shot. And don't be afraid to use a bit of film to be sure you get a really good-quality shot. Certainly the cost is nothing compared with the expense of getting the trophy in the first place.

If I am photographing something for a magazine article, I work on the basis that about one shot in ten will be good enough for reproduction. Take a series of shots from different angles and distances and use the technique called "bracketing." This means taking pictures one f- stop above and one below the internal or external light meter reading. Naturally, you can't do this with an inexpensive camera that doesn't offer shutter or f-stop adjustment, but nearly all the better types do.

Today, photography has become so bloody simple that I'm sure the average orangutan could get a good scrapbook from a safari, given the new "smart" cameras and superior film types on the market. Still, there's so much available that a wee bit of advice may yet be in order.

The type of camera you choose will obviously have a fair effect on the quality of your photos. It's not absolutely necessary to drop a lot of money into a sophisticated 35mm SLR. Most of the far simpler preset "pocket" cameras will give you good results provided you don't want to bother with distant pictures of game. If, on the other hand, you are interested in starting a collection of birds and animals on film, I suggest that you do choose the 35mm and, beyond a normal lens, invest in a zoom telephoto lens or individual longer lenses that will enable you to reach out for those shots that would appear as just indistinct spots on a normal snapshot. For this, you'll want either a series of lenses from 90mm to 400mm, or perhaps you'll choose one of the fine new zooms. I have had a lot of good results with a

100–300mm zoom for general game work but also carry a 400mm for bird shots where "filling the lens" is really crucial for a small subject. A wide-angle such as a 28mm is excellent for scenics. The real pros do a lot of work with 600–1000mm lenses, but these are extremely difficult to hold still, even with a rest, and are probably best left to the advanced shutterbug. Another excellent attachment is the "doubler" or 2x "sandwich" lens that will double the power of any focal length you happen to be using.

The best man to talk to is your dealer, who will be able to advise you on the current best buys and film types. I personally recommend you shoot color slides simply because of their flexibility of form. They are easily made into prints or converted to black and white for publication. A good dust-proof case is a must for your camera under safari conditions, even better if it's well reinforced against shock. By all means, don't forget a flash unit for poor light situations or camp evening shots.

Certainly, it's not possible for me to teach you to become a fine wildlife photographer, at least not in a chapter! There are some people who can, though, and I think the best place to start would be with the book *Wildlife Images—A Complete Guide to Outdoor Photography* by top professionals John Wootters and Jerry T. Smith (Petersen Publishing Co., Los Angeles, 1981, $17.95).

Before leaving cameras and photography, there is something else I notice to be a common waste of film with inexperienced wildlife photographers, and I can't call it anything but the rapidly-disappearing-arse shot. So often, and I suspect simply because it's *there*, people take pictures of the rumps of animals disappearing into the bush. Of course, when you get the film back home and have it processed, it's not much of anything. Thus, try to stick with the rule not to press the shutter release unless you have an animal at least at no lesser angle than sideways to you. Sorry if I imply that you are not precisely teetering off the top of the commonsense I.Q. scale, but I freely admit that I've done it hundreds of times myself.

An instant camera can be a very nice extra, especially for use with local people. However, in taking photos of picturesque rural Africans, you must be careful. The best approach is for your professional hunter to set up the deal if a lot of safaris go through some spots you'll be visiting. There are several possible results arising from unauthorized pictures of rural Africans. In this connection I experienced one of the most singularly unusual sights I have ever seen on a continent not known for the commonplace.

It was in Sidamo Province of Ethiopia, where I was hunting with Karl Luthy and Chris Pollet, I being the relative greenhorn. We were about to eat breakfast, a marvelous dry-ice sort of fog rolling off the golden pelt of shaggy grass around camp, when I noticed movement. With eyes like baseballs, I saw a fully armored knight on a whopping white *Rowland Ward's*-class charger riding slowly right through the edge of our encampment. Well, I'd had a few the night before, but certainly not *that* much. Lord, but he was magnificent! He carried a lance that would have served St. George perfectly on the opening day of dragon season; there was a bow and a full quiver of arrows on his back and a genuine, dead-ringer crusader broadsword on his hip! His armor, the chain type rather than plate, was as well oiled as I have been from time to time, and he certainly looked a very believable apparition to me.

I made a lunge for my camera but collected a look from yon paladin and a restraint from Karl, leaving no question that my ideas of any portraiture were not very well chosen. I most definitely did not take his picture but I sure wish that I had. He just rode on with hardly more than a glance until he was swallowed up by the fog.

Who was he? What was he doing there? I don't have a clue, but Karl suggested that Ethiopia had lone seekers after whatever; sort of modern Holy Grailers who, if they did nothing else, sure impressed the hell out of remote safari camps. I didn't try to photograph him but I know in my absolute soul that he would have implanted that hog-sticker in my spleen if I had. The point is that some pictures aren't worth it.

Being overenthusiastic with your camera can bring problems in places far more urban than remotest Ethiopia. Most tribal people familiar with the machines will demand payment and become mighty irate if it's not forthcoming. Far worse, many of the really primitive tribes have a solid belief that the taking of a photograph of them somehow either steals or depletes their souls or spirits, a situation you don't want to be on the wrong side of! There is a little device, called by several brand names depending on the manufacturer, which is a mirror-angled lens, permitting you to take portrait-quality pictures of somebody when actually at right angles to them. Since you are obviously not pointing your camera at them, there is no offense taken. The cost of such a doodad is reasonable enough to be worth the investment in space-age subterfuge that can give excellent pictures of real primitives.

The various aspects of game viewing are the largest tourist industry in Africa that I can think of. Although we're essentially interested in hunting, you will hopefully get a crack at a short time in a park, reserve or private reserve sometime during your trip. What is important to remember is that it's a long way from the etiquette required at the Bronx Zoo.

To draw up a program, there are basically three different types of game-watching trips. The first, arbitrarily, would be typified by a visit to one of the major parks such as the Kruger in South Africa, a tremendous and beautiful area bigger than several European countries. Although there are organized tours available, most people take their own cars and drive themselves around the immense warp and weft of maintained roads, having a look at whatever they come across. There are many overnight facilities available, provided one books a reservation well in advance and doesn't happen to collide with the local school holidays.

In private reserves, most of the viewing is offered as part of your accommodation with the lodge that runs the joint, such as Mala-Mala, also in South Africa. Here, you will be accompanied by an armed game guard who will (hopefully) avoid any misunderstandings that might arise with the toothier residents.

If you're really into naturalism, your best bet will be the "wilderness trail" approach to game viewing, which is normally a several days' foot safari through a park or reserve accompanied by a guide and at least one man with a very big gun. This is the closest you'll come to the real Africa beyond a shooting safari, as the reasonable but not tough treks between camps will give a much more realistic and intimate exposure to every level of wildlife than you could possibly get from the back seat of a minibus. If you want to look at animals and photograph them in the natural state, this, in my opinion, is the best bet. Any experienced agent will be able to give you a wide choice of locations. You will normally sleep in real bush accommodation and have the pleasure of campfires, hyenas and the whole schmaltz. If this were a tourist guide book, I'd give the wilderness-trail concept five gold stars.

As I have often observed elsewhere, for the sake of sweet Jesus and your own posterior portions, don't get the Green Peace idea that African park animals are somehow tame. They may be blasé but they still bite. In fact, probably the most dangerous animal in Africa today is the park lion, overfamiliar with humans through sheer exposure. If you are doing your own driving, don't under any circumstances get out of your vehicle and don't get too close to any of the big game. Elephants have bad days too, and what a nasty cow jumbo can do to the best that General Motors or Ford can whack out would leave you goggle-eyed, if not dead. It's their territory, so have a nice look, but always be in a position to retreat with grace and style, but more important, speed.

Although they are definitely not identical activities, game viewing and hunting do have common elements. If you are driving through a park and come across a cheetah, lion, elephant or anything else of interest, keep in mind that the merest sound of the human voice is as poisonous in the park as it is when hunting. Even a murmured "Oh, look at that!" won't give you much to look at for long. Use hand signals, if you must, but try to keep the anonymity of the motor vehicle as separate from the presence of humans as possible. In most places, except where it has been chased by motorized poachers, game doesn't associate cars with humans, which is why you can normally approach as closely as you do.

Equipment for park game viewing is really the same as that described for a hunting safari, although you won't be as far out in the blue as you would be on a shooting trip. Besides the camera and tape recorder we've discussed, the absolutely essential item without which your trip would be marginal at best is reasonable binoculars. They will make all the difference as to what you will be able to see. Attempting a game-viewing trip without them is a waste of time.

I find that the most practical powers of magnification are

either 7x or 8x, the field of view, if not ridiculously small, not as important as the quality of the optical image. The best I have ever seen—although I've never been able to afford them—were the Leitz Trinovid brand, but excellent Japanese glasses for well under the current price of $200 are no disadvantage. If you buy or borrow more powerful binoculars such as 10x or 12x, you'll find that you can't hold them still enough to see clearly under field conditions. I personally use very battered Bushnell 7x26 compact binoculars; this is not meant as an ad for Bushnell but surely, after eight years of field use, it's no denigration either. The previous binoculars I used when hunting professionally in the early years were another brand. The constant friction with the chest of my bush jacket actually wore the metal rings that held the eyepieces to the extent that the lenses fell out! You've got to walk a few miles with binoculars to have that happen!

Just before finishing off this bit on game viewing, let me add one more word of encouragement: Go to a park or reserve, you won't be sorry.

Appendix A

Safari Agents, Hunting Companies and Professional Hunters

The following is a reasonably comprehensive list of American safari booking agencies; bearing in mind that most travel consultants can book a safari for you, although it is not usually their speciality. I recommend that you consult the specialists in the field. As in any area of business, agencies are born, absorbed, merge and go bankrupt. These particular agencies have been chosen for inclusion essentially because they maintain one or another degree of advertising profile and my aim is to try to save you some time in spooking through the backs of hunting magazines for their ads, although you'll miss some great daydream reading if you don't.

The overwhelming majority of African safari operators are represented by agents in the United States. Majority, of course, doesn't mean *all*. The second part of this appendix offers a representative view of some firms that prefer to keep their own booking arrangements, either to save the commissions involved or for other reasons best known and kept to themselves. After all, if you can fill your safari season by yourself with old clients or personal references, why pay somebody a percentage to book clients for you? Logically, many firms use both agents and accept bookings on their own. The agents, for equally obvious financial reasons, don't supply local addresses of safari operators. Some of the larger firms, such as SafariSouth in Botswana, have their own booking office in Texas as, I would guess, it's easier to handle things from nearer the source of much of their business. Geoff Broom, who has an ultradeluxe two-country safari between Zambia and Zimbabwe, accepts absolutely no bookings from agents. One presumes he doesn't have to.

I imply no favoritism at all in choosing or using any of the following agencies, nor do I accept any responsibility for your choice. I have the pleasure and honor of knowing many of the agencies personally and hope all will excuse me from any partiality. If I were planning an African hunt, you can bet I'd write every last one of them.

Safari Booking Agents

ADVENTURE SAFARIS LTD.
Three First National Plaza
Suite 747
Chicago, Illinois 60602
Tel: (312) 782–4756

JACK ATCHESON & SONS,
INC.
3210 Ottawa Street
Butte, Montana 59701
Tel: (406) 782–3445

BOSTON SAFARIS LTD.
Shrewsbury Street
West Boylston,
    Massachussetts 01583
Tel: (617) 835–6057

BREAKAWAY SAFARIS (PTY.)
    LTD.
Matz Building, Suite 226
513 East Jackson Street
Harlingen, Texas 78550
Tel: (512) 423–8030

BUSHVELD SAFARIS
18 Winthrop Avenue
Pensacola, Florida 32507

GLOBAL OUTDOORS
85 Johanna Lane
Staten Island, New York
    10309
Tel: (212) 494–6011

INTERNATIONAL BIG GAME
   SAFARIS
100 South Waverly Road
Holland, Michigan 49423
Tel: (616) 392–6458

ISI WORLDWIDE
   ADVENTURES LTD.
72 West Adams Arcade, 1st
   Floor
Chicago, Illinois 60603
Tel: (312) 782–6456

JONAS BROTHERS, INC.
Safari Booking Service
1037 Broadway
Denver, Colorado 80203
Tel: (303) 534–7400

KLINEBURGER WORLDWIDE
   TRAVEL
3627 1st Avenue South
Seattle, Washington 98134
Tel: (206) 343–9699

JIM MACARTHY AD-
   VENTURES
4906 Creek Drive
Harrisburg, Pennsylvania
   17112
Tel: (717) 652–4374

SAFARI ADVENTURES LTD.
1929 Lone Pine Road
Bloomfield Hills, Michigan
   48013
Tel: (313) 851–1707

SAFARI CONSULTANTS, INC.
P.O. Box 14318
Gainesville, Florida 32604
Tel: (904) 378–3000

SAFARI OUTFITTERS, INC.
8 South Michigan Avenue
Chicago, Illinois 60603
Tel: (312) 346–9631

SAFARI TRAVEL
   INTERNATIONAL
3505 Hart Avenue
Rosemead, California 91770
Tel: (213) 288–2720

SAFARIWORLD TRAVEL, INC.
Dimension II Building, Suite
   108
8918 Tesoro Drive
San Antonio, Texas 78217
Tel: (512) 828–5629
(Associated with Klineburger
   Worldwide Travel)

SPORTING INTERNATIONAL
P.O. Box 25187
Houston, Texas 77265
Tel: (713) 526–3161

TROPHY HUNTERS SAFARIS,
   INC.
Quayside Town 1, Suite 1507
1000 Quayside Terrace
Miami, Florida 33138
Tel: (305) 893–1162

ERIC WAGNER SAFARIS, INC.
307 Northwest 3rd Street
Ocala, Florida 32670
Tel: (904) 732–0079

The disclaimer offered for the above list of agents applies to the hunting companies and professional hunters listed next. Their addresses were freely available so I feel that I can do no less than pass them on to you. You will at once notice that many of the famous and even historical firms are not listed for the reasons mentioned earlier, as agents handle their business. Thus, please presume no slight to any firm or individual not listed, as you will be able to obtain complete information by querying a selection of agents.

Safari Operators and Professional Hunters

GEOFF BROOM
   INTERNATIONAL SAFARIS
(*operating in Zimbabwe and Zambia*)
Private Bag 5930
Victoria Falls
Zimbabwe
Tel: Victoria Falls 33517

FRANZ COUPÉ
Avenue des Vergyz 14
1225 Chene-Bourg
Switzerland

DON GROBLER
10 Ruthleigh Drive
Westville, 3630
Durban, Natal 4000
Republic of South Africa

HUNTERS TRACKS (PTY) LTD.
P.O. Box CH 4
Chisipite
Harare 36697
Zimbabwe
Tel: Arcturus 27716

GARY KELLY SAFARIS
11 Surely Lane
Kloof
Republic of South Africa, 3600
Tel: (031) 741137

KGAMA SAFARIS
P.O. Box 1201
Mogwase 0302
Bophuthatswana
Southern Africa
Tel: 014292–2405

MR. P. A. JOHNSTONE
Rosslyn Safaris
Private Bag WK 5934
Hwange
Zimbabwe

MR. BRIAN MARSH
P.O. Box 4602
Harare
Zimbabwe

NUANETSI HUNTERS
(Don Price)
Private Bag 2008
Mwenezi
Zimbabwe

SAFARISOUTH (PTY) LTD.
P.O. Box 25114
Houston, Texas 77005
Tel: (713) 785–6681

VADOMA SAFARIS
545 Estes Street
Lakewood, Colorado 80226
Tel: (303) 237–2110

MR. C. T. WARD
P.O. Box 5564
Windhoek 9000
South-West Africa/Namibia

WILD LIFE SAFARIS CO.
P.O. Box 24
Khartoum
Democratic Republic of the
   Sudan

Appendix B

Suggested Equipment for a Twenty-One-Day Safari

The following gives a fair idea of what you should bring for a twenty-one-day safari in Africa. Shorter or longer trips can be catered for accordingly by making the adjustments you feel are necessary to the lists below.

Clothing and Personal Requirements

hunting shoes
camp shoes
socks (4 pairs)
underwear (4 pairs)
shorts or long trousers (3
    pairs)
bush jackets or hunting shirts
    (3)
windbreaker

warm jacket (cold climate
    only)
sweater
hat
pajamas
gloves (cold climate only)
belt
traveling clothes for trip
    overseas

ammo holder
dark glasses
prescription glasses (2 pairs)
toilet kit, shaving tackle
antimalarial prophylaxis
antibiotics
Bonamine or Dramamine
antiseptic powder or salve
tweezers
Swiss army knife
antihistamine
insect repellent

lip balm
eyedrops
Anbesol (for gum pain)
sun lotion
bathing suit
handkerchiefs (4)
pen and notebook and
   address book
Lomotil (for dysentery)
dry skin cream
small flashlight
small talcum powder

Documents and Financial Requirements

passport
visas
traveler's checks
tickets and reservations

interim reservations for
   hotels
cash

Shooting Equipment

rifle(s)
shotgun
sling with detachable swivels
telescopic sight with
   replacement if possible
scope mounts
7x or 8x compact binoculars
rifle ammo (160 rounds
   minimum—all same bullet
   weights, 100 soft, 60 solids)
No. 1 buckshot (2 5-packs)
rifled slugs (2 5-packs)
Nos. 6, 7, or 8 shotshells (as
   many as can be conve-
   niently taken, the rest
   ordered through the
   outfitter)

earplugs for zeroing
compact gun-cleaning kit
lens paper for cleaning
   binoculars and scopes
WD-40 (1 small aerosol can)
hard gun cases
shooting glasses
small screwdriver/tool kit

Additional Options

field guide to birds
field guide to mammals and
   reptiles
compact fishing tackle
small tape recorder/player
   and tapes

camera and camera
   equipment (see chapter 20)
instant developing camera
   with film
belt knife with sharpener

Appendix C

Trophy Price List

It might be simplistically observed by one who didn't understand the hunter's mind that the taxidermically prepared trophies resulting from the African safari are the whole basis and reason for the trip. They are, actually, the *tangible* result of a safari, but are really no different as a stimulus than the photographs on the desk of a banker or stockbroker of his wife and children. Both evoke very personal memories and are constant reminders of valued experiences. Trophies from a safari are a focal point, lingering from days past, that can bring back the smoke of a grass fire or the ringing, bellowing trumpet of a charging elephant. I suppose they are also seen, questionably, as symbols of a man's prowess, rather in the same way that having a wife with, let us say, ample proportions, proclaimed a good provider a hundred thousand years ago and still does in some cultures today. Certainly, the implication of prowess in a hunter's mounted buffalo head or lion skin is no different than a bowler's league trophy or an ex-soldier's sun-faded medal ribbons and souvenirs.

Well, whatever the psychological implication of the trophy collected by the hunter, there is still a mighty practical aspect to the process involved in having it field-prepared, documented, packed, disinfected, shipped and crafted into the final product that will glare, snarl or leer down at generations of your family to be, barring, of course, as with the frequent fate of Uncle George's moose head, an unsympathetic widow or divorcée with a penchant for garage sales.

The field preparation of trophies isn't the responsibility of the client in any way, thus there's no point in discussing the matter here. The specialized safari staff will take care of all this expert work as part of your safari costs. It's only after the ball is over that it becomes your responsibility, after the trophies have been dipped, packed, shipped and certificated with the export permits from the country of origin as well as a veterinarian's certificate and a list of packed contents. Now the really nasty work of paying for the shipment comes up.

Rather than spend a great deal of time and ink, as regulations are certain to change, let me suggest that you contact a taxidermy house *before* you leave and have a hard look at the procedures. Your safari company or, as mentioned earlier, your local African taxidermy firm, will arrange the formalities, but make absolutely sure, whomever you decide to deal with, that you haven't taken a leopard or other species in an area where he's locally legal but internationally taboo. The same applies to other species such as some rhinos, so make sure you didn't pay what it would cost to refloat the *Titanic* for naught.

I herewith express my deep appreciation to the ancient house of Jonas Brothers of Denver, Colorado, for their kind permission to reproduce a portion of their price list, which, you are advised, is subject to change without any notice and which will probably be changed by the time you read this book. The following figures are given to you simply for *relative* costing between one type of mount and another and are not represented as being currently valid. They are certainly not binding on any party. The particular price list partially quoted here dates from late 1983.

Many of my clients have chosen to have work done in Africa in such excellent establishments as that of Botswana Game Industries in Francistown, Botswana, as well as other smaller firms in South Africa, Zimbabwe and, although I am unfamiliar with any company names there, in Zambia. I have also seen some work that would bring tears to a statue of Diana for some of the butchery accomplished by unknowns. None of this was at the hands of any company mentioned. As in most things, you get what you pay for; if you're lucky, that is.

One of the specialities of Jonas Brothers, Denver, is their freight arrangements on shipping consignments of trophies from

African points to America at considerably reduced containerized rates. Naturally, this is very involved fare and requires your attention before you hie yourself off. I would recommend that you also look into this well before you go and then cross-check, no matter who your safari firm is, what arrangements they have found best from their particular shipping points. If there have been problems, you can count on their having heard about them.

Modern taxidermy, as I'm sure you are aware, has come light years in development from the old concept of sawdust-stuffed ragbags of the last century. Somehow, though, I doubt that you are going to have an irresistible urge to drop the $49,500 required—without shipping—to have your elephant done up life-size, or even the life-size, open-mouthed hippo offered by Jonas (your hippo, of course) for a piffling $17,950, as of this writing.

Most safari clients have their better antelope- and buffalo-type trophies done up in what is commonly known as a "shoulder mount" or "head mount," while such species as the cats and zebra are normally fated to be rugs, either hung on walls or laid on the floor.

There are many, many variations on the theme. Elephant feet make attractive and interesting artifacts such as waste-baskets, trays and stools topped with zebra-skin cushions, and there are hundreds of varieties of animal foot ashtrays, lamps, tables of elephant ear and tobacco pouches of unmentionable parts of Cape buffalo, which is probably why they're always glowering at their presumption of your intentions.

One thing you might consider if you're a bit short on your personal balance of trade would be to have your skulls and horns simply bleached and mounted on plaques rather than invest in the full shoulder mounts. It's much cheaper and, depending on your personal taste, stark and attractive without being ghoulish. Many of your skins can be simply tanned and dressed as you may have a use for the beautiful leather. So, without further ado, here's a selected price list of some of the taxidermy you can have done with your trophies, although I have not included prices of full, life-size mounts as these are relatively unusual, except for museums and institutions.

Selected Taxidermy—Heads

Baboon (open mouth)	$435.00
Buffalo (Cape and dwarf)	$895.00
Bushbuck	$395.00
Duiker	$325.00
Eland (common)	$935.00
Elephant	$8950.00
Gazelle (Grant's type)	$435.00
Gazelle (Thompson's type)	$395.00
Gemsbuck	$595.00
Gnu or wildebeest	$595.00
Hartebeest: up to	$595.00
Impala	$395.00
Kudu (greater)	$695.00
Leopard	$395.00
Lion (open mouth)	$375.00
Nyala	$495.00
Oryx (common or white)	$545.00
Rhinoceros (white)	$2195.00
Roan antelope	$655.00
Sable antelope	$655.00
Waterbuck	$595.00
Warthog (open mouth)	$655.00
Zebra	$655.00

Fur Rugs

Includes tanning, artificial teeth, lining, padding and double felt border in two colors. We do not use the natural teeth since artificial teeth are far superior and will last indefinitely.

Open Mouth Flat

Leopard	$750.00
Lion	$995.00
Size of Thompson's gazelle	$275.00
Size of impala	$325.00
Size of sable	$435.00
Zebra	$765.00

Novelties

Ashtrays, 1 foot only

Cape buffalo	$155.00
Eland, sable, hartebeest, sitatunga, and zebra	$135.00
Hippopotamus	$295.00
Rhino (Bookends one-third more each)	$295.00

Elephant feet

Serving tray	$395.00
Foot stool	$435.00
Metal-lined wastebasket	$475.00
Combination wastebasket and stool	$545.00
Liquor decanter	$595.00

Elephant tusks

In wrought iron or brass bases (each)	$535.00
In decorated wrought iron boxes (each)	$650.00

Capped and chained to hang on wall:

On wrought iron or brass (each)	$515.00
On black ebony bases (each)	$625.00

Horns on shields (including bronze, bleach or buckskin)

Size of duiker	$105.00
Size of Thompson's gazelle, impala	$145.00
Size of sable, hartebeest	$195.00
Buffalo	$325.00
Warthog skull	$255.00
Hippo tusks	$195.00
(Full European style 45% additional)	

Skulls—cleaned and bleached

Leopard	$105.00
Lion	$160.00
On panel (additional)	$ 75.00

Table lamps
> *Size of impala:*
> 1 foot $170.00   3 feet $245.00
> 2 feet $215.00   4 feet $275.00
>
> *Size of sitatunga, nyala:*
> 1 foot $195.00   3 feet $275.00
> 2 feet $245.00   4 feet $295.00
>
> *Size of sable, zebra, buffalo*
> 1 foot $245.00   3 feet $360.00
> 2 feet $285.00   4 feet $395.00

Gun racks
> Impala or Grant's gazelle feet (each) .... $ 93.50
> Zebra feet (each) $105.00
> On panel (additional) .... $ 71.50

Miscellaneous (using your own tanned skins)
> Zebra hoof pen set (1 foot) $255.00
> Coffee or end tables (rhino or elephant skin) $765.00
> Coffee table with map of Africa or painting . $925.00
> Map of Africa from elephant ear to hang
>   on wall (or painting) $875.00
> Pillows (skin on one side—zebra, etc.) $150.00
> Tobacco pouches (scrotums)... from $93.50 to $140.00

Index

12/24/84
To Jimmy Shaw
From Jerry Shaw